Praise for *The Breakout Principle*

P9-DOH-710

"For peak performance, serious athletes say they must 'get in the zone.' . . . To reproduce this calm concentration in your own life, [*The Breakout Principle*] guides you step-by-step through simple techniques, such as focusing on repetitive activities like walking or breathing. The book's practical advice, grounded in sound research, will help many people who long to stop struggling and start achieving."

—*Natural Health*

"Timely and profoundly insightful, this book takes us one more important step toward the possibility of enjoying life free of injurious stress."

—W. Timothy Gallwey, author of
The Inner Game of Tennis and *The Inner Game of Work*

"After clearing away the debris of anxiety with *The Relaxation Response,* Dr. Benson now teaches us to build a wonderful new structure of confidence in the clearing."

—Rabbi Harold S. Kushner, author of
When Bad Things Happen to Good People

"Anyone with inspiration and the desire to change will be guided in the right direction by the wisdom, experience, and words of Dr. Herbert Benson."

—Bernie Siegel, M.D., author of
Love, Medicine and Miracles and *Prescriptions for Living*

"*The Breakout Principle* is a breakthrough book. Herbert Benson is a leading-edge thinker, and the result of his teaming up with William Proctor is a book that is not only fascinating for its insights but also of great practical value, helping readers 'zone out' and view life from a totally new perspective."

—George Gallup, Jr., cochairman of The Gallup Organization

"Herbert Benson, M.D., and William Proctor have been enlightening pioneers in their studies of *The Breakout Principle*. Now their work can be shared by everyone, not just health-care practitioners. This imaginative book is highly recommended."

—Reverend Theodore M. Hesburgh, C.S.C.,
president emeritus, University of Notre Dame

"Dr. Herbert Benson and Mr. William Proctor have proven their top talents and diligence. Millions of people can benefit from *The Breakout Principle*."

—Sir John M. Templeton, founder of
the Templeton Prize for Progress and Templeton Growth Ltd.

The Break-out Principle

How to Activate the Natural Trigger
That Maximizes Creativity, Athletic Performance,
Productivity, and Personal Well-Being

Herbert Benson, M.D.,
and William Proctor

SCRIBNER

NEW YORK   LONDON   TORONTO   SYDNEY

SCRIBNER
1230 Avenue of the Americas
New York, NY 10020

First Scribner trade paperback edition 2004

SCRIBNER and design are trademarks of
Macmillan Library Reference USA, Inc., used under license
by Simon & Schuster, the publisher of this work.

For information about special discounts for bulk purchases,
please contact Simon & Schuster Special Sales:
1-800-456-6798 or business@simonandschuster.com.

Designed by Kyoko Watanabe
Text set in Sabon

Manufactured in the United States of America

1   3   5   7   9   10   8   6   4   2

The Library of Congress has cataloged the Scribner edition as follows:
Benson, Herbert, 1935–
The breakout principle: activate the natural trigger that maximizes creativity,
productivity, athletic performance, and personal well-being/Herbert Benson and
William Proctor.
p. cm.
Includes bibliographical references and index.
1. Mind and body. 2. Peak experiences. 3. Self-actualization (Psychology).
I. Proctor, William. II. Title.

BF161.B474 2003
158.1—dc21   2002030655

ISBN 0-7432-2397-7
0-7432-2398-5 (Pbk)

To Marilyn and Pam

Acknowledgments

So many people have contributed in one way or another to the publication of this book that it would be impossible to mention all by name. But we do want to express thanks to several who have made special contributions. These include:

Our editor, Beth Wareham.

Our agent, Vicky Bijur.

Our publisher, Susan Moldow.

We are also grateful for the incisive editorial suggestions of Stuart Woodward and Pam Proctor.

Finally, we must acknowledge the insights gained from the many individuals who have benefited from a Breakout, and whose experiences are recounted in the following pages.

Contents

Preface   xi

Part I: POWERING THE BREAKOUT

1 What Is a Breakout?   3

2 Anatomy of the Trigger   26

3 The "Spirit" of Peak Experience   46

4 Mapping the Creative Mind   69

5 The Ultimate Self-Help Principle   87

Part II: THE SIX PEAK EXPERIENCES

6 The First Peak—Self-Awareness   105

7 The Second Peak—Creativity   125

8 The Third Peak—Productivity   147

9   The Fourth Peak—Athleticism   182

10 The Fifth Peak—Rejuvenation   210

11 The Sixth Peak—Transcendence   233

12 The Power of Intrinsic Belief   257

The End . . . and the Beginning:
    Realizing the Promise of the Breakout Principle   283

References   289

Index   305

Preface

As indicated in the text, the conceptualization and writing of this book have been in process for several years. The conclusions and research represent the culmination of Dr. Herbert Benson's investigations during his career at the Harvard Medical School and the Mind/Body Medical Institute. In particular, the roots of the Breakout Principle lie in the relaxation-response research that Dr. Benson has been conducting for more than three decades.

The Breakout Principle also represents the next major step beyond the relaxation response and reaches into new areas of scientific inquiry and practical application. Specifically, the techniques developed by Dr. Benson for eliciting the relaxation response were primarily designed to enhance personal health—including cardiovascular and emotional well-being—through the reduction and management of stress. The Breakout Principle incorporates all these benefits, but moves well beyond the previous understanding and applications of the relaxation response.

First of all, a Breakout may be triggered by traditional relaxation-response techniques, such as silently repeating a word, prayer, or phrase—or engaging in a repetitive physical activity—while assuming a passive attitude. Or the Breakout may be evoked by other means, such as immersion in one's personal belief system, in acts of altruism, in a significant personal encounter, or in a mental state that we call *total abandon*.

Also, in contrast to the previous popular understanding of the relaxation response, a Breakout typically leads to additional experiences or states of mind, which can result in improved personal performance and the generation of life-changing insights. In all cases, the essential element for a Breakout involves the decisive breaking of prior thought and emotional patterns.

The methodology that has helped us identify and utilize the Breakout Principle falls into three distinct categories, which are highlighted throughout the text. First, a considerable body of historical and sociological evidence has emerged that delineates the inner emotional and mental responses of those who have enjoyed life-changing insights. This information has suggested directions for our inquiry and has also reinforced scientific findings in peer-reviewed studies conducted at the Harvard Medical School and other institutions.

Second, the Breakout Principle is based on a considerable body of scientific research in which Dr. Benson has participated. This research includes physiological and neurological measurements involving those who use standard relaxation techniques, brain-imaging using functional magnetic resonance imaging (fMRI) equipment, and in-depth studies and reviews of the literature on nitric oxide and other molecular and biochemical interactions.

Various scientific studies have established that nitric oxide, which is produced in cells throughout the body, is associated with significant health benefits. These include antibacterial and antiviral functions, enhancing of immune function, lower blood pressure—and even improved sexual function with Viagra! Among the foundational scientific literature on this topic is the recognized 2001 article in *Brain Research Reviews* coauthored by Dr. George B. Stefano of the State University of New York, Dr. Benson, and other neuroscience and medical researchers (v. 35, 1–19).

Third, the book's methodology has required interviews with those who have undergone a Breakout and an analysis of specific behavioral components in their experiences. Research has been conducted with a variety of individuals to evaluate precisely how the Breakout Principle works in various environments and fields of endeavor—including business, the arts, spirituality, athletics, and personal health programs.

The case studies and illustrations in the book are taken from interviews and the experiences of various study participants. However, because of the personal nature of the information, specific names and certain personal characteristics have sometimes been changed to protect the identity of patients and other interviewees.

Also, a word must be said about the use of the first-person singular, such as *I, my,* or *me,* which is employed throughout much of the text, and also the first-person plural, including *we, our,* and *us.* This is a coauthored manuscript, with both authors assuming equal status. But because the research described in the book and also a number of the case illustrations come from Dr. Benson's work and files, we have chosen on many occasions to employ the first-person singular to highlight his personal involvement in those areas. Depending on the context, *we* sometimes refers to the authors and the reader, sometimes to Dr. Benson's research colleagues, and sometimes only to the two authors of this book.

Finally, a word of caution for those who hope to make medical use of the Breakout Principle: Before you use any of the techniques described in this book with the intention of treating a disease or health condition, you should first consult with your physician.

HERBERT BENSON, M.D.
WILLIAM PROCTOR

Part I

POWERING THE BREAKOUT

1

What Is a Breakout?

Have you ever noticed that self-improvement books, tapes, and programs often promise the moon, but then don't deliver?

- Perhaps no matter how hard you study and practice, they just don't help you at all.
- Or maybe they work, but only for a limited time. Either they—or you—lack staying power.
- Or you are wrestling with some deep fear, grief, or other trauma—and the program doesn't take your concern into account.
- Or a particular self-help program may prove useful, but you still feel shortchanged because you need improvement in *several* areas—such as playing golf, public speaking, *and* developing a consistent prayer life. Yet you lack the time or inclination to concentrate on more than one routine at a time.

Most people have had such feelings and have wistfully concluded that what's really needed is an *ultimate self-help principle*. In the best of all worlds, you might like to find a single, one-size-fits-all solution to your personal needs and aspirations—a panacea that would combine every personal improvement concept into one all-encompassing, easily accessible formula. Also, ideally, this single concept would infuse you with the personal discipline to stick with the program year after year, as you transform your life for the better.

If you've ever found yourself longing for the self-help program to end all self-help programs, I have good news. After my more than thirty years of research at the Harvard Medical School, I've discovered that *a fundamental self-transforming principle does indeed exist*—a principle that has been firmly established in exciting new studies on the molecular, biochemical, and neurological levels. What's more, the benefits—which reach well beyond traditional notions of self-help and have the potential to revolutionize your entire life—can be accessed through a simple but extremely powerful concept that I call the *Breakout Principle*.

So What Exactly *Is* the Breakout Principle?

In a nutshell, here is our basic working definition:

> The Breakout Principle refers to a powerful mind-body impulse that severs prior mental patterns and—even in times of great stress or emotional trauma—opens an inner door to a host of personal benefits, including
> - greater mental acuity
> - enhanced creativity

- increased job productivity
- maximal athletic performance
- spiritual development

The most significant phrase in the above definition is "severs prior mental patterns." Many if not most of the problems we face in terms of blocked creativity and productivity, subpar athletic performance, flawed health, or even stunted spirituality can be traced back to unresolved destructive or negative thought patterns—such as nagging anxieties, stress-related emotional baggage, or circular, obsessive "mental tapes."

But there's more. You can actually learn to *turn on a natural inner switch to sever those past mental patterns and activate Breakouts that will transform your daily life.* My investigations, which have been published in numerous peer-reviewed journals, have convinced me that this accessible, biological-medical "trigger" can be used to power up creativity, deep philosophical insights, stress-reduction responses, and top-notch professional performance.

Learning to activate this trigger can also provide you with what superior athletes call the *physiology of zoning,* or *getting in the zone.* In postcompetition interviews, world-class baseball sluggers "in the zone" have reported that 95-mile-per-hour fastballs seemed to be moving in slow motion. Professional tennis players have said that their opponent's bullet serves seemed the "size of basketballs." And top basketball players have reported that when they shoot, they somehow *know* they are unable to miss.

These almost mystical mind-sets—which typically involve a sense of invulnerability or perfection, effortless activity, or extreme clarity of thought—certainly aren't limited to superior sports achievement. Public speakers, writers, and other professionals who have entered into similar high-performance states have described their experiences in similar terms.

In many ways, then, the Breakout concept does promise to open the door to an ultimate self-help principle that spans the secular to the spiritual. But to understand how the abstract definition applies in a real-life situation, let's consider the rather unusual creative experience of a top management consultant whom we'll call Jason.

The Needlepoint School of Management Consulting

Jason was facing one of the toughest challenges of his career. A leading management consultant, he had been asked by a major U.S. corporation to take charge of the search for a new chief executive officer. But the problem was particularly difficult and multifaceted.

Several top executives in the company were vying for the CEO position, and two had let it be known that they expected to quit if they weren't selected. Opinions on the board of directors diverged radically. Stockholders had even divided into factions over the pending succession—they knew that the value of their portfolios might be seriously damaged by the wrong choice.

Unfortunately, there was no clear front-runner. Even after exhaustive analyses by Jason and his firm, including numerous reports from a leading executive headhunter, the picture remained murky.

"To use a grammatical image, it's a compound-complex problem," Jason complained to a confidant. "Extensive research—but no solution. No obvious heir apparent."

So what was required to move the consulting forward?

"I need a 'shazam,' " Jason said. "A brilliant way out of my pickle. All the analysis and detailed matrices—all the research in the world isn't going to help now. Forget additional lists. No more pros and cons. The time's arrived for needlepoint."

Needlepoint was Jason's favorite way to escape the day's frustrations. Just as important, the pastime often helped him "think outside the box"—and come up with million- or billion-dollar solutions.

So that day he left the office building, settled down in his hotel room, and pulled out his latest needlepoint canvas—a cover for a pillow that he was doing in petit point. (Petit point, for the uninitiated, is needlepoint that requires relatively small stitches—for Jason, usually about twenty-four per inch.)

During his career, Jason had learned that monumental amounts of research were necessary to move toward a solution. But after finishing all the hard, plodding research and analysis, Jason often hit an inner wall that intense work and thought couldn't penetrate. In many ways, his experience provided a classic illustration of the Yerkes-Dodson Law, which, as we'll see in Chapter 2, says that efficiency increases with stress up to a point. But if stress continues *after* that point, efficiency will begin to decline steadily.

Although Jason had heard that traditional relaxation techniques were supposed to help control stress, he knew he wasn't the "meditator type." Still, he had found that through needlepoint, he could control his stress and position himself to receive a "shazam."

As it happens, Jason was in good company. A feature in the *Boston Globe* (January 31, 2002, H1, H4), published long after he had embarked on his petit point, disclosed that the male knitting underground included such notables as Oscar-winning actor Russell Crowe; Ethan Zohn, winner of the CBS *Survivor: Africa* contest; fashion designer Bob Mackie; and network TV executive Stu Bloomberg.

One reason for the surge in male knitting, the *Globe* surmised, was "a need for stress relief during anxious time" (H4)—which was at least part of the reason Jason pursued petit point. But the consultant was mainly interested in that shazam.

Seeking the Shazam

"The insight has to come from outside," Jason explained. "It's absolutely essential for me to get away from the job and coworkers. Put myself in a position where my mind can roam around in a completely different space. The best way for me to shift gears is needlepoint."

In particular, he had found that when he was working on a background canvas, with only one color and one type of stitch, the work was highly repetitive. Row after row, he executed exactly the same finger movements. As a result, he could "zone out." Most important of all, he could break all previous trains of thought—and let his mind wander and hover freely, over this or that.

"That's when I often get my shazam," he said.

But unlike the old superhero Captain Marvel, who had employed the magic word in the comic books Jason had read as a youth, the consultant knew intuitively that it was virtually impossible to *mandate* a shazam. He couldn't *force* a brilliant insight. Instead, he had to release any preconceived agenda and be perfectly willing to emerge on the other side of the stitching without any new insight.

"First of all, it's best for me to *forget* the problem—just let my mind zero out and become a blank," he said. "I'll allow myself to get carried away with mindless repetition. Focus on nothing but those stitches, doing one after the other. Then, the solution may drift into my mind."

If that happened, he would "float or hover above the facts. But I won't review them in detail. I'll just watch them, hold them in my head."

On this occasion, Jason settled into a comfortable chair in his hotel room and began to stitch a petit point background. As he labored quietly for about fifteen minutes, the activity lulled him into a kind of trance. Random thoughts about the CEO issue drifted into his mind—and without warning, a solution burst forth.

Jason suddenly saw an elegant way to fit together all the difficult, moving parts in the selection process. He concluded that a senior executive with nearly fifteen years in the company and who was only a couple of years from retirement should be given the CEO position. That would satisfy a board faction that wanted him in the top slot. The move would also assuage fears of stockholders and securities analysts who were worried about the continuity of the firm's policies.

Another leading candidate—a senior executive with the company known for his sophisticated, continental tastes—would be offered the position as head of the company's European operations. Given his predilections, this man seemed quite likely to accept the overseas job.

The third main candidate, who was currently working with another company, was in many ways the strongest of all. He would be brought in as second-in-command. Then, when the newly installed CEO retired after two years, he would move up into the top spot.

Finally, the fourth main candidate, a young female executive, was favored strongly by some on the board. At the same time, others felt she was not quite seasoned enough. So she would be moved up to third-in-command. This would position her to take over after about ten years—when the second CEO retired.

By deftly moving these executive "chess pieces" around, Jason saw that *all* the strong candidates could become a vital part of the company for the foreseeable future, with the skills of each fully utilized. Also, none would be sent a signal that he or she was being pushed out or passed over. The result would be a stronger company than now existed, with the CEO succession settled for years to come. Having the major outlines of his solution in mind, Jason was now ready to plunge back into the high-pressured corporate environment and hammer out the details.

Although this unusual idea-generating technique worked well for Jason, the same approach obviously won't fly for those who lack a passion for needlepoint. Fortunately, there are other ways to trigger Breakouts and their creative benefits—not only in business but also in sports, the arts, religion, and an almost limitless range of other pursuits.

The Incredibly Broad Range of the Breakout

The Breakout phenomenon has emerged in such wildly different circumstances as these:

- Lisa, an avid tennis player, typically played at the top of her game during most of a match—then fell apart.

  In the early games, she often found herself playing

with effortless, winning strokes. But in the last point or two, when the final outcome was on the line, she hit easy balls out and double-faulted when she was serving for the match. By using a variation of the Breakout mechanism, she was able to stay "in the zone" even when the pressure was greatest.

- Rebecca, a novelist, periodically found herself confronting seemingly insuperable roadblocks in her plots.

  To break through a barrier that was preventing her from getting one of her characters out of a tight spot, she resorted to her usual method of triggering creativity: she stopped work, donned her sneakers, and walk-jogged to a favorite seaside vista near her home. As she strolled and gazed out over the water, an insight popped into her mind that enabled her to make significant progress in her plotting. Without knowing the scientific explanation, she had made effective use of the Breakout.

- Ted's primary goal in life was to deepen his spiritual awareness—but the stresses of life kept getting in the way.

  Ted found that his faith fell short in helping him manage the cares of daily life. But a study of works by the Counter-Reformation mystic Archbishop Fénelon and St. Augustine caused him to revamp his approach. He determined that when he confronted a crisis in his family, banking job, or volunteer activity, he would "let go" of his worries and accept the difficulty as an opportunity to cultivate his prayer life. As a result, his anxieties began to give way to increasing inner peace.

- Sheila, who was extremely sensitive to stress, had chronic high blood pressure averaging 160/95, a level serious enough to require medical intervention.

  Dietary manipulation and counseling for high-stress family problems failed to bring her readings down to acceptable levels. So her physician prescribed antihypertensive medication—an ACE inhibitor—to correct the problem. But then Sheila began to practice a daily mind-calming technique that enabled her to cut her drug dosage significantly.

  Specifically, the first thing every morning, she would spend ten to fifteen minutes focusing sequentially on tensing and then relaxing every main muscle group in her body, beginning with her feet and moving up through her legs, trunk, arms, and neck. Also, whenever she experienced a tense situation during the day, she would concentrate on breathing regularly and silently, repeating the word *peace* on the outbreath.

  After she had employed these techniques for about six weeks, Sheila's doctor recommended that she cut back on her antihypertensive medication, and eventually she went off drugs entirely. She also found that her family difficulties became less burdensome—largely because triggering these health-enhancing "micro-Breakouts" during the day enabled her to manage her responses to pressure more effectively.

- Robert, a trial lawyer, was suffering an almost unbearable case of nerves.

  As Robert prepared to wind up an important courtroom presentation, he feared that he would be physically unable to make his final appeal to the jury. Even during preparation for the trial, he had suffered occasional irregular heartbeats, insomnia, and panic attacks. But as he rose for his summation, an unexpected wave of calm swept over him—the result of a "stealth Breakout," as I have come to call certain surprise forms of the experience. As a result, he spoke with exceptional fluidity and eloquence.

The full stories of such individuals—which will be related later in our narrative—could easily provide the starting points for a series of quite useful, though entirely separate, self-help books. Yet my most recent research at the Harvard Medical School has revealed an astonishing paradox: These seemingly dissimilar incidents—and others like them—are all part of the same story.

Specifically, dramatic insights and personal breakthroughs—or Breakouts, such as those described above—are rooted in the same underlying medical and biological phenomena. Furthermore, even though the challenges and circumstances may be quite different, each Breakout event is triggered in precisely the same general way.

In short, if you can grasp what has helped you improve your tennis serve, you'll understand what it takes to strengthen your speaking ability. And if you can learn how to stimulate creativity on the job, you will be able to take giant steps toward improving your health—and even comprehending the biological foundations of your spiritual life.

During the past three decades, I've been able to do some original scientific work at Harvard—such as identifying the relaxation response and exploring the impact of personal beliefs and spiritual practices on human health and well-being. The Breakout concept represents the culmination of these years of medical research.

A Bird's-Eye View of Breakout Science

How is the Breakout Principle related to my previous work on the relaxation response? The Breakout is rooted not only in the previous physiologic research on the relaxation response, which measured cardiovascular and respiratory responses, but also in a wide range of new scientific methodologies and disciplines, such as brain imaging, molecular biology, and biochemistry. Furthermore, the Breakout Principle incorporates all the health benefits of the stress-reducing relaxation response. At the same time, it opens the door to entirely new applications—such as in creative breakthroughs, spiritual insights, greater productivity at work, and enhanced athletic performance.

Several fundamental scientific principles underlie every Breakout. Although subsequent chapters will go into more detail, this summary of Breakout science should provide a useful starting point.

Principle #1: A Breakout begins with your natural power to maximize health, mental ability, and physical performance.

Before a self-improvement program can work effectively, significant emotional roadblocks—such as deep phobias, debilitating stress, or other emotional traumas—must first be swept away. In other words, you cannot hope to maximize your ability to think creatively at work, lower your handicap in golf, or succeed with any other self-help system if you're preoccupied with depression, anxiety, or overwhelming grief.

Sometimes, these inner obstacles are so serious that they must be dealt with professionally, either through counseling or medications. But in many cases, interfering emotional barriers can be minimized or eliminated automatically through the Breakout mechanism. The reason for this is that every Breakout is rooted in our innate, self-healing, stress-reducing biological and biochemical package, which inspired the great Greek physician Hippocrates to extol the natural restorative abilities of the human body. In ancient Latin, these inherent powers, which we possess from the womb, were called *vis medicatrix naturae*—or the "healing power of nature."

We now understand that this natural healing and energizing capacity works remarkably well on several fronts. For instance, only about 25 percent of medical complaints that bring patients to health care professionals can be diagnosed and treated effectively by drugs, surgery, or other scientifically based medical procedures. Most of the remaining 75 percent will eventually improve as the body responds on its own, without medical intervention.

The Breakout Principle is rooted in these same self-healing powers. The innate physiology that promotes better emotional and physical health has also been associated with enhanced self-awareness, creativity, job productivity, intimacy in relationships, athleticism, and spiritual transcendence. Or to put this another way, you have been born with an array of biological triggers that you can "pull" to activate life-changing Breakouts.

Principle #2: The same mind-body mechanism operates in every Breakout trigger.

The fundamental mechanism for activating every Breakout can be stated rather simply:

To trigger a Breakout, you must sever completely your previous train of thoughts and emotions.

This decisive disruption of prior mental patterns will enable you to shift your focus into new and more productive directions. Achieving such a break in your old mental tapes is an absolute prerequisite if you hope to experience dramatic new spiritual insights, creative breakthroughs, or leaps to new heights of professional or athletic achievement. Chapter 2 will provide a much more detailed description of how the relatively simple but extremely powerful mechanism of the Breakout trigger works.

A common corollary to the basic Breakout Principle is that to break prior mental patterns, it will often be necessary to *quit concentrating on yourself.* You must disregard the way *you* are performing, or the way *you* are appearing to others—and dwell instead on what's happening *outside* your narrow orbit of self-interest.

Sometimes, you may have to find a way to replace your chronic egocentricity with altruism. Or it may simply be necessary to shift your focus from old, negative mental habits to promising new possibilities—even if you still don't quite know the exact nature of those possibilities.

A personal reflection

Years ago, I believed that to do a good job in a lecture, I had to stay tied to a script. As a lecturer in physiology at the Harvard Medical School, I would write out my entire talk, go into the amphitheater the night before my presentation, and practice the whole lecture out loud.

Then one day, a student said, "You're such a great teacher

when you're one-on-one. But why are you so stiff when you speak to a group? Drop your notes!"

After another professor gave me substantially the same advice, I finally decided to take a chance on their counsel. I threw away my notes entirely for one lecture just to see what would happen. From then on, my public speaking was never the same. As I abandoned my fears of making a mistake and focused instead on my listeners, my anxiety disappeared and I discovered I could communicate with great freedom.

More recently, as the keynoter at a convention of several thousand psychotherapists in Los Angeles, I felt literally at one with the entire group. It almost seemed that my mind melded with theirs. As I scanned the sea of faces, I understood exactly what they needed to hear from me, and the words came out effortlessly, as though someone else were speaking. A standing ovation confirmed that, somehow, I had connected with them on a deep plane—and without relying on a single note.

Although I didn't understand at the time what was happening, I realize in retrospect that, during that address, I had experienced a dramatic Breakout. Just as important, as I related with that audience on a profound emotional level, I was caught up in a genuine peak experience—one that bordered on the mystical and would enrich my life for months and years to come.

My secret to unlocking these benefits was simply to dare to challenge my fears, throw away my notes, and look my audience in the eye. But a vast number of other pursuits may also help you leap out of an unproductive mental or emotional track—and trigger Breakouts of superior achievement, insight, or creativity, which in turn lead to life-changing peak experiences.

A few such triggering activities that I've observed in my research include walking, jogging, swimming, artistic expression, showering, housework, a relaxing meal, helping others, and traditional prayer. Or who knows? You might even use something as unlikely as needlepoint skills to produce a Breakout.

Principle #3: As a Breakout begins, your body and mind move through a series of distinct, identifiable stages.

Typically, the Breakout Principle encompasses an inner process that consists of four distinct stages:

- The process begins with a *hard mental or physical struggle.*

For a businessperson, this may be a concentrated problem analysis or fact-gathering. The serious athlete may engage in extensive and demanding physical training. The person on a spiritual quest may plunge into concentrated study, a "dark night of the soul," or intense prayer, meditation, or soul-searching.

Sometimes, this initial, struggle phase may begin involuntarily, as a result of some traumatic outside event. For example, I've encountered numerous people who have been devastated by the death of a loved one, a deep-rooted phobia, or an outside calamity, such as the 2001 terrorist attack on the World Trade Center and the Pentagon.

The classic Holmes-Rahe "social readjustment scale" lists those life events and changes that are most likely to cause stress. According to this measurement, the top five in descending order of impact are death of a spouse, divorce, marital separation, a jail term, and death of a close family member (*Journal of Psychosomatic Research* 11 [1967]: 213). Victims may not choose these assaults on their emotional well-being, but they *can* choose to begin to deal effectively with them—through the Breakout process.

- The second stage involves *pulling the Breakout trigger.*

This event, which directly follows the struggle, has been variously described as "letting go," "backing off," or "releasing" your mind from the hard-work mode. The most important characteristic of this second stage is that pulling the Breakout trigger *must completely sever prior thought and emotional patterns.* Our research has demonstrated that characteristic biological and molecular responses occur when the trigger is pulled.

- The third stage in the Breakout process is the *Breakout proper, coupled with a peak experience.*

The Breakout will always be accompanied by a greater sense of well-being and relaxation. In addition, this new, unstressed mind-set will often lead to such peak experiences as the creative business insight that came to Jason after his needlepoint retreat. Inevitably the peak will involve something unexpected—a surprise that produces unanticipated new ideas or higher levels of performance.

- Finally, the Breakout cycle finishes with a fourth stage, which involves *returning to a "new-normal" state— including ongoing improved performance and mind-body patterns.*

In other words, those who have enjoyed a Breakout must always reenter the world of struggle and stress. But having undergone the experience, they are now in a much stronger position to rise to greater achievements, or to generate more profound ideas and insights.

The following visual sequence represents our attempt to picture these four stages, but as you consider this pattern, remember this: The Breakout Principle, which arises from highly complex neurological, biochemical, and physiologic interactions, cannot be captured fully in two-dimensional diagrams, or even in technical language. As we will see in later chapters, the Breakout mechanism involves nonlinear mental processes that might be depicted more appropriately in some multidimensional matrix or hologram.

But despite these limitations, this picture should provide you with a better understanding of how the Breakout sequence may flow inside your mind and body. Also, further details and insights will emerge as we will continue to build upon this basic diagram in our later discussions.

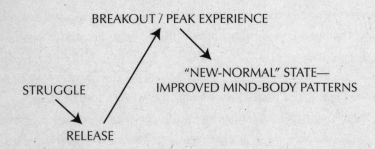

As suggested earlier, certain biological responses will accompany these stages. The struggle may include physiologic signs of anxiety and stress, such as increased blood pressure, heart rate, and brain activity. In contrast, during the release stage, mind and body quiet down to open the way for a Breakout and peak experience.

For example, fMRI (functional magnetic resonance imaging) graphs in studies I've done with neuroscientists led by Sara Lazar at the Massachusetts General Hospital and Harvard Medical School have revealed a shift to a remarkable calming of body and brain during relaxation exercises (*NeuroReport* 11 [2000]: 1581–85).

Principle #4: Activating the trigger appears to cause your body to release puffs of nitric oxide—a response that counters stress hormones that can impede a Breakout.

Perhaps the most startling scientific concept to explain the Breakout mechanism is that the calming response—or "release"—that typically precedes a Breakout may cause the body to *release increasing amounts of nitric oxide* throughout the body. This nitric oxide (NO), in turn, counters the negative effects of the stress hormone norepinephrine (noradrenaline). Among other things, norepinephrine causes a racing heart, high blood pressure, anger, anxiety, and greater vulnerability to pain. The benefits of an increase in nitric oxide were discussed in a 2001 article that George Stefano, Gregory Fricchione, Brian Slingsby, and I coauthored (*Brain Research Reviews* 35 [2001]: 1–19).

The overall calming of the mind and body—which I identified in scientific studies almost three decades ago as the relaxation response—is also associated with a number of stress-reducing events that extend well beyond the brain. These include reduced blood pressure, lower heart rate, and an overall lowering of the metabolism.

I sometimes refer to the gaseous puffs of NO—which have been described in the above coauthored article—as the biological analogue to the Hebrew theological concept *ruah (ruwach),* or the Greek *pneuma.* These terms, which are used extensively in the Old and New Testaments and are translated as "spirit," "breath," or "wind," are often associated with the divine presence that instills spiritual confidence and inner peace.

The full implications of our ongoing studies on nitric oxide, which have sparked considerable interest in the scientific and medical communities, will be presented in some detail in Chapter 3.

Principle #5: A "peak experience" often follows a Breakout.

The late, noted psychologist and Brandeis professor Abraham H. Maslow—writing forty years ago, before modern neuroscience had burst on the scene—did some preliminary exploration of the concept of the "peak experience" in his descriptions of a human "hierarchy of needs." These began at the lowest level of "physiological needs" (e.g., oxygen and nutrition) and moved up to the highest plateau of "being needs," or "self-actualization."

Maslow argued that the greatest personal creativity, well-being, and philosophical understanding became possible when a person moved up to the highest, self-actualization level. Furthermore, at the level of self-actualization, the individual was more likely to have a "peak experience," characterized by great insight, freedom from fear and anxiety, and a sense of being unified with an infinite or eternal dimension of reality.

When he died in 1970, Maslow was still in the early stages of formulating his peak-experience concept—which is actually a common theme that runs through most of the world's great religions. At times, he got off track, such as by suggesting that psy-

chedelic drugs might be a valid way to trigger these phenc
But he was quite correct in contending that most peop.
capable of having "plateau" and "peak" experiences, which may
range from creative insight to mystical transport.

In an insight consistent with our more recent research findings related to the Breakout, he also saw that these experiences
required a "shift in attention" or "attention-change" that broke
prior trains of consciousness. But Maslow remained at a loss
about how to trigger high points of human consciousness, and he
conceded that further research was required. I believe we now
have the necessary research at hand to take the next step: We can
actually begin to teach practical strategies to trigger Breakouts,
which will open the door to various peak experiences.

The six peak experiences that we'll be exploring in Part II
include:

- *The Peak of Self-Awareness*—a new level of self-
  understanding that provides the solid inner platform for
  all self-help efforts (Chapter 6).
- *The Peak of Creativity*—which allows you to surmount
  mental roadblocks and experience new insights in your
  work or avocation (Chapter 7).
- *The Peak of Productivity*—which can provide an
  infusion of personal energy that will exponentially
  increase stamina, endurance, and strength at work or at
  home (Chapter 8).

    In this chapter, we'll not only explore individual
    productivity but also introduce ways that teams in an
    organization can combine their individual creative
    abilities into an even more powerful force that I call a
    Breakout Network.

- *The Peak of Athleticism*—which results in much better achievement in sports, exercise, and other physical activities, including the possibility of entering the "zone" of superior performance (Chapter 9).
- *The Peak of Rejuvenation*—which will provide you with better health and protection against disease (Chapter 10).
- *The Peak of Transcendence*—which encompasses the possibility of experiencing deeper spirituality (Chapter 11).

Finally, as we conclude our discussion in Chapter 12, you'll encounter a recurrent theme that may be the most important factor of all for triggering many Breakouts and peak experiences. I'm referring to the *power of personal belief*.

The Mysterious Power of Personal Belief

A complete explanation of what happens with many Breakouts may be possible only if we import insights from the "theological," "religious," or "spiritual" realm—a domain that has far too often been maligned by Western scientists.

Many people have reported to me that only after prayer or an encounter with a divine presence have they experienced the kind of powerful Breakout that can produce an *ongoing* state of improved health, self-awareness, or more productive relationships. For example, many of those who have found lasting ways to overcome serious problems with substance abuse, such as drugs or alcohol, have started their road to recovery through a Breakout event. Also, these individuals typically understand their personal transformation in spiritual terms, such as being sustained by a Higher Power.

It may be hard, if not impossible, to explain in the limited terms of Western science how an amorphous "spiritual" force might contribute to human self-improvement. But significant efforts to link science and the spirit continue at Harvard and elsewhere. In discussing the peak of transcendence, I'll share with you the results of our latest studies that employ scientific tools and techniques to probe the mysteries of prayer and "intrinsic belief"—or the profound kind of faith that completely transforms lives.

Some may find our observations and studies on prayer and belief puzzling or even disturbing. A few may even become angry with some of our findings. But I trust that most readers will come away with the clear impression that modern science and the "spiritual" realm are really complementary, and not competitive. Also, as we use scientific tools to probe the domains of religion and spirituality, I feel confident that thoughtful readers will agree that, given the difficulties inherent in such an inquiry, complexity and profundity must consistently prevail over the simplistic explanation or the easy answer.

Now, let's move beyond this brief overview and begin to explore the Breakout experience in more detail—including the precise ways in which the all-important trigger can be activated.

2

Anatomy of the Trigger

At some point—when you've been racked by debilitating stress or faced an overwhelming obstacle at work or in your personal life—you've probably been advised to "let go" or "back off" or "release it." At first, such counterintuitive counsel may seem useless. But in fact, our research shows that "backing off" is far more effective for solving problems and generating creativity than we might ever have imagined.

To put this another way, you will recall that the fundamental principle that drives the Breakout Principle is the *ability to break away from prior mental and emotional patterns*. In other words, it's necessary to sever your consciousness completely from negative "mental tape recordings." This change of inner direction will automatically turn on an inner switch, which will enable you to generate regular Breakouts and peak experiences that can transform your entire life.

Although this basic trigger mechanism may appear deceptively simple, the process is actually rooted in complex biochemical interactions that occur throughout the brain and elsewhere in the body. As we'll see in the next chapter, for instance, my research suggests that the effective "letting go" of a problem triggers the internal release of nitric oxide, which has been linked to the production of neurotransmitters such as endorphins and dopamine. These neurotransmitters are chemical agents that are produced in brain cells and are sometimes called the body's "natural tranquilizers." They include morphinelike components that enhance feelings of well-being and help mask pain.

Also, the Breakout-related neurotransmitters are associated with positive mental and emotional states, as well as greater creativity, learning ability, memory, and productivity. Such molecular events can be tracked with highly sophisticated medical research tools, such as the fMRI brain-mapping procedures, and innovative techniques of blood analysis.

Even though the Breakout Principle biology is extremely complex, the process can be jump-started by one or more easy-to-understand triggering techniques. But what exactly is this Breakout trigger? How does it work? And most important of all, how can you activate your own internal triggers and open inner portals that may lead to significant personal benefits?

What Is the Breakout Trigger?

You'll recall from the previous chapter that the Breakout trigger is not some isolated event but, rather, constitutes the *second step* of a distinct four-stage process—(1) struggle, (2) release, (3) Breakout/peak experience, and finally (4) return to a "normal" but enhanced level of insight or performance. In fact, it's extremely difficult, if not impossible, to trigger a Breakout unless you go through that first step, which I've called the struggle.

To facilitate our discussion of the four-step Breakout process and to clarify the role of the trigger, I've reproduced below the diagram from the previous chapter, with a few minor revisions.

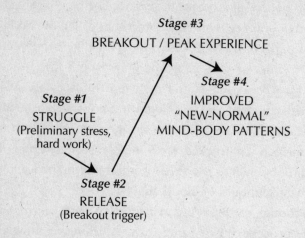

Stage #3
BREAKOUT / PEAK EXPERIENCE

Stage #4
IMPROVED
"NEW-NORMAL"
MIND-BODY PATTERNS

Stage #1
STRUGGLE
(Preliminary stress,
hard work)

Stage #2
RELEASE
(Breakout trigger)

In this revised diagram, you can see that the struggle and release stages now emphasize an important truth about the Breakout process:

A preliminary period of stress is necessary to trigger the benefits of a Breakout—but the stress should increase only to a certain point.

The struggle stage usually entails extensive preparation, hard work, or comprehensive training. As we saw in the previous chapter, this initial stage may begin voluntarily, as with the decision to embark on a difficult project at work. Or it may be initiated entirely involuntarily, as with a traumatic external event such as the death of a loved one or a national calamity. But regardless of how the process begins, significant stress will be involved in the early stages.

Easily understood illustrations of this phenomenon can be found in any field of endeavor—from business management . . . to scientific research . . . to writing fiction . . . to religious disciplines . . . to competitive sports.

Basketball can provide us with a simple illustration of how the Breakout trigger works. For an accomplished shooter to get "in the zone" in a game so that he begins to sink baskets practically every time he attempts a shot, he must first have countless preliminary workouts. Of course, even if a player has logged in extensive hours of practice, he or she may still have a bad game. But the struggle phase will put the player in a much stronger position to experience a Breakout—as the experience of Cathy demonstrates.

The "go-to" guard

Beginning when she was only nine years old on a community league team, Cathy, a shooting guard, spent many hours on the basketball court. By the time she reached high school, she had taken thousands of practice shots from every conceivable angle and position on the court. As the years went by, she gained a reputation as the best outside shooter on her middle school and junior varsity high school teams.

Finally, after working her way into a starting position on the varsity in her junior year, Cathy became the "go-to" player who was expected to score regularly in double figures and hit crucial shots that could make the difference between a win and a loss. At first, however, the pressure of this role didn't lead to superior performance.

In one of her early junior-year games, on orders from the coach, Cathy took thirteen shots from the field—and missed every one. She ended up with only three points, all of which came from the free throw line. To make matters worse, her team lost by a wide margin. Depressed by her performance, Cathy began to wonder if she had picked the right sport. The constant weight of responsibility for her team's performance caused her to tighten up even more in subsequent games, and she continued to shoot erratically.

About halfway into the season, a trusted adult adviser who was a teacher, helped Cathy put the situation in perspective. The teacher encouraged her to try to understand that "basketball is not life." The man approached the girl's problem with a two-part strategy. First, he emphasized that friendships, family relationships, and "higher personal values" were more important in the long run than a high school sport. Second, he suggested that Cathy focus on the performance of the entire team, rather than just on her own statistics.

"Remember there are always four other players out there on the court," he said. "Try thinking about them more than you think about yourself. Try forgetting yourself for once! By placing your importance in front of everything, you're getting in the way of a successful outcome."

This was a classic statement—rooted in a particular spiritual tradition—in the principle of "letting go," "backing off," or "releasing" the stress and pressure that accompany every preliminary struggle experience. So before Cathy would play in a game, she got into the habit of invoking what her teacher called an "altruistic moment." She consciously placed a mental image of each team member at the forefront of her mind and gently turned away from thoughts of herself.

Finally, Cathy's teacher did some periodic personal cheerleading to reinforce her newly emerging, outward-looking mind-set. For example, he would say, "Come on, Cathy! Let it go! Give it over! We both know basketball is just a game. It's the members of the team—those friends of yours out there on the court—who really count. So when you get out there, have fun, and see what happens!"

With such adult encouragement, Cathy's stress declined to manageable levels, and her shooting during games improved markedly. But paradoxically, the most powerful factor in her transformation seems to have been her new selfless attitude, which resulted in dramatically improved teamwork. She found that she was constantly being set up for easy shots because her teammates were now thinking of her almost as much as she was thinking of them.

In a regional play-off game during her senior year, Cathy turned in an almost unheard-of performance in basketball: a near perfect shooting game. She sank eight out of eight free throws and seven of eight field goals, including several three-pointers, and led her team to the next round of the state play-offs.

Throughout the game, Cathy sensed that she could do no wrong, either in her shooting or ball handling. Somehow, she was at one with the basket and with her teammates. In other words, she was playing "in the zone." Yet this peak experience had become possible only because she had successfully negotiated the struggle phase of her training and then "pulled" the Breakout trigger with an altruistic, "let go" attitude.

This story has a happy epilogue. The tape of this play-off game was a decisive factor in Cathy's being recruited by several college coaches, and she went on to play varsity basketball in college.

To sum up, then, years of sweat and struggle will typically precede a Breakout, which has the power to transform your life. Without preliminary hard work and stress, a superior performance in *any* field of achievement—and especially a *series* of superior performances—is unlikely. Sweat must always precede release.

But far from being just a restatement of some superficial self-help formula, the dynamic movement from struggle to Breakout is backed up by a long tradition of scientific research—which has implications that reach far beyond the sport of basketball.

The Science Behind the Struggle

In the annals of modern medicine, one of the earliest statements of how the struggle stage works came from Robert M. Yerkes and John D. Dodson, two researchers who worked in the Harvard Physiologic Laboratory almost one hundred years ago.

They demonstrated conclusively in 1908 that as stress increases, so do efficiency and performance. In other words, in the initial phase of any project, we need to prepare, work hard, and analyze to be maximally productive. But *the link between pressure and performance persists only to a certain point.* When stress becomes too great, performance and efficiency tend to decline, the Harvard researchers discovered.

Most of us have experienced this "backfire" quality of stress when such factors as excessive hard work, anxiety, or insomnia begin to cut significantly into the potential for superior achievement. This often-overlooked Yerkes-Dodson Law can be expressed in the following diagram:

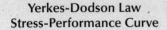

Yerkes-Dodson Law
Stress-Performance Curve

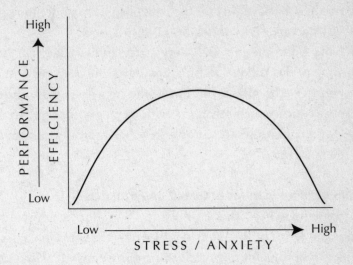

For years, scientists have been intrigued by the simple yet profound conclusions of Yerkes and Dodson. For example, Indian researchers, testing the relationship between menstrual stress and decline in performance on intelligence tests, affirmed the basic operation of the Yerkes-Dodson findings (*Psychological Reports* 78 [1996]: 51–58). Moreover, a Swedish study explored the application of the Yerkes-Dodson Law to impairment of memory in eyewitnesses who are under excessive stress (*Psychological Bulletin* 112 [1992]: 284–309).

Over the years, I have also made some contributions to the Yerkes-Dodson concept, especially as the law applies to business leaders. For example, in an article I coauthored in the *Harvard Business Review* with Robert L. Allen, former executive director of the Henry P. Kendall Foundation, we used the Yerkes-Dodson Law as a springboard to discuss ways by which executives could balance stress to achieve maximum productivity in a corporate setting. Our basic message was that those under significant stress at work must back off before the stress begins to undermine productivity and creativity (*HBR* 58 [1980]: 86–92).

In the end, the person who successfully balances stress according to the Yerkes-Dodson Law will be in a strong position to experience a Breakout. But those who hope to trigger a Breakout must educate themselves, as with any new concept, so that they can recognize the circumstances that typically accompany this phenomenon.

Becoming more alert for Breakout opportunities

I sometimes hear this complaint: "I'm not accustomed to thinking in terms of Breakouts—so I worry that I may be missing chances to become more creative or improve myself. How can I take better advantage of my Breakout possibilities?"

Plunkitt of Tammany Hall once said, "I seen my opportunities and I took 'em!" A similar mind-set will work with Breakouts if you can condition yourself to recognize and exploit situations during the "struggle" phase that have the potential to trigger these experiences. One way to become more alert is to compile your own personal checklist of situations or problems that may lend themselves to a Breakout response. For example, we immediately begin to look for a Breakout solution in situations where the person:

- Confronts a particularly knotty problem at work— particularly one that demands a creative or out-of-the- box solution.
- Meets a seemingly insurmountable challenge in family or personal life.

- Encounters a person who is especially hard to get along with.
- Wrestles with a spiritual issue.
- Faces any situation that heightens anxiety.

In considering potential Breakout scenarios, we advise dividing the possibilities into one of two types of situations, which were mentioned earlier:

1. A struggle that begins *voluntarily* with an act of the will.
2. A struggle that is *imposed involuntarily,* usually by some outside event.

When the Breakout process begins in a mostly voluntary way—such as in business management, scientific research, or serious athletic competition—you must usually *decide at the outset to put in a significant amount of preliminary hard work and training.* In other words, it will take a firm prior commitment and solid preparation before you can hope to build a platform from which a Breakout can occur. Conversely, if you don't work and train sufficiently, a Breakout will probably never happen.

But sometimes—such as with a family tragedy, the loss of a job, a spiritual crisis, or a community disaster—the initial stress may be thrust upon you. In such situations, you don't have a choice whether to deal with a problem. Circumstances have generated turmoil and angst.

But even such involuntary stress can lead to the trigger of a Breakout—especially Breakouts that lead to profound self-awareness. As the following illustration shows, you can respond to the unwanted pressure in a way that increases your chances of triggering a Breakout and an accompanying resolution of the problem.

Triumph over national tragedy

In the wake of the horrific terrorist attacks on New York City and Washington, D.C., on September 11, 2001, Chuck, a former New Yorker whom I have known for many years, was beset by inner turmoil. Because he was in touch with many friends in Manhattan who were dealing with the disaster, he found he had trouble focusing on his work or sleeping at night. Also, he worried about the future of the American economy and political stability.

As Chuck contacted his New York acquaintances, he found many of them far more numbed, grief-stricken, and disoriented than himself. To varying degrees, they were experiencing post-traumatic stress disorder, which may follow exposure to war, a serious crime, or other physical attack.

Some wrestled constantly with their fears that the terrorists might strike again. Others were afraid to return to their offices in other Manhattan skyscrapers. Still others, in their efforts to explain events in a comforting way to their frightened children, became frustrated as they dug deeply into their spiritual and emotional resources for answers. They sometimes found that these reservoirs of strength were much shallower than they had ever suspected.

Worried about the anguish of his friends and the future of American society, Chuck felt immobilized for days after the disaster. Even though he now lived far away from New York City, he periodically lapsed into tears for no obvious reason—a probable sign that he was grieving. But then two experiences helped stabilize his emotions by moving him into the Breakout process.

The first Breakout occurred after a particularly intense phone conversation with a friend in Manhattan who had lost a business associate in the World Trade Center collapse. That discussion, plus exposure to ongoing television reports about the disaster, left Chuck wide-eyed on his bed that night, with anxious thoughts rushing through his mind.

But then he remembered a familiar passage from the Psalms that he had always found comforting—"The Lord is my shepherd . . ." (Psalm 23). Following advice I had given him years before, he began to repeat this phrase silently over and over to himself. The comforting repetition of the passage soon broke Chuck's train of worried thoughts, and he drifted off to sleep. The next morning, he felt more at peace and sensed he had somehow tapped into spiritual resources that were stabilizing his emotions and enabling him to deal with the tragedy.

To maintain his more tranquil feelings of self-awareness (see Chapter 6 on the "peak experience" of self-awareness), Chuck continued to repeat the line from Psalm 23 regularly during the day. But he still remained concerned and confused about what the terrorist attacks meant for the future of American society and the economy.

In the midst of one of these confused periods, an unexpected event—President George W. Bush's address to a joint session of Congress and the nation on September 20, 2001—triggered another important inner change in Chuck. Because Chuck had a strong sense that a higher, divine power was at work in the crisis, several sections in the president's speech resonated with him, almost as a liturgical reading might provide "comforting words" in a religious service:

- "I ask you to live your lives and hug your children. I know many citizens have fears tonight and I ask you to be calm and resolute, even in the face of a continuing threat."
- "Please continue praying for the victims of terror and their families, for those in uniform and for our great

country. Prayer has comforted us in sorrow and will help strengthen us for the journey ahead."

- "Even grief recedes with time and grace."
- "The course of this conflict is not known, yet its outcome is certain. Freedom and fear, justice and cruelty, have always been at war. And we know that God is not neutral between them."

After the speech, Chuck felt a peculiar inner comfort. He sensed that even though the future might be uncertain, forces were at work that had the power to resolve the crisis. In effect, the speech of a political leader, communicated over his television set, had severed prior negative thought patterns and produced another Breakout.

Caution: In Chuck's situation, as well as in other experiences that incorporate a spiritual dimension, I want to make this clear: I am in no way attempting to minimize the possible presence or operation of some force outside the individual— a divine force, if you will. As scientists, we are limited in what we can measure. I *do* know from brain-mapping and other physiologic tests that a biological mechanism is involved in these Breakouts. But I would *never* deny that a scientifically unmeasurable transcendent force may also be at work in bringing about certain beneficial changes.

As you can see from Chuck's experiences, Breakouts that have the power to move you through life's rough spots can be triggered in a variety of unexpected ways. In fact, in light of ongoing recent research, I now realize that, so long as the basic, underlying biochemical release mechanisms are engaged, literally *countless* triggers can produce Breakouts. These Breakouts can, in turn, open inner doors to life-changing peak experiences, such as the increasing sense of inner stability and self-awareness that Chuck discovered. Now, let's explore how you might select a trigger that will best suit your problem and personality.

Selecting Your Trigger

Although it's impossible to draw up an exhaustive list of every activity or setting that may produce a Breakout, each of the triggers mentioned below has worked well for at least some individuals. In other words, they represent categories that have demonstrated the power to stimulate the biological changes commonly associated with Breakouts and peak experiences.

As you read through these options, stop at each one and ask: Is it possible that this approach, or something like this approach, would work for me?

Also, arrange to have a pen and paper, or better yet—a personal journal—close at hand. When you are reminded of a particular activity or event in your life that's similar to the one listed, jot the memory down for later reference. From now on, you'll be compiling data that you'll use to formulate your personal Breakout strategy. In the end, you'll discard much of what you record, but a few of your thoughts in the next few minutes—perhaps just one or two—may very well constitute your first step toward a Breakout.

Above all, remember your ultimate objective!
What you're trying to do in these pages is to gather information and formulate guidelines that can revolutionize your life.

You're searching both for the secret to transforming your life fundamentally, and also for the inner staying power that will render that transformation permanent.

Furthermore, as you begin to seek the release mechanism that will automatically throw an inner Breakout switch, you are embarking on the first, or "struggle," phase of this personal experiment. That is, you are studying, thinking, and analyzing— laying the necessary groundwork so that step two can occur. When the time is right, you'll "back off" and begin to trigger important Breakouts in your life.

Finally, don't worry about coming up with definitive answers at this point about exactly what trigger or triggers to employ. Your objective right now is simply to begin remembering and evaluating the events and experiences in your life that *may* have the potential to trigger a Breakout. This exercise will firmly fix in your mind some practical tools you can use to switch on this experience.

Now here are some of the broad categories of activities or interests that can trigger a Breakout in your life—and some illustrations of specific activities that may utilize that trigger. Any of these could break prior mental patterns and lay the groundwork for a Breakout.

Spiritual Triggers

- Prayer, as defined by your religious tradition
- Meditation, as understood by your tradition
- Contemplation, as understood by your tradition
- "Eastern" triggers, such as tai chi, chi gong, or yoga
- Repeating for several minutes any positive or meaningful word or phrase
- Sitting quietly by yourself or with a group in a chapel or house of worship

MUSICAL TRIGGERS

- Listening to your favorite music
- Listening to Mozart or Bach, even if you're not used to the experience
- Playing or singing music with which you are familiar

CULTURAL TRIGGERS

- Viewing a work of art, such as a painting or a sculpture
- Reading or listening to poetry or a particularly stirring speech or prose passage
- Sitting quietly in a tranquil building or other architectural space

WATER-RELATED TRIGGERS

- Taking a long shower
- Soaking in a bathtub or hot tub
- Sitting or floating in a quiet swimming pool or other water

REST-ROOM TRIGGERS

- Shaving
- Putting on makeup
- Grooming with a repetitive routine

ATHLETIC TRIGGERS

- Walking, jogging, bicycling, or performing any other repetitive exercise for at least fifteen minutes
- Becoming absorbed *visually* in a sport—such as by focusing intently on a tennis ball or a basketball, or watching closely the players' movements on the court or field without thinking analytically about it

- Combining repetitive mental exercises, such as prayer or meditation, with sports characterized by irregular movements, such as tennis (e.g., counting strings on a tennis racket or meditating silently between points)
- Golfing alone
- Repetitive practice (e.g., golfing range, batting cage)

REPETITIVE-MOVEMENT TRIGGERS

- Needlepoint (see the example of Jason in the previous chapter)
- Regular, conscious breathing
- Slowly beating a drum

NATURE TRIGGERS

- Sitting quietly in a garden
- Gazing over a seascape or a mountain range
- Strolling silently through the woods
- Fishing

HOUSEWORK-YARDWORK TRIGGERS

- Doing the dishes
- Gardening
- Doing repair work around the house or apartment
- Cooking
- Folding laundry

SURRENDER TRIGGERS

- Relinquishing control over a personal or a job problem
- Imagining and accepting a "worst-case scenario"—or the worst possible thing that could happen to you in the circumstances

Restaurant Triggers

- Eating at a quiet restaurant, either alone or with one other person with whom you feel entirely comfortable

Animal/Pet Triggers

- Sitting quietly with your pet
- Humming to, speaking quietly to, or otherwise communicating with or rubbing a calm animal
- Observing fish in an aquarium

Altruistic Triggers

- Becoming involved in some significant way in helping others
- Turning from a focus on yourself and your problem to the responses and needs of your companions or coworkers (see the example of Cathy above)

Brainstorming Triggers

- Sharing ideas with an occupational or volunteer group about a common problem
- Free-associating with one or more family members or friends about a common concern
- Forming and relying on a Breakout Network to solve certain problems at work or in volunteer activities (see below)

At first blush, these activities may seem totally different from one another. In fact, they all have one major factor in common: *the power to sever prior mental patterns*—and that's what the Breakout trigger is all about. In most cases, it's best to "pull the trigger" alone. But as the final example above suggests, in some circumstances the most effective Breakouts result from a team effort—or what I call Breakout Networks.

A Preliminary Word About Breakout Networks

Although much of this book focuses on the application of the Breakout concept to the individual, groups can also play a broad and powerful role through a Breakout Network.

These networks—which typically involve three to eight participants—may work in business and volunteer organizations, as well as in families and other intimate personal relationships. In these small groups, several people work and think together to break prior unproductive thought patterns. This joint process sets the stage to trigger new ideas and insights in individuals or groups that can provide broad benefits to all.

Later chapters will deal in more detail with the operation of these Breakout Networks. In the meantime, to understand the variety of ways that these networks can work, consider this summary of possibilities:

- A "moonshine shop"—or freewheeling idea-and-innovation team—may work in unconventional ways at odd hours to create new possibilities in a business organization.
- A college admissions committee may go for a walk together and, during the outing, find a new, more productive way of evaluating prospective students.
- A church or synagogue board may use a spiritual retreat to break administrative logjams.
- A dysfunctional or troubled family may work through

serious interpersonal problems while relaxing on a quiet beach.

- A husband and wife on the verge of divorce may repair their marriage by putting aside all talk and spending a weekend at a resort.

Those who succeed in learning to break prior negative thought patterns, either individually or in groups, and who understand the principles of the Breakout trigger, are more likely to move automatically into a life-transforming peak experience. When this happens, certain biochemical responses begin to occur in the body—including responses that involve what I call the "spirit" of peak experience.

3

The "Spirit" of Peak Experience

Many times, those who have a dramatic creative insight, a deep spiritual transformation, or some other peak experience find that they have great difficulty describing the event—and rightly so.

For one thing, the subjective impact is often ineffable: Words cannot quite encompass the extreme exuberance and excitement surrounding the occurrences. Or as T. S. Eliot put it in his *Four Quartets:*

> . . . *Words strain,*
> *Crack and sometimes break under the burden,*
> *Under the tension, slip, slide, perish,*
> *Decay with imprecision, will not stay in place,*
> *Will not stay still.* . . .

Another problem in finding the right words is that our conscious, subjective responses during a brilliant flash of insight—or a "peak experience"—arise out of a highly complex, biologically embedded network of biochemical and physiological interactions, which, in the past, scientists have been unable to understand. Now, however, thanks to research related to the Breakout, we are moving into a scientific era that promises to unveil the mysteries of the peak experience.

To illustrate how the Breakout biology works, let's consider for a moment the classic ancient prototype for the "eureka event"—the apocryphal story involving the Greek philosopher and mathematician Archimedes.

Interpreting the First Eureka Event

By some accounts, Hieron II, the king of Syracuse in Sicily in the third century B.C., asked Archimedes to determine the relative amounts of gold and silver in a decorative wreath.

Archimedes thought hard about the issue and even carried the wreath into his bath. While he sat and contemplated the headpiece for a while in the water, the answer finally came to him. He supposedly sprang out of the water, cried *"Heurēka!"* (or more popularly in English, "Eureka!"), which means "I have found it!" Then he streaked naked through the streets of Syracuse to broadcast his insight.

Although the actual facts may be shrouded in legend, many still credit Archimedes with discovering the method for finding the proportion of gold and silver in an item by weighing it in water. But what exactly occurred *inside his mind* to produce this insight? Although Archimedes certainly didn't understand the specific biological interactions that gave birth to his tremendous idea, we are now getting glimmers of an answer.

This ancient tale has all the earmarks of a classic Breakout process. First, Archimedes was confronted with a difficult problem and struggled to find the answer. Then, when he had gone as far as he could with his rational analysis, he moved to the second stage: he "released" the matter by relaxing in a tub of water. As we saw in the previous chapter, a shower or bath may be a powerful setting for triggering a Breakout.

In fact, as Archimedes soaked away in his tub and allowed his previous thought patterns to drain away, a Breakout did occur. Furthermore, if the details of the legend are to be believed, the experience was so overwhelming that he could signal his insight only with a brief, exuberant shout—the famous "Eureka!"

If Archimedes had understood as much as we now do about what was happening inside his body and brain, he would probably have had a great deal more to say—and a multitude of questions to ask. I'm sure he would have wanted to explore the myriad molecules and chemicals that his neural circuits released during his Breakouts. He would have marveled at the changes in his brain that showed up during brain-mapping tests.

Yet I'm also sure he would have been surprised to learn that his earth-changing scientific insights might ultimately have been traced back to his exceptional ability to trigger the release of simple puffs of a special gas in his blood vessels—a gas that we now call nitric oxide.

Puffs of Insight

It seems that almost anywhere you look these days in the scholarly or popular scientific literature, you are likely to run into nitric oxide (chemical designation: NO). The Breakout phenomenon is just the latest entry in a long line of NO highlights and triumphs.

For example, in the summer of 2001, news organizations reported that researchers at Tufts University and Brigham and Women's Hospital in Boston had discovered that nitric oxide switches on the glowing light emitted by fireflies (*New York Times,* July 3, 2001, D4; *Boston Globe,* June 29, 2001, A1).

At the other end of the spectrum, researchers in artificial intelligence at the University of Sussex in Great Britain have been exploring ways to develop "virtual nitric-oxide gas" computer nets in robots so that they can "think" more quickly and efficiently when confronted with new situations. The British scientists have programmed the computers in robots to simulate the action of the human brain's nitric oxide. The ultimate objective is to enable robots to grow and develop on their own, and ultimately to become autonomous (University of Sussex media release, December 21, 1998, www.sussex.ac.uk/press_office/media/media42; and *BusinessWeek,* October 8, 2001, 99).

But the most important work of NO occurs in the human body and brain. As an unusually small molecule, NO is not limited by many of the rules that control most biochemical interactions in our systems. In effect, nitric oxide is a highly active oxygen "radical" that serves as a "gaseous diffusable modulator."

In lay terms, NO consists of message-carrying "puffs" of gas that course through the entire body and central nervous system. Certain of these messages move back and forth in the brain through the medium of the gas, even though the brain's neurons may not be linked physically or electrically to one another.

This versatile NO molecule can provide an incredibly wide range of health benefits for you and your family. For example, various studies suggest that nitric oxide may:

- Enhance memory and learning by functioning as a neurotransmitter between synapses in the brain. In effect, the NO acts as a "modulatory transmitter" to help other neurotransmitters in the brain operate more efficiently.
- Enhance the output of neurotransmitters such as dopamine and the endorphins, which promote a sense of well-being and may play a role in a number of peak physical experiences. These include the "runner's high" and the sense of being "in the zone" during high-level athletic competition, musical performance, speaking engagements, and other demanding activities. Also, dopamine has been linked to many health benefits, such as improvements in Parkinson's disease patients.
- Regulate blood flow throughout the body.
- Improve the impact of estrogen replacement therapy, especially in treating depression in postmenopausal women.
- Help newborn babies overcome pulmonary (lung-related) hypertension.
- Serve as a therapy for a deficiency of oxygen to the brain (ischemia) that is related to stroke.
- Widen (vasodilate) blood vessels to increase blood flow to the heart—an especially important function after coronary bypass surgery.

- Counter septic shock (serious bacterial infection).
- Relieve impotence.
- Bolster the immune system.
- Provide the biochemical foundation for the relaxation response and the placebo effect—phenomena that we will explore in some detail below.

But these benefits just begin to describe the potential of this powerful natural gas. In fact, as suggested in research reviews I've published with other scientists, the whole NO mechanism may somehow be connected with what we think of as the "mind."

A Mind-NO Connection?

The mind, which philosophers and scientists have been trying to define for centuries, is an elusive entity that refers to the unifying consciousness that enables us to think through, control, and regulate the many functions that our brains perform every second of every day. Without such integration and control, we couldn't evaluate and cope with complex problems, make decisions that we expect to have an impact on the future, or otherwise perform our distinctly human mental and volitional functions.

Of course, we may never fully understand what the mind really is. In the end, we may even conclude that the mind involves qualities or forces that transcend the physical brain. But still, there seems little question that the mind is rooted at least in part in the biochemistry and physiology of the brain. And increasingly, the evidence points to nitric oxide as an important, integrating factor in the operation of some of our highest mental operations, including the Breakout.

To understand the precise linkages between the Breakout and its underlying biochemistry and physiology, it will be helpful to retrace in more detail my own scientific odyssey—which began with my exploration of the relaxation response and the placebo effect.

A Personal Odyssey

My journey toward an understanding of the Breakout mechanism began nearly three decades ago, when my research at the Harvard Medical School identified a physiological response that was characterized by decreased metabolism, heart rate, blood pressure, and rate of breathing (*Psychiatry* 37 [1974]: 37–46).

This phenomenon, which came to be known as the relaxation response, is the opposite of the stress, or fight-or-flight, response, which is accompanied by excess production of such stress-hormone secretions as epinephrine (adrenaline), norepinephrine (noradrenaline), and cortisol. The potentially destructive stress response typically occurs *automatically* when an outside stressor—such as pressure at work, fear, or anxiety—causes the body and brain to go on full alert. Animals and humans share this stress-response characteristic.

The relaxation response, in contrast, is peculiarly human in that it tends to arise from a specific *act of volition* or a *conscious relaxation strategy*. For example, the individual may decide to focus on the cadence of footfalls during running. Or she may engage in some other repetitive or mentally absorbing activity, such as prayer, meditation, yoga, tai chi, chi gong, or progressive muscle relaxation.

Although I believed my discovery of the relaxation response

was potentially significant, the reaction in both the scientific community and the general public took me entirely by surprise. My book based on the findings, *The Relaxation Response,* became the top nonfiction bestseller of 1975. More recently, the winter 2000 issue of the *Harvard Medical Alumni Bulletin* described my work as the latest in a century-long research trend at Harvard, featuring such figures as Oliver Wendell Holmes, William James, Walter Cannon, and A. Clifford Barger. Soon, practical programs based on the relaxation response sprang up to enable patients to deal with various forms of stress and related problems, including insomnia, hypertension, headaches, backaches, and a host of other complaints.

From the relaxation response to the placebo effect

But even as others were recognizing my work and using it to improve the health of patients around the world, I sensed increasingly that the relaxation response was just one piece of a much broader phenomenon. In particular, both my research and my clinical experience with individual patients had convinced me that there was a strong link between the relaxation response and deep personal belief.

Often in medical research, the power of belief has been limited to what has sometimes derisively been called the placebo effect. The term *placebo,* which is the Latin word meaning "I shall please," has been associated with dummy or sugar pills. If the patient believes that these inert treatments will work, the result may be improvement in certain health problems, at least for a time. In fact, in one review I did of studies involving the placebo effect, I found that placebos resulted in significant improvement in more than two-thirds of patients with angina pectoris (chest pains associated with lack of oxygen in the heart), asthma, herpes simplex, and duodenal ulcers (*New England Journal of Medicine* 300 [1979]: 1424–29).

Some scientists have suggested that the placebo effect is a figment of the imagination—that it really doesn't exist—but such a conclusion flies in the face of clear medical evidence. Consistently, such studies ignore the complete scientific definition of the placebo, which can be stated this way:

The *placebo effect* refers to the healing power of belief, which consists of three components: (1) the belief of the patient or person being healed; (2) the belief by the physician or healer; and (3) the positive and trusting relationship between the patient and the healer.

If all three of these components are in place, healing or at least significant improvement in a health condition is much more likely to occur. To avoid any misunderstanding, I have proposed that this comprehensive definition of the placebo effect be renamed *remembered wellness*—or the positive memory of how good health feels.

But as my research proceeded, I continued to wrestle with a fundamental question: What connection, if any, might there be between the placebo effect and the relaxation response?

In a number of my studies, I noticed that many people were able to establish a beneficial connection between the relaxation response and the placebo effect. For example, I frequently encountered people who were suffering from hypertension (high blood pressure) or complaining of insomnia or various aches and pains. Following our scientifically established protocols, I would recommend that they evoke the relaxation response with the standard technique, which was to assume a comfortable sitting position, close their eyes, and repeat silently on the outbreath a neutral word, such as *one,* for a ten-to-twenty-minute period. They were instructed to turn away from or gently ignore any extraneous thoughts that might interrupt their inner repetition.

Usually, the conditions of these patients would improve temporarily, but sometimes they failed to comply with the program after a few sessions. As a result, they would relapse into their original problem or complaint. So I suggested increasingly that instead of just repeating a neutral word, the patient should use a word or phrase that was rooted in his or her belief system. A Jewish person might choose to repeat *shalom* (peace), for instance, while a Christian might pick *Jesus loves me.*

Overall compliance among many patients clearly got better with this approach. Also, I noticed that plugging in belief-based words resulted in a greater *degree* of individual improvement. One African-American patient, for instance, showed much faster stress-reduction benefits, including lower blood pressure and heart rate, when she repeated phrases with deep, positive roots from her faith background, such as *Lord have mercy,* and *precious Lord.* In other words, the relaxation response and her human belief system seemed to be working together to magnify the beneficial impact on her health.

Even more exciting, I began to observe that not only was the health of my patients getting better, but some of them were also enjoying other benefits, such as greater productivity and creativity at work. Soon, I suggested that the athletes among my patients try combining their beliefs with their relaxation-response technique while on the court or playing field. Many reported that with this method it was much easier to get rid of debilitating anxiety or even to enter the "zone," where they felt they could do no wrong in pursuing their sport.

A scientific "tiger's tail"?

As I mulled over this evidence, which was a combination of anecdotal observation and controlled scientific research, I became convinced that I truly had a scientific "tiger by the tail." I seemed to have stumbled upon a biological mechanism that somehow encompassed the dynamics of human belief, the creative process, the essence of physical and mental performance, and even spiritual experience.

Yet to take the next step and really nail down these observations scientifically, I knew that I needed to join forces with experts from other disciplines. As a cardiologist and researcher specializing in the relaxation response and the placebo effect, I was confident I could oversee significant aspects of many projects. But to shift my focus to the operation of the brain, biochemical interactions, and other highly specialized areas of investigation, I clearly needed help. As a result, I entered into ongoing collaborations with leading researchers in neuroscience, brain-mapping, and biochemistry.

On one front, I embarked on an exploration of the biochemical and molecular foundations of the relaxation response and the placebo effect with the molecular chemist George B. Stefano and the psychiatric researcher Gregory L. Fricchione. One of the first and most important breakthroughs in our collaboration was an extensive review study that linked the body's output of nitric oxide to both the placebo effect and the relaxation response.

Our work culminated in a 2001 review article in *Brain Research Reviews* (35, 1–19), which one peer referee called a "seminal work" and "brilliant." Another referee said that our study contained concepts of "monumental significance" with "enormous" potential.

To understand what we proposed—and the significance of our understanding for the Breakout Principle mechanism—join me now in a brief "biochemical tour" of the human system. This journey should suggest what happens inside your own body and brain as nitric oxide is released and peak experiences occur.

The Incredible NO Scenario

As you proceed through a Breakout Principle scenario, the outward manifestations you can observe and feel are dramatic. But if you could somehow shrink to the size of a molecule and enter your own brain and bloodstream, you might think that you had entered a futuristic chemical lab. The hidden biochemical fireworks going on in your body closely track the conscious, four-stage Breakout sequence that we have already discussed. Here is a simplified version of the most likely biological scenario:

Stage One: Stress hormones increase during the struggle phase

At the outset, various factors, such as outside pressure, hard work, analytical thinking, or intense training, will put you under stress. At this stage, fight-or-flight hormones related to the stress response, such as epinephrine (adrenaline) and norepinephrine (noradrenaline), flood into your system from the adrenal glands, situated above the kidneys. Your blood vessels constrict, your blood pressure often goes up, your heart rate increases, and other changes identified with the fight-or-flight response occur.

These high-octane secretions raise your body and mind to a

high level of readiness and alert—a state that was absolutely essential when our prehistoric hunter-gatherer ancestors were on guard against predators. Furthermore, these same responses are necessary even in our more civilized society for top-level performance, creativity, or other peak experiences.

Remember the Yerkes-Dodson Law: Stress *must* increase to a certain point if you hope to achieve your maximum potential. But after that "certain point," the stress hormones become counterproductive or even dangerous.

Stage Two: Pulling the Breakout trigger releases body chemicals that counter the stress hormones

When you've wrung the maximum benefit from the "good" stress that your body has generated, you must escape the influx of "bad" stress. Otherwise the overflow of norepinephrine and other fight-or-flight hormones will drag you down into mediocre performance and perhaps even damage your health or kill you.

How can you tell when you've reached the top of the Yerkes-Dodson bell curve—and stress has begun to work against you? An effective subjective test is an inner shift from feeling a "good edge" and forward momentum in your work or thinking, to sensing that the pressure is beginning to work against you. Warning signs may include excessive anxiety or fearfulness, anger, a tendency to cry, frustration, boredom, forgetfulness, a block on creativity, or physical symptoms such as headaches, backaches, or insomnia.

To make your escape from this downward spiral into destructive stress, you can "back off," "let go," or "release" the pressure that is bearing down on you by switching on the Breakout mechanism. As we have seen, that may mean soaking in a tub of water, taking a walk in the woods, listening to a Bach concerto, or retreating for some solitary prayer. In every case, pulling the Breakout trigger effectively requires at least one of the following three approaches. Each of these has the power to break prior patterns of thought, and each requires at least ten minutes and preferably twenty minutes of your time:

1. Do or think something that is firmly rooted in your belief system (i.e., the placebo effect, broadly understood). You might spend some time in your chosen house of worship pursuing activities or disciplines linked to your faith. For example, you might contemplate some religious principle or figure, listen to music, or focus on a liturgical reading. Or if you are a committed nature lover, you might sit or wander in a soothing natural setting, such as in the woods or at the seashore.

2. Participate in some repetitive activity (i.e., evoke the relaxation response). This may mean jogging, walking, listening to your favorite music, or repeating an uplifting phrase, such as a snippet of poetry.

3. Combine (1) and (2) in some fashion—such as by reciting a repetitive prayer or repeating a deeply held philosophical belief as you jog.

Pulling the Breakout trigger in any of these ways will sever past patterns of thought and emotion. At the same time, a series of helpful biochemical "explosions" will begin to bubble up inside your body and brain.

First of all, according to our conclusions in the *Brain Research Reviews* article, those puffs of nitric oxide that we've been talking about begin to increase. As the NO gas permeates your brain and body, levels of the stress hormone norepinephrine increase briefly.

But then the NO counteracts the norepinephrine and other stress secretions. Simultaneously, as the NO puffs billow forth in the brain and body, the brain releases calming neurotransmitters, or "mental message-carriers," such as dopamine and endorphins. As a result of these secretions, the blood vessels dilate or open up, the heart rate decreases, the stress response fades, and inner tranquillity takes over.

Endorphins, which are soothing, pain-reducing, morphine-like secretions, have been associated with the experience known as the runner's high. When an experienced runner exercises for a few minutes, these endorphins begin to provide a highly pleasurable sensation. Later in the run, the impact may become so intense that the athlete actually begins to enter a mystical state.

Dopamine, another neurotransmitter associated with nitric oxide, has been linked to feelings of well-being and happiness, as well as to improvement in a number of medical conditions such as Parkinson's disease. Furthermore, a possible connection with the Breakout mechanism—specifically with the placebo effect— emerged in an investigation published in the August 1, 2001, issue of *Science* (1164–66).

Researcher Raúl de la Fuente-Fernández of the University of British Columbia and several colleagues, using positron-emission tomography (PET) with Parkinson's patients, compared the effect of a placebo medication with normal drugs used to treat the disease. In the PET technique, the patient is placed in a chamberlike device that can identify subatomic particles (positrons) emitted by the brain. The PET scanner then arranges these emissions into a computer picture that shows blood flow in the brain.

These researchers found that the placebo provided benefits

comparable to those of therapeutic doses of levodopa or apo-morphine, which are the common medications used to treat Parkinson's disease. In fact, they concluded that in some patients, *most* of the benefits from the active drug might be caused by the placebo effect.

Finally, the investigators determined that the operation of the placebo effect in these patients was linked to the release of dopamine. In other words, human belief—including the *expectations* for healing fostered by such belief—had the power to release significant quantities of the powerful dopamine neuro-transmitter, which could then improve the condition of Parkin-son's patients.

In addition to dopamine and endorphins, our ongoing research suggests that the NO-related "cast of biochemical characters" includes many other players. For example, we have found that mood-enhancing, antibacterial, and immunity-bolstering mole-cules, such as enkelytin, increase in the body as the human belief system and the relaxation response go into operation.

In other words, when you trigger a Breakout and nitric oxide begins to increase in your body, you can expect an incredibly wide range of physical and psychological benefits. These include greater protection from various diseases, an increased sense of well-being, and faster and more complete recovery from stress-related physical or emotional complaints. Furthermore, these benefits not only begin when you pull the trigger, but also con-tinue throughout the entire Breakout process.

Stage Three: The Breakout paves the way for a peak experience

After the many biochemical events associated with a Breakout have occurred, the way will be paved for you to undergo one or more of the "peak experiences" discussed in Part II. This is because the release of nitric oxide, positive neurotransmitters, and other biochemicals has created an inner platform where creativity, superior performance, and profound spirituality can thrive.

Of course, there is no guarantee that a peak experience will follow every time you engage your personal belief system or the physiologic changes we call the relaxation response. But at least the stage has been set for dramatic, stress-relieving Breakouts, and the likelihood of your benefiting from some life-changing insight or new performance plateau will greatly increase.

Stage Four: Returning to an improved, "new-normal" mind-body pattern

Typically after each Breakout and peak experience, you return to an ongoing higher level of achievement and insight than before the Breakout occurred. The difference between the former and the latter states may not be so clear after just one Breakout. But after multiple Breakouts, you'll find your typical performance tends to stay well above the pre-Breakout level.

There are several reasons for this "new-normal" state, which is characterized by greater staying power at an improved level of performance. In the first place, the more Breakouts you trigger, the more expert you will become in achieving and controlling them. The Breakout is a *learned skill,* which requires regular practice in a variety of circumstances.

You will also be able to maintain the new-normal state because of the *force of habit.* The more you trigger Breakouts, the more "natural" it will seem to use them when you need greater creativity, new insights at work, greater productivity, or stress reduction. Anything that becomes a part of your daily routine is more likely to become a long-term part of your life.

Furthermore, continuing high levels of performance become possible because the Breakout mechanism *becomes firmly rooted in your personal belief system.* This is a brand of belief built on personal experience. As you succeed time after time with a Breakout, you'll find that your confidence in yourself and your potential begins to soar. You actually begin to *expect* ongoing improvement.

Finally, your increased use of the Breakout in your new-normal state should *magnify the biological benefits,* including the ongoing release of neurotransmitters, and those extra "puffs" of nitric oxide.

A "Nitric Oxide Lift" for a Marketing Executive?

A marketing executive was having problems making effective presentations to a management group at work, largely because of her lack of confidence in her communications skills. So at our suggestion, she decided to employ the Breakout as she prepared one presentation. Specifically, she studied, analyzed, and thought intensely for several hours. Or in Breakout terms, she immersed herself in the struggle stage. Then she left the office and headed for the local art museum.

From her Breakout instruction, she knew that it was now necessary to sever her current mind-set from her prior linear, analytical thought patterns. As she walked, she actually began to picture the nitric oxide increasing throughout her cells, like some beneficent creative spirit. Soon, her mind began to disengage from her work concerns, and she experienced a total release from her prior thought patterns as she sat in front of one of her favorite paintings, a Picasso, and contemplated the artwork for about fifteen minutes.

Before long, the executive's thinking returned to her marketing presentation. But this time, undoubtedly as a result of the effects of the *real* nitric oxide and neurotransmitters she had been generating, she regarded the challenge from an entirely different perspective. She saw that she had been trying to cover too many topics and had failed to hone in on the one overriding concept she wanted to get across to the group. So she reorganized her presentation with great confidence around that single central idea.

After she had spoken to the group the next morning, she was praised for giving not only her best oral report, but also one of the best her managers had ever heard. As a result, her belief in herself increased dramatically and gave her more confidence when she made her next presentation. In effect, the biochemical resources she had tapped into in the first Breakout became even more accessible in the next.

Of course, many of us have had such experiences. But too often we fail to see that we can create the circumstances where these Breakouts can occur regularly in our lives. In the past, we have simply failed to understand that an underlying biological mechanism makes possible such ongoing, dramatic improvements in individual performance, creativity, and personal insights.

This nitric oxide scenario should provide some idea of what goes on deep in the brain and blood vessels of an Archimedes or an Einstein, as well as in a top athlete, business leader, or artist who is experiencing a Breakout. Furthermore, the science of the Breakout may even help us understand more fully what happens inside the body during a spiritual experience.

A Biology of the Spirit?

The weight of scientific research now shows that spiritual experiences arising out of deep faith and religious discipline—including meditation, prayer, and regular worship—may involve biological mechanisms similar to those associated with the runner's high, the artist's creativity, the businessperson's insight, or the scientist's "Eureka!"

In some ways, our recent scientific research into nitric oxide carries us full circle, back to some of the earliest theological descriptions of how spiritual peak experiences occur. For example, the Hebrew and Greek terms used to describe the working of God's Spirit in both the Old and New Testaments provide us with some rather suggestive spiritual analogues to proven biological processes.

Just as nitric oxide seems to be a kind of internal "wind" that facilitates many of our most complex and creative mental processes, as noted in Chapter 1 the Hebrew word in the Old Testament for "spirit," *ruah*, can also be translated as "wind," "breath," or the animating principle of life. In various contexts *ruah* may refer to the Spirit of God. Similarly, in the New Testament, the Greek word for "spirit," *pneuma*—from which we derive such English words as *pneumatic* and *pneumonia*—may mean "wind," "breath," the immaterial part of human beings, or the Holy Spirit.

Such comparisons remind me that we scientists may develop a certain undeserved sense of self-importance about our discoveries as we scramble and scrape our way up the sheer face of difficult scientific research. Robert Jastrow, a noted astrophysicist and agnostic—reflecting on the dilemma confronting scientists who venture onto ground that overlaps with spiritual studies—

has provided us with this much quoted observation, which comes at the end of his book *God and the Astronomers* (New York: W. W. Norton, 1992/2000):

> For the scientist who has lived by his faith in the power of reason, the story ends like a bad dream. He has scaled the mountains of ignorance; he is about to conquer the highest peak; as he pulls himself over the final rock, he is greeted by a band of theologians who have been sitting there for centuries.

As we touch on the scientific implications of religious experiences and spirituality, let me offer still another word of caution. I'm *not* suggesting that biochemical interactions—such as the release of nitric oxide—or any other exclusively physical explanation will ever be able to describe the totality of a given spiritual experience. In fact, I believe that for the foreseeable future, and perhaps forever, the space-time laboratory tools we employ in our scientific experiments will remain far too limited to measure the full range of spiritual expression. Much of what we often refer to as the spiritual realm—such as prayer, mystical visions, and the like—seems to me more akin to what theoretical physicists and mathematicians refer to as "extradimensional" reality than the everyday reality we quantify and evaluate in our scientific experiments.

Furthermore, absolutely nothing in my research precludes the idea that a spiritual experience may be initiated from some source *outside* the body and brain. This outside causative source may, in turn, cause changes in our physiology and biochemistry—such as the release of nitric oxide and various neurotransmitters—which we can then measure with our instruments. In other words, the events may begin outside the mind and body, but they culminate in physical ways that we can track with our instruments.

The late Oxford and Cambridge don and medieval scholar, C. S. Lewis summed up this possible interaction of space-time and extradimensional reality rather nicely in his classic work *Miracles:*

> A miracle is emphatically not an event without cause or without results. Its cause is the activity of God: its results follow according to Natural law. In the forward direction (i.e., during the time which follows its occurrence) it is interlocked with all Nature just like any other event. Its peculiarity is that it is not in that way interlocked backwards, interlocked with the previous history of Nature. And this is just what some people find intolerable. The reason they find it intolerable is that they start by taking Nature to be the whole of reality. And they are sure that all reality must be interrelated and consistent. I agree with them. But I think they have mistaken a particular system within reality, namely Nature, for the whole. (New York: Touchstone, 1976, 81–82)

To put Lewis's argument in the context of our recent studies at Harvard, we may actually detect significant brain and body changes in a person who is pursuing meditation or another practice related to the individual's deepest personal beliefs. But even if the physical changes are clearly measurable, the ultimate *source* of the changes may remain a mystery and may well arise from some "spiritual" realm or dimension, as we will consider later in Chapters 11 and 12.

* * *

The release of chemicals and molecules during a Breakout, then, is not only a solid scientific finding that is firmly rooted in peer-reviewed studies. It is also a phenomenon with implications that reach far beyond the laboratory, with a potential that can change your life in many different ways.

At the same time, nitric oxide is only a part of the research picture that has emerged in the last few years. As we'll see in the following chapter, brain-mapping studies and other highly sophisticated medical research tools are also revealing some startling support for—and explanation of—the Breakout Principle phenomenon.

4

Mapping the Creative Mind

Years ago, while watching a particularly gifted person think through a difficult problem, I would try to picture how those hidden brain circuits were working. At times, I would imagine particularly vivid cerebral scenes, as different sections of the individual's brain—connected by an unbelievably complex network of synapses, dendrites, and axons—flashed and exploded here and there, firing messages back and forth, until finally some significant thought or insight emerged.*

Of course, I knew I was indulging in fantasy. What I didn't realize was that someday, through such tools as brain-wave measurement, we would actually have the means to observe firsthand those inner events that occur when creative juices begin to flow.

---

*In brief, an axon is a relatively large extension of a neuron, or nerve cell; a dendrite is a much smaller branch of a nerve cell; and synapses are the connections between axons and dendrites.

Furthermore, I wasn't prepared for the surprises that other new medical technology would bring, both to my own research involving the relaxation response, and also to my work in developing the Breakout Principle.

One major eye-opener for me emerged during the sophisticated research technique known as functional magnetic resonance imaging (fMRI). This procedure showed that the complete calming of the brain during prayer, meditation, or relaxation exercises was a myth. Instead, the fMRI, which is able to measure precise brain activity through blood flow in different regions of the brain at specific moments, showed that the brain combined areas of quietude with cerebral activity.

The Power of the Dynamic Mind

For many years, I had assumed that when a person evoked the relaxation response, the events in the brain automatically tracked the physiologic calming in the rest of the body. In other words, I thought that the *entire brain* became less active as the calming activity—such as meditation, muscle-relaxing exercises, or the like—lowered blood pressure, metabolism, heart rate, and output of stress hormones.

But my assumption about the calming of the brain was only partially correct. Our new research at the Harvard Medical School has shown that effective relaxation response exercises—and by inference the "release," or inner calming phase, that must precede a Breakout—typically usher in a dynamic mental state, which may best be described as creating a *paradox of calm commotion.*

The paradox of calm commotion

In a pioneer study reported in the May 2000 issue of *Neuro-Report*, and also in the November 23, 1999, issue of the *New York Times*, our team, led by Sara W. Lazar, used a functional MRI scanner (fMRI) to study responses of several Sikhs during meditation. (Sikhism is a monotheistic Indian religion founded in the late fifteenth century A.D. that combines principles of Islam and Hinduism.)

For me, this study was particularly exciting because of the new scientific tools at our disposal. In the past, I had been able to measure cardiovascular and other metabolic and respiratory changes and also to catalog subjective emotional responses during interviews. But now, as a result of breakthroughs in neuroscientific research, I could watch actual brain alterations occur as the subjects elicited the relaxation response. Also, I reasoned that the fMRI pictures were recording neurological patterns associated with the Breakout trigger.

Before launching the actual experiment, my colleague Dr. Lazar asked the subjects to practice their meditative technique under study conditions. They were cautioned that they would *not* be sitting by themselves in a quiet room, as they usually did. Instead, they would have to deal with a clanking fMRI machine, technicians and researchers who were moving about, and other potential distractions. In some ways, they were being forced into a situation that included all the distractions that might be found in a typical office or other real-life environment.

To simulate this atmosphere, the participants engaged in practice sessions at home while listening to a tape with the clanking sounds. Also, they adjusted their relaxation sessions to conform to the procedures established for our scientific study. Specifically, they followed this agenda:

For an initial six-minute control period, the participants directed their thoughts toward naming animals, such as *cat, dog,* and *bird.* Then they were instructed to focus on repeating silently, on the inbreath, the term *sat nam,* a meaningful religious phrase they typically used during meditation. On the outbreath, they repeated silently *wahe guru,* another meaningful phrase. In this way, they enhanced their physiologic and mental benefits by incorporating their deepest, intrinsic beliefs into their activity. In other words, they combined the repetitive impact of a relaxation response exercise with concepts from their personal belief system.

Several minutes into the meditation a number of changes— both expected and unexpected—occurred in their bodies and brains. As was the case with many studies I have conducted over the past few decades, an overall calming and slowing of the breathing occurred. But the neurological measurements turned up some new information, including a few surprises.

The fMRI brain mapping showed that most sections of the entire brain became dramatically less active. Interestingly, however, we couldn't identify the *source* of this overall, marked quieting with the fMRI device. In other words, this operation of the mind *might* have arisen from somewhere inside the brain, but it might also have originated from outside the brain, perhaps in a separate "mind dimension."

Furthermore, as the general brain quieting occurred, isolated areas of the brain—especially those associated with attention, space-time concepts, and "executive control" functions, such as decision-making and choice of mental focus—became *extremely active*. But once again, we were unable to identify the root cause of these changes. They might have arisen from within the physical brain, or from some outside location.

During the meditation exercises we also observed significantly increased blood flow in the limbic system and brain stem, the "primitive" parts of the brain that control the autonomic nervous system, including blood pressure, heart rate, and breathing rate. Our research team's separate physiologic measurements, which I referred to above, confirmed that the practical result of this increased activity in the brain stem was actually to lower respiratory rate.

Finally, the fMRI showed that a particularly remarkable phenomenon happened at the very end of each meditation period. The subjects were asked to stop their formal meditation and fix their attention for three minutes on a spot on a screen in front of them. During this exercise, their overall brain activity increased dramatically.

So to sum up, our scientific study with the Sikhs demonstrated clearly that during deep relaxation—including the significant release of stress that typically occurs just before a Breakout—*a complex, dynamic series of events, encompassing both calm and tumultuous commotion, occurs in our minds and bodies.*

At first blush, this "calm commotion" phenomenon may seem contradictory. But in fact, both the calming and the highly active dimensions appear to be essential to personal health and well-being. In particular, those who have used relaxation techniques and have experienced this paradoxical calm-commotion phenomenon have consistently reported relief from high blood pressure, insomnia, mild and moderate depression, premenstrual syndrome (PMS), and symptoms of cancer and AIDS.

Our brain-mapping investigation with the Sikhs also suggests that a healthful and productive dynamism occurs at a crucial stage of the Breakout. Specifically, it seems that in the release stage—as prior mental and emotional patterns are broken and the Breakout trigger is pulled—these events typically take place:

- Overall activity in the brain becomes quieter.
- Simultaneously, activity increases in those sections of the brain associated with autonomic regulation of blood pressure, heart rate, and rate of respiration.
- Activity also increases in regions of the brain linked to attention, awareness of space-time concepts, and executive control of decision-making.

With this neural and physiological platform in place, the Breakout proceeds automatically and, I believe, paves the way for a peak experience. So now, when I observe or hear reports about someone going through the Breakout process, I find that I no longer have to fantasize about what is going on in the brain and body. Instead, I can be confident that any outward or conscious activities and thoughts I may be watching are merely the tip of a vast brain-body "iceberg," which is supporting the unfolding peak experience.

But even though the basic biological events behind every Breakout are the same, the outward events or thoughts that trigger this phenomenon are quite varied, and sometimes surprise me—as is evident in the following illustration involving Robert, a prominent attorney who succeeded after failing to follow my suggestions.

How Robert Won by Breaking My Rules

When I ran into my friend Robert several years ago, he was embroiled in a major crisis—with many of the medical danger signals of excessive stress: incapacitating anxiety, occasional irregular heartbeats, insomnia, and frequent bouts of the cold sweats. I knew that a recent medical exam, including an electro-cardiogram, had shown that he was in no immediate danger. But the encouraging report didn't relieve his emotional and physical discomfort or give him a good night's sleep.

Robert was a good attorney who sensed he might be on the verge of becoming great. So he felt under tremendous pressure as he prepared for one of the most important cases of his life. Barely forty, he had already achieved a fine reputation, but if this trial went well, his career could soar to significant new heights.

Unfortunately, Robert wasn't handling the spotlight well. He was edgy and nervous and felt himself becoming so distracted that he feared the quality of his trial presentation would suffer.

I sensed that unless he found a way to decompress, he might push his body and mind so far that he would face serious medical consequences. As a result, I suggested a series of practical "rules" of stress reduction that I knew had helped others in similar situations. Also, I suspected that by reducing his stress, he might lay the groundwork for a Breakout that could dramatically improve his legal performance. Unfortunately, as an independent self-starter, Robert wasn't particularly receptive to my suggestions about how he might escape or cope with the stress—and thereby break the destructive inner mental and emotional patterns that were plaguing him.

First of all, I asked if he might consider trying a repetitive, nonreligious meditation technique to lower his anxiety. After all, this approach had worked beautifully for thousands of my patients and others around the world who had read my books and articles.

His response was a little deflating: "Those never help me. My mind doesn't work that way."

So I tried a different tack: Could he postpone the trial for a week or so—and maybe take off a few days to relax?

"Impossible. Too many delays already."

Okay. If he was adamant about going ahead with the trial, could he at least get his cocounsel to take some of the load off his shoulders?

"I'm the only one who can do it."

Clearly, Robert was dead set on handling the entire show himself—and staying firmly embedded in his familiar but extremely anxious thought patterns. Sure enough, when the trial began, he seemed to deteriorate emotionally.

As I followed the proceedings, I fully expected the worst. I was sure that Robert would become increasingly confused and out of control during the public proceedings, and that his image would suffer. I even worried that he might undergo some medical crisis. After all, he had been exposing himself to extraordinary emotional stresses and strains for most of his career.

But I was in for a surprise—and so was Robert. The climax of this little drama occurred just before he rose to deliver his summation, his closing argument to the jury.

"What followed didn't make sense," he recalled. "The tension was overwhelming, and I was a mess. My heart was pounding, and I could hardly breathe. I was sure I wouldn't be able to get a word out."

Yet as he related later, just before he stood up to face the jury, he felt overcome by a sense that "none of this really matters." He had become so fatigued by the stress he was bearing that he could no longer proceed a step further under the emotional load. So, in effect, he "threw up his hands," at least symbolically, and abandoned his conviction that everything depended on him. Simultaneously, the worries that had been weighing him down seemed to fall away. On a purely physical level, he became conscious that after an initial, burden-releasing sigh, his breathing became regular and easy.

"Suddenly, I felt very light, and this strange inner calm gripped me," he recalled. "As I spoke, the words came out naturally and fluently. I had absolutely no need to refer to my notes. I connected to my listeners amazingly well, as though I had merged with them at some deep level. I sensed they could understand my thoughts as well as I did."

In the end, Robert won his case, and his career and professional reputation got a considerable boost. But as a mind-body specialist, I remained puzzled by his report.

Robert had apparently taken none of the usual steps that I had identified to evoke the relaxation response or to bring about a Breakout. For example, he had not relied on a repetitive word or movement, and he had not employed any form of meditation or prayer. Yet he had apparently still experienced a Breakout, along with the same remarkable mental quietude that is associated with disciplined meditation.

As I reflected on his description of his experience, I finally realized that his unexpected inner tranquillity had occurred because he had chosen to *abandon all control over his situation.* This state of total abandon had effectively broken his prior negative mental and emotional patterns and caused his anxiety to disappear.

Perhaps most important of all from Robert's viewpoint, his inner sense of calm had moved him directly into successful action. The stress and anxiety associated with the struggle phase gave way as the tranquillity of the release took over. Finally, the sense of abandon triggered the Breakout and his peak performance in the courtroom.

Certainly, I had been aware in the past of "surprise Breakout" cases similar to Robert's, but I had always considered them exceptional. Now, I have begun to *expect* Breakouts in unexpected places—even in those circumstances where the individual undergoing the Breakout may be resisting the experience.

But even though individuals who are surprised by the Breakout Principle will almost always benefit, our ultimate objective should be to learn how to harness the impulses evident in Robert's story so that they can be called into play on command. That way, we can exercise more control over our high-performance faculties and, more regularly, put ourselves in a position to gain the greatest personal and psychic rewards. In fact, Robert's experience of total abandon is one of the six basic triggering mechanisms for a Breakout—which we will introduce a little later.

But now, let's take a closer look at the amazing biology of the Breakout by taking a brief tour of the workings of the human brain.

A Brief Journey Along Robert's Mind-Body Highway

I like to think of the process that Robert was experiencing as a cascade of inner impulses and events, which were hurtling along the network of cerebral channels of the mind-body continuum. Countless thoughts, ideas, and fragments of ideas transmute, crystallize, and finally *break forth* into a dynamic set of concepts, such as the ones that changed the course of Robert's courtroom experience.

As we take this journey, it won't be anatomically or neurologically accurate to try to divide the brain up into clear-cut centers of activity, because in most situations, the cerebral messages and instructions whip about in nonlinear patterns through many parts of your neural network. So as we enter Robert's brain, imagine that we are always on the move, being swept along on a flow of molecular currents that can't be measured or described easily with normal space-time technology.

In the simplest terms, here is what seems to have happened when Robert began to experience anxiety, fear, irritation, or some other disruptive emotion during the struggle phase:

As he plunged into gathering information to prepare his legal case, the cerebral action began in a general region that might be called the *thinking brain*. This physical area encompasses what many other researchers have included in the neocortex and controls such functions as attention, analytical thought, artistic skills, and sophisticated memory and learning. These abilities are a large part of what distinguishes humans from other creatures.

In these thinking-brain regions, Robert formulated his courtroom strategies and also did all his basic legal research. Unfortunately, his analytical thinking and awareness became overly engaged. If he had been hooked up to one of our fMRI scanners, the parts of his brain that controlled such thinking and language skills would have been lighting up on the pictorial printouts.

Instead of the blinding insights that Robert had expected from such hard work, he started to experience "mental roadblocks." These obstacles and frustrations in turn produced anxiety, irritation, and other uncomfortable emotions in other regions of his brain, which is sometimes called the *primitive brain*. The brain stem, which is situated at the top of the spinal cord, and the cerebellum, located at the base of the skull, are the physical seats for much of this primitive brain activity. Robert's primitive brain houses his autonomic nervous system and is also the source of primeval feelings and emotions, such as fear and anger. This region represents a combination of what scientists in the past have called the *reptilian brain*.

At this level, reptiles, mammals, and humans share many characteristics. But humans have special problems because of their higher intelligence. For example, out-of-control analytical thinking—including an obsession with horrendous worst-case scenarios, which periodically plagued Robert—can stimulate stress-related responses in the brain stem and related regions. Such responses may result in negative health consequences, including cardiovascular problems such as heart abnormalities or hypertension. These physical responses will typically stymie creative thought and productive work. Robert's case was a prime example of this negative fallout.

Robert's stressful physical responses presented him with a number of difficulties as he sank deeper and deeper into fear and anxiety about the prospect of failing with such an important case. His overawareness of the possibilities, both good and bad, caused excessive arousal of his brain stem and autonomic nervous system, to the point that he practically became immobilized.

Remember the Yerkes-Dodson Law!

It's helpful at this point to recall the bell curve of the Yerkes-Dodson Law. According to that principle, too much negative activity in the thinking, analytical part of the brain will overload the body with stress. The result will be a steady *decrease* in productivity, not to mention such side effects as higher blood pressure, heart rate, breathing rate, and metabolism. Breakouts simply cannot occur in such an overheated mental environment—as Robert discovered.

So what was the solution to Robert's mind-body bottleneck?

Breaking Through Robert's Mind-Body Bottleneck

Robert's destructive mental patterns were short-circuited when he stumbled upon the Breakout mechanism. In effect, he gave up on his attempt to control and solve everything by analysis—and thereby severed the prior thought and emotional patterns that were holding him back.

We can infer from a medical and biological perspective that a number of good things now began to happen in Robert's brain. When an unexpected, indefinable "something" clicked inside him, he decided that he was tired of worrying so much about the case. Simultaneously, he saw that nothing was to be gained through such anxiety. He had done all the preparation he could. What was going to happen was going to happen, regardless of any further concern he might feel.

"So what do I have to lose by refusing to worry?" he thought. "I've had it! From now on, I'll just go with the flow."

In this simple attitude shift, Robert completely *abandoned* his need to control the legal case—and was surprised with a Breakout. Specifically, when he backed off from his intense legal analysis and preparation, he found that he was able to sit quietly at his counsel's table just before his summation. The new attitude of abandonment and release of control had succeeded in "cutting off" the negative patterns that had blocked a free flow of constructive mental messages through his mind-body highway. Finally, his mind was free to operate in more creative ways.

To put this in terms of brain research, as Robert released his anxieties and any expectations about how the trial would come out, his brain moved into that paradoxical calm-commotion state recorded in our brain-mapping studies. In a flash, the primitive brain regions sent calming signals to his cardiovascular and respiratory systems and his body's metabolism. As a result, even though thoughts and words from his summation were flowing fluidly through his mind, he experienced a lowering of heart rate, blood pressure, breathing, and output of stress hormones.

Robert began to feel so relaxed and confident that just before he stood up to speak, he actually put aside his written notes. His thoughts had stopped churning, and his breathing came easily and regularly. His feelings of stress decreased still further as he turned away from anxiously focusing on himself and his performance and instead concentrated on the judge and the jury.

From a medical viewpoint, what had most likely happened at this point was the scientifically measurable phenomenon that I've called calm-commotion. In other words, most of Robert's overall brain activity had quieted down—marked by a significant reduction in blood flow throughout the brain. At the same time, activity increased in his learning and memory centers, his concentration centers, and areas controlling his rate of breathing.

When Robert finally stood to give his summation, this stimulated activity in his brain stem and related regions, with a resulting stablilization of his cardiovascular functions. He found himself at a maximum level of mental alertness and sharpness, but not so much on edge that unproductive stress and anxiety would once again take over.

As he opened his mouth to speak, Robert, like any seasoned public speaker, knew the first words that would come out of his mouth. He understood the supreme importance of simply getting started. But he had cast aside any concerns about what he would say after that. With his creative mind firmly in charge, he floated lightly over his subject matter. The initial calming effect also prepared him for the next phase of the Breakout process—a peak experience.

As Robert proceeded with his summation, he found that he could connect in almost a telepathic, mind-to-mind manner with his listeners. While speaking, he could simultaneously read their responses and adjust his words to meet their needs. The intensity and persuasive power of his closing argument increased until finally, almost before he knew it, he had completed perhaps the most powerful summation of his career.

The Mystery of the Mind

Robert's experience and that of many others who have experienced significant Breakouts point to an important ongoing issue in mind-body research—a question that will probably never be resolved satisfactorily in scientific terms. I'm referring to the precise nature of the mind, and the relation of the mind to the brain.

For many years, scientists have argued about whether the mind is entirely a part of the physical brain or is some sort of separate entity that may transcend the confines of biology and space-time. Most neuroscientists these days believe that the mind is simply a function of the physical brain. They argue that, although we cannot currently measure or explain such phenomena as artistic creativity, human self-consciousness, the experience of space-time transcendence, or spiritual insight, it doesn't mean we will never have the tools to make such measurements.

But I'm not so sure. One factor that gives me pause is that my investigations have caused me to accept the possibility of an "extradimensional reality"—or if you prefer, a "spiritual" dimension—which transcends the brain's ability to recognize the four dimensions of space-time. In contrast, much modern scientific and medical research has been based on the reductionistic assumption that, either now or at some point in the future, all reality will be measurable and understandable with the tools of human science.

On the other hand, if an extra dimension or other reality beyond space-time does exist—and if we are making use of some inner faculty that enables us to interact with such an extradimensional realm—then it's inevitable that at some point we will reach our human limits. In effect, we will arrive at an impenetrable intellectual wall, beyond which our ordinary mental abilities cannot take us.

To put this another way, what we perceive as the human "mind"—including such distinctive human features as our self-consciousness, creativity, and spiritual capacities—may reach into regions that lie beyond space-time. In other words, because of the physical brain's inherent limitations, the workings of the mind may ultimately lie outside our capacity to measure, analyze, and comprehend. Some evidence for such a radical conclusion may be the simple fact that we clearly have the awesome capacity to reason and speculate about transcendent qualities and possibilities. Other evidence may be emerging in our scientific studies involving fMRIs, PET scans, and the like.

Of course, I'm in no way suggesting that the mind doesn't interact with human biology. Our studies with the Sikhs and other brain-mapping research projects demonstrate clearly that the mind and the brain profoundly influence each other. But at the same time, it's not at all clear that the mind is completely defined by or contained in the physical brain. In fact, such studies as the one with the Sikhs, which we published in the May 2000 issue of *NeuroReport,* seem to call into question the normal laws of causality, which state that the intangible cannot affect the tangible. That particular study showed through brain scans that it's possible that an intangible mind, perhaps arising from or influenced by a source outside the physical brain, can apparently affect the tangible, physical brain and body.

Although the idea that the mind and the brain may in some way be separate entities remains a minority view, a number of prominent scientists and philosophers have been intrigued by the concept. The Nobel Prize winner Sir John Eccles has made a number of strong arguments in favor of an active, searching, self-conscious mind that is distinct from the physical brain. He has even gone so far as to acknowledge the existence of a human soul outside human biological systems (see John C. Eccles, *Evolution of the Brain: Creation of the Self* [London: Routledge, 1989], 178, 203–5, 216, 226, 236, 237–38).

The British mathematical physicist, theologian, and Templeton Prize winner John Polkinghorne goes even further, believing that God may interact with the creation, including human beings, by inputting information into the "open physical process" of the universe (see his *Quarks, Chaos, & Christianity* [New York: Crossroad, 1994], 71). Similarly, the University of Pennsylvania scientist and physician Andrew B. Newberg and his colleagues, who have used PET scans in their research, argue that a "real" realm of the spirit lies beyond our brains and biology. But they believe that God uses our mental processes to break through to us (see their *Why God Won't Go Away* [New York: Ballantine Books, 2001], 38, 164).

It seems quite possible to me that some part of the mind—perhaps what theologians may refer to as the "spirit" of human beings—may be linked to a dimension beyond the physical matter, DNA codes, cell structure, and other limitations of our brains and bodies. Certainly, at the very least, as we suggested in our discussion in our 2001 *Brain Research Reviews* article (35, 3–4), the mind must be a "unified entity" or "unified consciousness" capable of highly developed cognitive strategies and integration processes. In the end, of course, we may never pin down precisely every source of the mind with our scientific instruments. But the important thing is that no matter what your mind may consist of, it can work for you in ways that you may never have understood or even imagined.

Sometimes, you may be lucky enough to be surprised by a life-changing Breakout, as Robert was. But why just rely on luck? To enjoy the full benefits of this phenomenon, why not learn to trigger Breakouts and peak experiences at will? If you can develop this skill, you may very well find that you have also discovered an "ultimate self-help principle" that has the power to transform your entire life.

5

The Ultimate
Self-Help Principle

Although we've focused in the last two chapters on complex medical research and some weighty philosophical issues, you do *not* have to be a scientist or a philosopher to take full advantage of the Breakout. Certainly, the fact that established biology lies behind the Breakout should give you confidence as you embark on the program. But in the end, the Breakout is not about research or theory. Rather, it's rooted in practical techniques and everyday activities that have the potential to change your life.

As a scientist, I guard against wild promises. But my research and study have convinced me that the Breakout Principle does indeed transcend other self-transformation claims, to the point that it constitutes a kind of "ultimate self-help principle" that can carry you to significantly new levels of performance and achievement.

The six peak experiences described in Part II suggest the range of possibilities. But before we launch into a discussion of those peaks—and how you can enjoy each of them by triggering a Breakout—I want to provide you with a little more detail about six basic mechanisms that are involved in many Breakout triggers.

The Basic Triggering Mechanisms

As we have already seen, a wide variety of activities or thought patterns may trigger a Breakout. These include such pursuits as walking, jogging, eating with a compatible companion at a favorite restaurant, sitting quietly in a worship center or a natural setting, meditating, sewing, or just allowing one or more of your senses to fill your mind with some dominant, overriding impression.

But why exactly do these triggers work so well? Typically, they operate successfully to produce a Breakout because one or more of the following powerful natural mechanisms are also operating deep in your biological system:

- *The first mechanism:* engaging in a repetitive physical or mental activity that breaks prior thought patterns.
- *The second mechanism:* becoming immersed in some expression of your personal belief system.
- *The third mechanism:* surrendering yourself to an experience or sense of what I call "total abandon."
- *The fourth mechanism:* participating in some significant, absorbing personal encounter.
- *The fifth mechanism:* becoming deeply engaged in an altruistic activity.
- *The sixth mechanism:* filling your mind with one dominant sensory impression—such as a particular sound or sight.

The first of these mechanisms—the repetitive mental or physical activity—is perhaps the easiest to understand and describe, while the others may involve a considerably more complex set of internal dynamics.

Note: With each of these six mechanisms, I will assume that before trying to pull the trigger, the individual has completed the first "struggle" phase of the Breakout process or an intense period of work or preparation, which has probably involved significant emotional or physical stress.

The First Triggering Mechanism: Practicing a Repetitive Mental or Physical Activity

Throughout much of my career, I have emphasized the benefits of evoking the relaxation response, which research has proven can produce important stress-reducing physiologic benefits. What I didn't know until relatively recently is that the same simple techniques used for the relaxation response can also be used to trigger a Breakout.

To help you understand exactly how this first mechanism works in the context of a Breakout, it's important first to understand the simple, proven technique that I have recommended to many of my patients.

Step 1: Choose a meaningful word or short phrase that can be repeated silently on a single exhalation, or outbreath.

If possible, the word or phrase should be solidly rooted in your personal belief system. Remember, by combining repetition with your personal beliefs, you may enhance the impact of the exercise by incorporating the placebo effect. This combined repetition-belief exercise is what I have referred to in my previous writings as the "faith factor."

So if you are Jewish, you might say *shalom*. If a Sikh meditator, you might use *sat nam*, as the participants in our previously described study did. If a Christian, you might choose *Jesus is Lord*. Or if you affirm some nonreligious belief system, you might select a line from a favorite poem or philosophical work. On the other hand, if you don't have a particular personal philosophy, any neutral or uplifting word or phrase will do, such as *one, peace,* or *love.*

Step 2: Assume a comfortable sitting position, close your eyes, breathe easily and regularly, and repeat your chosen word or phrase silently on the outbreath for ten to twenty minutes.

Step 3: Don't fight or be upset with distracting thoughts or interruptions—just gently turn away from them and return to your silent repetition.

It's normal for your mind to wander, especially when you are just getting used to this exercise. The important thing is not to become uptight or begin to feel you have failed. Rather, just sigh and say, silently, "Oh, well," and return to the repetition.

Step 4: After the allotted ten to twenty minutes have passed, open your eyes, sit quietly for a few minutes, and allow everyday thoughts to enter your mind.

It's at this stage of the exercise that you are most likely to experience a Breakout. Physiologically, your body is releasing extra amounts of nitric oxide, along with neurotransmitters associated with feelings of well-being and protection from stress. Also, your brain has undergone a general quieting, but with heightened activity in the attention and executive-control centers.

The repetitive activity has broken the prior thought patterns of your conscious mental state—a precondition for the "release," "backing off," or "letting go" experience that will typically precede a Breakout and peak experience. But even though you have broken those old thought patterns and have reduced your stress levels, the research, facts, and analyses you have performed are still resting there in the background, ready to be rearranged and reassembled into new, more creative configurations.

In essence, Breakouts and peak experiences often involve new ways of looking at old problems and fact patterns. The trick is to find a way to step outside or "float above" the previous, dead-end trains of thought—and that's what this rather formal, repetitive Breakout triggering mechanism is all about.

Alternatives to Formal Mental Repetition

The repetitive triggering mechanism can also be engaged in a less formal fashion than the above four-step process. For example, if you like to take long walks, jog, play the drums, or do needle-point, you may achieve the same result. What's important is that the repetitive activity be nonstressful and sufficiently regular and long-lasting to enable you to break those former, limiting mental patterns.

But effective repetitive activity is only one possibility for triggering a Breakout. Many people have found that becoming deeply immersed in some manner in their personal belief systems is just as effective.

The Second Triggering Mechanism: Immersion in Your Personal Belief System

This second mechanism is just as powerful as the first, but it operates more subtly. In fact, you may miss the creative benefits from this experience completely if you fail to understand how it works.

First, the operation of this second mechanism assumes that you do really have a deep personal belief system. Those beliefs should be life-changing and life-influencing. In the case of a deep philosophical, political, or moral position, it should be the primary source of meaning in your life.

For example, I have known many people who were committed to preserving the environment. But in most cases, a simple philosophical or political position probably won't serve as this kind of triggering mechanism. In other words, it would take more than occasional contributions to the Sierra Club for an environmental belief system to qualify as a worldview.

Instead, environmental beliefs that have the power to trigger a Breakout tend to be those that encompass most aspects of a person's life. Environment-driven voting, volunteering, and even proselytizing would typically characterize the life of a truly committed environmentalist. A few people may actually develop a quasi-religious worldview, perhaps with a belief in animistic spirits in trees, plants, and animals, or in some cases, a belief in the whole of nature as a living and conscious entity.

Such a deeply committed environmentalist might experience a Breakout this way:

- Stress builds up in her life as she tries to work through a problem with a relationship at work.

- She reaches a dead end in trying to analyze or "fix" the problem.
- During a contemplative solitary hike, she finds herself sitting in total stillness near the top of a peak, gazing over the mountains and trees in the distance.
- She has a sense that she is becoming one with the woods, the sky, the rocks, and other natural surroundings. This feeling is consistent with her belief that, somehow, human beings are at one with all nature—though she recognizes that, often, we violate that essential unity by failing to show respect to the environment.
- Prior, stressful thought patterns and emotions fade away, and new thought patterns drift into her consciousness. In other words, she experiences a Breakout.
- An entirely new way to approach the work relationship emerges in her mind. Among other things, she finally accepts that she can't change the other person.

Similarly, a belief system may be rooted in a traditional religious faith, but according to various researchers, the convictions held should be *intrinsic,* as opposed to extrinsic. In other words, the individual's beliefs should permeate his life and actions and not just be pigeonholed in one part of his life.

Typically, such an intrinsic faith will involve not just lip service or intellectual assent to certain articles of belief but, instead, a commitment of time and effort to regular belief-related activities or outreach efforts. The person's entire life in some way expresses the faith that is being articulated. Also, an intrinsic faith will emerge in regular spiritual habits or disciplines, such as contemplation, meditation, or prayer. These may be practiced in a variety of settings, including the quiet of a personal room, a natural setting, or a worship center, such as a cathedral, mosque, or synagogue. (For more on intrinsic belief, see Chapter 12.) Also, these spiritual disciplines may be pursued *with or without* the repetition of triggering mechanism number one.

In medical terms, the ability of personal belief to heal is sometimes called the placebo effect, though I have coined the term *remembered wellness* for this effect in an effort to suggest a far broader impact than the older term. Our 2001 *Brain Research Reviews* article on nitric oxide suggests just how powerful the placebo effect, or remembered wellness, can be in countering stress-related health conditions and diseases.

Of course, this belief-based mechanism can trigger Breakouts in all the areas we discuss in Part II—including creativity, productivity, athleticism, and spirituality. In other words, if you can learn to trigger regular Breakouts through your personal belief system, you will not only enhance your health but also open the door to profound improvement in many other areas of your life.

The Third Triggering Mechanism: Surrender to a Sense of Total Abandon

Sometimes, you may trigger a Breakout when you just give up or surrender yourself to the flow of circumstances and events, without trying to control them. This sense of total abandon can effectively sever your bondage to past, destructive thought patterns and serve as a release switch to move you up to a new plane of insight and performance.

In effect, this is what happened with my attorney friend Robert, whose story we discussed in the previous chapter. Sitting nearly exhausted and resigned at his courtroom counsel's table, he sensed that he had struggled and worried all he could. He concluded he could do nothing more to control or influence the outcome of the case. At the deepest levels of his being, he realized, as the old song says, "*qué será, será*"—what will be, will be.

Also, at the back of his mind was the ultimate worst-case scenario, complete failure and even damage to his reputation. But he had arrived at the point where he could accept even that. This sense of utter abandon and surrender paradoxically freed him to perform at a peak level when he rose to deliver his summation. With a who-cares, here-goes-nothing attitude, he dazzled the jury and won his case.

Many times, engaging this particular mechanism may be quite difficult on a conscious, planned level. Those trying to employ it may find that they become immobilized as they try to convince themselves that they don't really care about the outcome of a challenge or as they focus on a worst-case scenario. It may simply be impossible to talk yourself into such a state.

More often, the experience of total abandon, with the release that leads to a Breakout, seems to occur by surprise, as happened with Robert. But occasionally, I do encounter an individual who can move into this state at will. If you are in this category, this mechanism can become a powerful instrument in your Breakout tool chest.

The Fourth Triggering Mechanism: Engaging in a Significant Personal Encounter

In a number of interviews for this book, individuals have reported the breaking of patterns of old "mental tapes" during a relaxing or stimulating personal interaction. One woman, for instance, described having become creatively paralyzed during a particularly stressful workday.

She had gone home early because, as an amateur songwriter, she had promised to produce some original material for an important community volunteer fund-raising production. Usually, she would come up with a concept for a song, write the lyrics, then compose a melody to fit the words.

But because she was close to emotional exhaustion, she found that she couldn't take even the first step. The basic idea on which she hoped to build a song just wouldn't come to mind. So she tossed aside her pencil and paper, closed the piano near her chair, and went out to eat with her husband.

During that meal in the secluded corner of a rather quiet, softly lit restaurant, she and her spouse began to chat about some nonstressful, cheerful activity of one of their children. Gradually, the conversation turned to the exhaustion she had been feeling at work, and her frustration at not being able to come up with an idea for a song.

At that moment, a fresh idea hit her. She brainstormed briefly with her husband, and then devoted about five minutes to scribbling not only the idea but also the first few lines of the lyrics and the melody for the song on a paper napkin. When they returned home, she finished her draft within a few minutes, and by the end of the evening, she actually had the finished product ready to e-mail to her community group.

This woman's experience illustrates the power of the fourth triggering mechanism. Specifically, interacting with a suitable companion in a favorable setting of almost any type can provide a wonderful platform to stage a Breakout. But there is an important precondition: As you interact, you must succeed in turning *completely* away from the day's anxieties and frustrations. The change of scene, the smell and taste of good food, and the diverting conversation must have the power to shift your attention from the mental and emotional shackles of the immediate past, to the tremendous potential of the future.

On the negative side, I'm reminded of one man who was trying to think "out of the box" while on a business trip. He went out by himself to a quiet restaurant intending to free-associate, but he soon got into an altercation with a surly waiter over a poorly cooked entrée. Needless to say, he left the restaurant without any new ideas—but with plenty of dark thoughts about the waiter.

So don't assume that there is a rote, automatic way of successfully engaging any of these triggering mechanisms. The prerequisite is always that the old, destructive mental patterns must be released and a new inner state of relative peace and calm ushered in—not that one state of worry or preoccupation be substituted for another.

The Fifth Triggering Mechanism: Becoming Altruistic

This fifth Breakout triggering mechanism involves turning away from yourself and toward others. In other words, becoming more altruistic may actually improve your performance and creativity in different activities.

Many times, negative thought patterns exist because we focus mostly or exclusively on ourselves—how *we* appear to others, how *we* may benefit from certain actions or events, what *we* have done or accomplished, or how *we* can prevail over someone else. At the same time, we tend to ignore completely how we can help or enhance the interests of other people.

In the midst of such egocentricity, it's easy to become nervous, self-conscious, anxious, depressed, or in the grip of some other inner emotional state that will almost always serve as an absolute barrier to a Breakout. So in a counterintuitive twist, self-absorption may actually detract from your ability to improve yourself.

In other words, you will become overly concerned and focused on your own performance or image. The resulting negative emotions will then block your ability to achieve new levels of performance or self-transformation. On the other hand, if you back off or release yourself from that self-centeredness, you will place yourself in a much stronger position to experience a Breakout and possibly a beneficial personal transformation.

The Sixth Triggering Mechanism: Filling Your Mind with a Sensory Impression

This final Breakout triggering mechanism can be particularly powerful, as the individual's attention is riveted—and past thought patterns are broken—by intense stimulation of one or more of the senses. For example, if you tend to become enthralled by the beauty of nature, such as a blazing sunset or the play of the wind on trees, you may be able to use such impressions to break prior thought patterns and set the stage for a Breakout. Other people obtain similar results when they listen to a moving symphony.

Many athletes rely heavily on an acute, concentrated visual sense to focus totally on the ball or on the movement of competitors in a game. Such focus is a prerequisite for accurate basketball shots, a high baseball batting average, and consistent tennis strokes. As we'll see in Chapter 9, this extreme visual focus helps the athlete shut out the noise and distractions of the brain's thinking. At the same time, the visual sense puts the body's motor memory in *direct* touch with the ball that must be struck or thrown, or with the movements of competitors that require a split-second response or countermovement—as frequently happens on a basketball court or football field.

Engaging other senses may also help trigger a Breakout. Here are a few illustrations:

- *Smell:* If you feel blocked creatively, overwhelmed by stress, or otherwise in need of the benefits that the Breakout Principle can provide, immersing yourself in a pleasant-smelling environment may help. For example, some people find that prior mental and emotional patterns are severed when they visit a bakery, or when they smell a certain perfume or other favorite scent.

- *Hearing:* A number of people find that their mental patterns automatically shift when they hear a certain kind of classical or popular music. A particular rhythm or beat may also help trigger a Breakout.

- *Touch:* Some people crave a massage because it enables them to forget their worries and cares for a few minutes. You may find that the right masseur can be your ticket to a Breakout. Others achieve the same result by soaking for several minutes under a hot shower or in a steaming tub.

- *Sight:* Many people find that a favorite movie or TV show—regardless of how many times they have seen it— can help them break prior negative thought patterns. Some of the favored films and shows we have encountered include Hitchcock mysteries, the first *Star*

Wars trilogy, *Chariots of Fire, I Love Lucy* reruns, and Cary Grant's romantic comedies.

Can These Triggering Mechanisms Work Together?

As you reflect on these six mechanisms, it should be obvious that they will often not be mutually exclusive. In other words, a particular mechanism will often work well with one or more of the others, and together they may even produce a powerful, exponential effect.

For example, many people I know combine mechanisms one and two by repeating a word from their personal belief system. Those who use this technique are much more likely to have staying power using a formal repetitive technique because they enjoy a deeper meditative experience when their personal philosophy is engaged.

Other people may enjoy a walk or a jog (the repetitive activity of mechanism one) in the company of a sympathetic companion (mechanism four). The result may be an increased chance of severing past thought patterns, which will lead to a Breakout.

In a particularly creative synergistic application of *three* of these mechanisms, a woman volunteered through a mentoring program at her worship center to work with young schoolchildren in a low-income area. She looked forward to drilling the youngsters on math and spelling because she found that the combination of the repetition, *plus* the altruism, *plus* the opportunity of doing outreach work that arose from her deepest religious convictions produced an exhilarating mental and emotional change of pace for her. Many times, after these volunteer sessions, she found that she returned to her daily life considerably more productive, creative, and joyful.

But this is just the beginning of the benefits that the six triggering mechanisms can provide for you. To understand the full range of possibilities, let's now embark on an in-depth exploration of the six peak experiences, any of which may lie on the other side of any Breakout.

Part II

THE SIX
PEAK EXPERIENCES

The First Peak— Self-Awareness

It has become something of a cliché to say that the modern world has flooded us with so much information and activity that we have lost the opportunity—or even the ability—to be reflective and contemplative. Unfortunately, the cliché contains more than a kernel of truth.

One of the most common complaints I hear from patients suffering from stress-related illnesses is that their lives are in constant confusion and chaos. When I question them further, they sometimes reveal that their anxieties and agitation result from generalized worries about their health, which they have simply not taken time to resolve. Or they may confront other problems related to their careers and relationships that also stem from overscheduling or overwork.

Because of their chronic busyness, they fail to plug in periods of personal withdrawal from daily life, which might provide them with an opportunity to get some perspective on their concerns. Yet all significant, long-lasting personal change must usually begin in a quiet space that promotes reflection, which in turn leads to self-awareness. You *must* withdraw from the hullabaloo of life from time to time to give yourself an opportunity to look within and explore those areas that need transformation.

Part of the power of the Breakout is that the concept is rooted in a recognition of our basic need to periodically cease outward activity and turn away from the inner noise of agitated thought patterns and worries. These moments of inner rest, which allow us to put aside the cares of the world, will often lead directly to a fundamental change of outlook and the opportunity to take steps that can change our lives.

This shift will typically lead to enhanced self-awareness. Such self-awareness can then provide the groundwork for long-lasting, productive changes in other, more specific areas of life, such as your health, business, athletics, creative endeavors, personal relationships, or spirituality. In other words, a profound experience of self-awareness may become the first stop on the way to other peak experiences.

The First Stop: Self-Awareness

As we use the term, *self-awareness* refers to the state of knowing, or at least sensing to some degree, who you are and how you fit into the world around you. Those who are self-aware typically spend time in introspection, or in mulling over the basic direction and meaning of life, their personal value system, or their future.

As suggested above, self-awareness isn't necessarily a spiritual, philosophical, or religious end point, nor does self-awareness automatically lead to some deep spiritual insight. Rather, becoming self-aware may mark the first stage in moving toward such an end point. In other words, those who begin to explore the Breakout phenomenon may first move through some sort of self-awareness "Eureka!" before they can open those inner portals that lead to other peak experiences.

How does the peak experience of self-awareness work in practice? The answer revolves around what I call the *self-awareness question*.

Asking the Self-Awareness Question

Typically, in undergoing a peak experience of self-awareness, you pass through several stages. Initially, you may run into some kind of barrier or dead end in your daily life. For example, you may find that your usual activities, achievements, or values are inadequate in some way. Or your worldview falls short of being able to provide you with solid answers in a personal crisis.

As a result of this impasse, you move into a second phase of inner exploration and begin to look into ways to overcome the particular barrier that is blocking your forward movement. Often, you will first ask and then try to answer a fundamental question about your own existence, such as the following:

- Who am I?
- What's the meaning of my life?
- What am I really good at or meant to do with my life?
- Are my personal values on the right track? If not, why not? If so, how can I live more consistently with them?
- What will I be doing ten or twenty years from now?

- What is the single most important thing to me?
- What do I think about death?
- Why do I lack the self-discipline to change a particular bad personal habit?
- What am I doing wrong in my relationships with others—and how might I change?
- Are my basic attitudes harming my health—and if so, what can I do to change?
- How can understanding the meaning of a particular tragedy or catastrophe help me conquer my fears?

Finally, after you have framed your particular self-awareness question and begun seriously to investigate possible answers, you will be ready to experience a Breakout—which may move you a step closer not only to understanding more about the meaning of your life but also to solving other problems you face.

A Beatle's Journey toward Self-Awareness

When the Beatle George Harrison died, the *New York Times* ran a front-page story that highlighted his inner journey. The paper said that he "served as an anchor" for the Beatles, "leading the others on a spiritual quest toward Eastern philosophy that influenced their music in the latter part of the 1960s" (December 1, 2001, A1). In one of his most telling observations before he died, Harrison said:

Everybody dreams of being famous, rich and famous. Once you get rich and famous, you think, "This wasn't it," and that made me go on to find out what it is. In the end, you're trying to find God. That's the result of not being satisfied.

And it doesn't matter how much money or property or whatever you've got, unless you're happy in your heart, then that's it. And unfortunately, you can never gain perfect happiness unless you've got that state of consciousness that enables that. (A24)

Although Harrison continued to delve into Eastern philosophy, including Hinduism, it's not clear that he ever completely found what he was searching for. But it *is* clear that he became acutely self-aware. In effect, after taking time out from his busy schedule for philosophical reflection, he went through an experience that had all the earmarks of a self-awareness Breakout.

According to various reports, Harrison concluded after this experience that he and the Beatles were part of a bigger creative, cultural, and spiritual picture. This insight encouraged him to continue his spiritual explorations in greater depth, and to relate his inner journey to his music. In the end, in the opinion of a number of observers of the pop music scene, Harrison's search had a profound impact on many of his songs, such as "My Sweet Lord," "Here Comes the Sun," "Something," "That Is Life," and "The Art of Dying."

Self-awareness, then, may constitute a peak experience in its own right. But at the same time, it may become a first step toward subsequent Breakouts, which can produce other, more specific creative breakthroughs and achievements.

With George Harrison, personal self-awareness seems to have been linked not only to his broad spiritual search but also to his musical creativity. With you, the next step after self-awareness could involve better performance at work, new insights into your relationship with your spouse, or some health consideration such as lower blood pressure or permanent weight reduction. But how exactly might you trigger a Breakout that results in a peak of self-awareness?

As we have already seen, to effect any Breakout you must do or think something that has the *power to break past emotional and thought patterns*. Any of the six triggering mechanisms described in the previous chapter will certainly work with a peak of self-awareness.

But perhaps the most commonly used mechanism is the second—*becoming deeply immersed in exploring your own personal belief system*. To understand how this mechanism might work in practice, let's reexamine in more detail a few of the self-awareness questions listed above.

Paul Asks: "Who Am I?"

Sometimes, the Breakout sequence begins just by asking and contemplating a serious philosophical question, such as "Who am I?" or "What does my life really mean?"

I'm reminded of Paul, a single man in his early thirties, who had succeeded beyond his dreams at an investment banking firm. After only a few years in the business, he had begun to make huge sums of money. For a while, the excitement of putting together big deals and outwitting competitors was so exhilarating that he gave no thought to where his work was taking him personally. He lived from day to day, savoring his immediate victories, but ignoring thoughts of his ultimate destination.

All that changed one evening after he returned to his apartment following a particularly contentious day of negotiations with venture capitalists. He found himself sitting alone in his well-appointed living room. But for some reason, he didn't feel like turning on the television and listening to the news or one of those inane sitcoms that usually provided him with mindless relaxation after a particularly rigorous workday. Instead, he found himself savoring the quiet of his apartment in a way that he had failed to do for weeks, if not months.

Almost involuntarily, his thoughts shifted to his work. But he found himself focusing not so much on the details of his current deal-making as on the overall movement of his career.

"Where exactly am I going?" Paul asked himself. "Where will I be in five years? Or in ten? Will I have a spouse or children? Will I contribute anything of lasting significance to the world? What kind of person am I becoming?"

Although Paul dated almost every weekend, he had rarely bothered to consider what it would mean to settle down and start a family. He just didn't have the time for such matters—or at least, he hadn't made the time to think about them. Certainly he never reflected on what influence he might exert on people or events outside the limited orbit of his work.

But this evening, he allowed his imagination to project further into the future than ever before. "What will I be doing when I'm fifty, or sixty, or seventy?" he asked. "Will I be alone? Will I be happy? For that matter, will I even live that long?"

Those were difficult concepts for him to grasp. He didn't even know if he would be alive at such a seemingly "advanced" age. But the more he contemplated the distant future, the more uncomfortable he became because he realized that what he was doing now wasn't providing him with adequate emotional or psychic preparation for the years to come.

Although Paul was making a great deal of money, he had already discovered that there was a limit to the satisfaction that money could buy. He could travel just so much and accumulate just so many adult toys. As he sat there quietly in his chair, he sensed strongly that there was more to life than his career and income. But what exactly did this "more" consist of?

Paul is still searching for the answers to these questions, but that doesn't diminish the significance of his self-awareness Breakout that particular evening. As with so many others who have experienced similar insights, he didn't immediately understand where the next steps on his inner journey would lead him. But he did know now that he was firmly on the way to further discoveries about himself and his place in the world.

Most people I've encountered in Paul's age range haven't yet become particularly philosophical or reflective. Thoroughly absorbed in their day-to-day careers or family concerns, they haven't taken the time to step back or "retreat" from everyday life, so that they can reflect or philosophize on their condition and direction. As a result, advancing years and age may catch up with them before they realize what has happened. Paul was a refreshing exception. After his Breakout—even though he knew he didn't have all the answers—he at least had the potential to deepen his inner life in ways that had previously been impossible.

Rachel Asks: "Why Do I Lack the Self-Discipline to Lose Weight?"

Rachel, who consistently weighed in at about thirty pounds more than her ideal weight, had tried many different diets. In a few cases, she had actually succeeded in losing most of the excess poundage and getting within five or six pounds of her goal. But every time she did, she would succumb to the "yo-yo syndrome": the temptation to start overeating again—especially by giving in to the siren song of desserts during business and travel meals. She always put the lost weight back on again.

"I just lack the self-discipline to deal with this," she confided in resignation on more than one occasion to friends and family members.

In fact, Rachel was quite correct in bemoaning that, given her usual emotional state, she lacked sufficient self-discipline. For years, she had become entangled in the stressful, "struggle" phase of trying to fight her way through to an ultimate, permanent solution to her weight problem. But she had always failed.

What Rachel desperately needed was to move beyond her usual anxieties and low self-esteem, break those prior negative mental patterns, and position herself to experience a Breakout. Only through a transforming experience or insight could she hope to gain a new perspective on her health and image. She especially needed to acquire a fresh view of herself and her personal potential. This heightened self-awareness could then *empower* her to deal with the specific problem of her excess weight.

The breakthrough came unexpectedly as Rachel was embarking on yet another weight-loss program. She had known for years that an important first step for long-term weight reduction was a personal fitness program. For one thing, getting some reasonably vigorous exercise before a meal would burn up extra calories. In addition, she knew that various studies had shown that premeal workouts could suppress a person's appetite.

But Rachel had always resisted exercising for several reasons. In the first place, most of the programs she had tried had recommended an approach that for her seemed too demanding. She responded negatively even to walking a half hour or more several days a week.

An underlying problem was that Rachel was mostly sedentary and drove everywhere and did everything she could to avoid physical movement, even in shopping malls. She hated even the hint of perspiration and hard breathing. Usually, because she became too tired during the first stages of the activity and too sore the next day, she quickly gave up.

Also, a strong lack of self-confidence led her to resist exercise. In the past, whenever she had attempted to launch a program, she had usually felt excessively self-conscious, as though "everybody's looking at me and laughing." She didn't see herself as physically active or athletic, and such activity felt profoundly threatening.

Then Rachel stumbled upon a new program that promised to overcome most of her objections to exercise. The basic idea was to start out by walking only about five minutes. After that, she was instructed to add a minute every session until she reached ten minutes.

She was to continue to walk only for ten-minute periods for a couple of additional weeks, and then gradually add minutes until she reached sessions of twenty minutes. After that, she could lengthen the outings as much or as little as she wished.

Rachel liked this strategy because she could finish a session before she started feeling bad about her fitness level or about the way she imagined she was coming across to anyone who might be watching. Also, the early stages of the program were easy enough to prevent her from becoming exhausted or getting sore.

So Rachel went out for her first short walk feeling quite confident and free of anxiety about her image or her ability to perform. And she got more benefits than she had bargained for.

The street in front of her house was quiet and deserted at her chosen time, and she immediately found herself enjoying the early-morning sun and the breeze. She became so preoccupied with pleasant thoughts that she forgot to glance at her watch to see if she had put in her required minutes. When she finally remembered the time, she was startled to see that she had been walking for almost ten minutes. She felt so good that she was almost tempted to keep going. But then, recalling her previous experiences with fatigue and soreness, she turned back toward home—and that was when it happened.

The repetition of the walking, plus the peaceful natural setting, had provided the mind-body mechanism to break Rachel's prior emotional and thought patterns. She had become so exhilarated by exercising without pain or anxiety that she almost began to feel that she had turned into a different person. Immediately after this near mystical change in her outlook, she sensed that she might not be the exercise-averse person she had always assumed she was. She had been given a glimpse of what she might become, at least physically.

For a few minutes, her imagination took flight. She saw herself not only taking off those extra thirty pounds, but also developing an entirely new body. She imagined she was moving from a walk to a jog, and then to a run. She even flirted with the notion of becoming a competitive runner. At the same time, she saw what might happen to other parts of her body if she embarked on a serious strength-training program. In her mind's eye, her energy levels began to soar. She even imagined that her aging might be slowed and might in some respects even begin to operate in reverse.

As these thoughts flitted through Rachel's consciousness, time actually seemed to stand still. When she reached home, she discovered she was unable to remember any of the familiar neighborhood landmarks she had just passed. By any measure, she had experienced a dramatic Breakout, which had led her up a peak of self-awareness.

This experience provided strong motivation for her exercise and diet regimen in the months ahead, but the impact reached far beyond the physical. Rachel had been given a view of herself and her potential that had a major, permanent influence on her self-assurance and her sense of her possibilities.

Katie Asks: "Are My Basic Attitudes Harming My Health— and If So, How Can I Change?"

Katie, a young artist, suffered from extensive swelling of her left knee during times of stress. Although she probably suffered from rheumatoid arthritis, her symptoms failed to clearly fit any medical model. After trying various treatments, she finally came to me because she suspected that the roots of her problem might lie "in her head" and not be susceptible to ordinary medical diagnosis and treatment.

Many times, in cases involving pain or other clear physical symptoms, I introduce the patient to a repetitive relaxation technique designed to evoke the relaxation response. But in Katie's case, I realized that more was required. I sensed that a large part of her problem lay not only in her inability to manage the stress in her life, but also in her somewhat restrictive mind-set. Among other things, she failed to understand or believe that her mind could actually affect her body in a wide variety of physical ways.

"In fact, there is a mental component in many of our physical problems—but it's much more complex and comprehensive than you think," I explained. "The links between the mind and body are so extensive that, often, the best way to deal with a health problem is actually to begin with medical strategies designed to influence the operation of the mind. In any event, it's frequently advisable to combine traditional medication or surgery with mind-body or stress-reduction techniques."

As we talked, I could sense Katie's dawning awareness of the true nature of the mind-body linkage, which had completely escaped her before. It became evident that she now understood that she could take control of her body by using certain simple mental techniques, such as those that evoked the relaxation response.

So I instructed her in the simple repetitive technique of repeating silently to herself a positive word when she exhaled, over a ten-to-twenty-minute period. She chose the word *love* and followed all the other standard instructions, including the assumption of a comfortable sitting position, closing her eyes, and gently turning away from distracting thoughts when they entered her mind.

After her first session, which she completed in my presence, her swelling decreased markedly in two weeks. Her initial experience of using a repetitive technique to achieve a Breakout enabled her to sever prior negative thought patterns—including her ignorance about how the mind can influence the body. Her new self-awareness about her health led directly to a positive physical result—the decrease in swelling around her knee.

Furthermore, the swelling eventually disappeared and did not return. She continued to practice the relaxation technique periodically, but clearly the most important factor in her recovery was that she had become acutely aware of the tremendous power that her mind could exert over her body. She claimed she "knew" she was cured and would remain free of the swelling.

I should note that Katie's case was unique. I've never encountered a similar cure before or since, and I would certainly not suggest her experience as a paradigm for everyone who suffers symptoms of arthritis. On the other hand, Katie's experience always sticks in my mind as a compelling illustration of how physical problems may be mitigated or even overcome by a Breakout involving a peak experience of self-awareness.

A Manhattan Family Asks: "How Can We Deal with Our Fears?"

Raising and responding to profound questions of self-awareness may also help trigger beneficial Breakouts when a person is unable to deal with some outside traumatic event, such as a death in the immediate family, a divorce, the loss of a job, or a national disaster.

In the wake of the devastating attack on the Twin Towers of the World Trade Center in New York City on September 11, 2001, patients came into our offices and other medical facilities around the country with a common set of complaints. They reported they were suffering from heightened anxiety, fears, and insomnia, which are associated with post-traumatic stress disorder, or PTSD.

The impact on one Manhattan couple and their eleven-year-old daughter is a case in point. Gazing through her bedroom window, the girl had actually watched the Twin Towers collapse on that fateful day. Then, because her parents wanted to keep abreast of every detail of the latest news developments, she was exposed constantly to television accounts of the disaster and the aftermath.

Shortly after the event, the telltale symptoms of possible PTSD began to appear first in the girl and then in her parents, and they continued for more than a month. Many medical experts warn that PTSD symptoms that continue beyond a month may signal more serious, long-term effects. Typical symptoms of PTSD include mental flashbacks of the traumatic event;

nightmares; insomnia; inability to concentrate on ordinary daily tasks; unusual sensitivity to loud or sudden noises; and an excessive tendency to avoid any situation or thought that might be a reminder of the event.

All three family members were having trouble getting a good night's sleep, and their anxiety levels had noticeably increased. In addition, each person suffered individual PTSD-related problems. The little girl frequently "acted out" her feelings with excessive whining and misbehavior. The mother was afraid of going to work because another airplane might plow into her office building.

The father, who had to travel frequently to other parts of the country, found that his fear of flying, which had been a mild problem before, had now become a major phobia. He was much more inclined after September 11 to make excuses for canceling trips. When he absolutely had to schedule an out-of-town meeting, he usually found himself fighting back classic panic attacks, with shortness of breath and a general sense of terror.

"We can't keep living like this," the mother finally said to her husband. She was especially concerned about the long-term impact on the child, and the husband agreed something had to be done.

"What do we do?" he asked. "Family therapy? Medications? Move out of the city?"

They acknowledged that any of these solutions might be in order, and they also agreed it was probably best not to discuss the problem in front of the girl until they had formulated a plan. But after a particularly tense evening meal, they couldn't contain themselves. The subject of the terrorist attacks came up, and each family member began spontaneously to express deep-rooted feelings.

The child poured out her worries about her parents. She disclosed her fear that one or both of them would enter their office building and never return because an airplane had crashed into the skyscraper.

"You're not alone," the mother confessed. "I worry about the same thing. It was horrible to see those two towers come down before our eyes. I guess we can't expect to forget something like that overnight." But she didn't leave the matter there: "Still, we can't go on living like this. Each of us probably has years to live and enjoy one another, and we simply can't keep being paralyzed by fear."

The father, relieved that the matter was on the table, felt that a load had been lifted from his shoulders. "We're all in this together," he said. "We have a problem, but we all love one another and we're a reasonably smart family. So why don't we work together to find a solution?"

The girl, happy to be accepted as a team member in an effort to resolve their common problem, immediately brightened up. "So what can we do?" she asked.

"The other day, Daddy and I were going through the possibilities, such as going to a family therapist," the mother suggested.

"I don't have time for that," the girl said, apparently thinking of the demands of school and soccer practice.

"Or we could move out of the city," the father suggested.

"No way," the girl said. "What about my friends? Besides, the terrorists could get us there too."

"Or medications," the mother said only half-seriously.

"Ugh."

"I think the best approach would be first to try to figure out what we're *really* afraid of," the father said. "Maybe there's one main thing, one underlying fear that's bothering all of us. What could it be? If we can figure it out, maybe we can find a way to deal with it. If we can't, we may have to seek outside help."

"So what do you think this big fear is?" the girl asked.

"You tell me," the mother responded.

The eleven-year-old thought for a few moments and replied, "Being hurt. Losing one of you. Being killed like the people in the buildings."

"I feel sort of the same way," the father replied. "I'm not so afraid of being hurt, but I can't stand the idea of losing one of you."

"Or leaving either of you behind," the mother said.

"So it's death," the father replied. "What we all seem to be afraid of in one way or another is death."

"That's deep," the mother replied uncomfortably.

"And not easy to deal with," the father said. "Who has the answer to death?"

"You should come with me on the weekends," the girl said. She reminded her parents that this very subject had come up during religious instruction classes at a local worship center, where they deposited her every weekend just before they went out to enjoy a cup of coffee. In those sessions, the teacher had dealt with a variety of theological issues, including death and the afterlife.

"Out of the mouths of babes," the mother quoted.

The family didn't resolve all their problems at this family summit. But by beginning to talk out their fears and concerns, they had taken a major step in dealing constructively with post-traumatic stress disorder. Therapists sometimes call this special state of self-awareness "learning to process your traumatic experience in a safe environment."

As the family continued to talk about their feelings and fears over the next few days, each member moved quite naturally into a constructive action plan. The parents joined their daughter at the worship center and joined an adult discussion group that was held at the same location. At these meetings, they encountered other parents who were going through some of the same challenges that they faced. As a result, they obtained advice and insights that helped them deal more effectively with their daughter, not to mention their own inner turmoil.

The girl sensed significant support and encouragement from her parents. She was relieved when they announced that they were going to severely limit the family's exposure to television newscasts about the disaster and the terrorist investigation. Also, in family discussions, the parents continued to demonstrate that they respected their daughter's views and input, and they made it clear that she had been instrumental in causing them to look for help in the worship center. As a result, the girl had a definite sense that she and her parents were in the crisis together and were working arm in arm toward a solution. Almost immediately, she found she was able to get a good night's sleep, and her tendency to act out her anxieties disappeared.

The mother and father kept working through their own respective symptoms of post-traumatic stress disorder with some success. Limiting exposure to news reports helped them as well as their daughter. The father actually consulted a therapist, who recommended a desensitization program to help with his intensified fear of flying. The mother also went through desensitization training at a group session with a psychologist, whom her company had made available. Soon, her fear of entering her office building became less of a problem.

Overall, the parents' anxieties didn't recede as quickly as did those of their daughter. But they were now able to cope more effectively and function quite well in the new post–September 11 social and political environment in New York City.

The Breakout connection

Now let's pause for a moment and ask what this family's experience might teach us about the Breakout phenomenon. A major lesson that strikes me is that the inner turning point for each of the three family members occurred as a result of what I have called a Breakout Network.

In other words, they didn't operate in isolation. Instead, they *worked together* toward a solution to the problems they were facing. At the outset, their frank three-way discussion about the worries and fears they were experiencing enabled them to proceed *jointly* to sever the prior anxious emotional patterns that were blocking each of them from dealing with their respective problems.

Furthermore, each person moved into a new state of self-awareness. This fresh perspective on their situation enabled them in individual ways to understand that their fears were really rooted in a basic fear of death, and that it was possible for them to develop effective tools to deal with the challenge. Or to put this in terms of our basic thesis, they experienced a joint Breakout, which then led to individual peak experiences of self-awareness.

As you can see, the peak experience of self-awareness may benefit you in two possible scenarios. On the one hand, the experience may prove to be extremely useful as a *onetime, life-changing phenomenon*. That was much the situation with Paul, who experienced a turning point in his apartment, and then began to view his career and values from a broader perspective. Similarly, my patient Katie underwent significant healing after broadening her understanding and belief about the power of her mind over her body.

On the other hand, heightened self-awareness may also serve as a *first step* that leads to a broader process of personal transformation. Self-awareness may get things started, and then merge naturally and imperceptibly into other Breakouts and peak experiences.

In this vein, the Manhattan family, in dealing with their post-terrorist emotional traumas, first experienced a new self-awareness about life and death. Then, in individual ways, they dealt with their respective fears and anxieties. Similarly, Rachel needed greater self-awareness about her physical potential before she could move ahead with her weight-reduction and exercise-training programs. In these two cases, a more general type of self-awareness came first. Specific decisions, insights, performances, or programs—some of which involved subsequent Breakouts—followed.

Many times, however, a separate peak of self-awareness isn't necessary at all. You may be able to move *directly* into a Breakout involving a specific peak performance, achievement, or insight. As we'll see in the next chapter, for instance, many people may undergo a Breakout and then move immediately into a significant breakthrough in personal creativity.

The Second Peak—
Creativity

Creativity is a quality everyone admires and desires, but few feel they can generate regularly. I can't count the times I have heard friends or patients say, "I'm just not a creative person." In fact, *anyone* can become more creative simply by understanding and learning to access the underlying biology of creativity. The secret lies once again in understanding and utilizing the Breakout Principle.

Creativity begins with the freeing of your mind to move in unaccustomed directions. Bestselling author Stephen King provided a capsule description of how this process works in his book *On Writing*. He said that when he was writing his novel *The Stand*, he reached page 500 in his draft and smashed into a creative wall.

"I had come to a place where the straight way was lost," he

said. "I wasn't the first writer to discover this awful place . . . this is the land of writer's block" (*On Writing* [New York: Scribner, 2000], 102).

In an effort to break the literary logjam, he began to take long walks along familiar neighborhood paths (203). Finally, King's dogged perseverance and understanding of his peculiar creative process paid off. In his own words, here is how his Breakout occurred:

> For weeks I got exactly nowhere in my thinking—it all just seemed too hard. . . . I had run out too many plotlines, and they were in danger of becoming snarled. I circled the problem again and again, beat my fists on it, knocked my head against it . . . and then one day when I was thinking of nothing much at all, the answer came to me. It arrived whole and complete— gift-wrapped, you could say—in a single bright flash. I ran home and jotted it down on paper, the only time I've done such a thing, because I was terrified of forgetting. (203)

Several telling points jump out of King's description of his creative experience. First, he fought hard to find an answer to the proper direction of his narrative. As he says, he beat his fists and knocked his head against the problem, but nothing came to him right away. This is a classic description of the struggle phase of the Breakout process. All or most avenues of preparation and analysis are often exhausted before the startling insight can occur.

Second, when he was blocked, he resorted to walking—one of the highly effective repetitive activities for breaking prior thought patterns and laying the groundwork for a complete turnaround in mind-set. As he walked, his concentration shifted from his work to the familiar natural setting. When you are hoping to receive a flash of insight, repetition and familiarity can be much more effective in setting the stage for a Breakout than mental activities that distract or stimulate.

Finally, as we would expect from our observations of the Breakout, King says that one day, "when I was thinking of nothing much at all," the answer came "whole and complete . . . gift-wrapped . . . in a single bright flash."

In other words, probably as a result of the repetitive walking plus a conscious "letting go" or "total abandon" of his problem, he finally reached a mental state where a Breakout occurred. You'll recall that these two strategies—repetitive activity and total abandon—are among the six basic mechanisms that have the power to trigger any Breakout.

The result was his creative "flash," which allowed him to move ahead and finish the story—and provide the public with yet another of his spine-tingling bestsellers. Obviously, we can't all expect to achieve the creative level of a Stephen King. But we *can* look to his experience as a useful, practical model for a Breakout that opens the door to a peak experience of creativity. To understand more fully just how powerful the creative Breakout can be—and also how the biological mechanisms operate—let's reflect for a moment on the science that underlies the creative process.

The Biology of Creativity

As you would expect, the creative process is linked directly to the basic Breakout biology that we have already discussed. In other words, at the beginning of a Breakout that produces a creative insight, we would look for such responses as:

- Overall quieting of the brain.
- Heightened activity in the attention and executive-control centers of the brain.
- Increased release of nitric oxide and accompanying neurotransmitters of "well-being," including dopamine and endorphins.

Other studies have suggested that even more may be involved with the biology of creativity—including an increased tendency of several regions of the brain to interact more completely in a process known as coherence.

From "coherence" to creativity

A report in *Brain Cognition* (40 [1999]: 479–99) suggests that both the left and right hemispheres of the brain contribute to verbal creativity in highly creative people. In contrast, less creative people use mainly one hemisphere of the brain.

A 2000 study by scientists in Slovenia backed up this conclusion with an investigation involving an electroencephalogram (EEG) (*International Journal of Psychophysiology* 36 [2000]: 73–88). They found that "coherence," or the ability of different parts of the brain to work together, was necessary for high levels of creativity. Among other things, they saw increased cooperation between hemispheres of the brain, including regions of the brain that lie distant from one another.

Another report by the same Slovenian scientists, published in *Brain Topography* (12 [2000]: 229–40), evaluated the EEG activity in 115 student teachers in a resting state, both with their eyes open and with eyes closed. Measuring the brain activity of their subjects for coherence, they again found a strong correlation between mental coherence and creativity.

Other EEG studies have established that mental functions associated with creativity are characterized by similar brain patterns. In an Austrian study, a series of EEGs were conducted on people performing a variety of mental tasks involving visual perception and imagery, listening to and composing music, verbal and visual creativity, and alterations in mood (*International Journal of Psychophysiology* 26 [1997]: 77–97).

The researchers found clear differences in the EEG results depending on the tasks performed. Specifically, they discovered special responses in coherence, or the way different areas of the brain cooperate in performing mental tasks. Because most of the tasks were related in some way to creativity—such as in the composition of music, or verbal and visual creative expression—we have another strong indication that the mind works in distinctly different ways when creativity is involved.

A related study from the same laboratory found that creative thinking—whether verbal, visual, or musical—is characterized by increases in coherence between occipital and fronto-polar electrode sites (*International Journal of Psychophysiology* 24 [1996]: 145–59).

Coherence, then, is emerging as a distinctive feature of the mind that is operating creatively. It is also likely that a similar kind of coherence occurs in the latter stages of the Breakout process, as peak experiences of all types occur. So we can expect increased mental coherence during peaks of athleticism (including the experience of getting into the zone), productivity, rejuvenation, and spirituality.

A "creative intelligence" paradox?

Another line of studies, conducted at Lund University in Sweden, has shown differences in regional cerebral blood flow between one group of subjects who had low scores on a creativity test, and another group with high scores (*Neuropsychologia* 38 [2000]: 873–85).

Cerebral blood flow was measured as the study participants engaged in various verbal tasks. In accordance with the predictions of the scientists, the highly creative subjects showed significantly increased or unchanged blood flow in the anterior prefrontal, fronto-temporal, and superior frontal regions of the brain. The group that got lower scores on the preliminary creativity test showed mainly decreases in cerebral blood flow in those areas.

Interestingly, on standard *intelligence* tests measuring logical-inductive abilities and perceptual speed conducted before the cerebral blood-flow evaluation, the less creative subjects scored *higher* than the creative group. On other sections of the intelligence tests, which focused on verbal and spatial abilities, the groups were at the same levels.

These results show not only clear differences in cerebral blood flow in creative and less creative people, but also suggest that conventional, analytical intelligence isn't a prerequisite for creativity. In fact, creativity appears to operate through mental channels outside of those associated with logic and perceptual speed.

Clearly, many distinctive physical changes occur in the brain during creative thought, but how do you get the process started? How do you turn on that inner biological switch?

Ultimately, it will be necessary to rely on one of the triggering mechanisms that have the power to produce a Breakout. But first, to increase your chances that the Breakout will lead to a peak of creativity, you may find it helpful to alter some of your expectations about exactly what creative thinking "feels like."

To this end, let's explore the extent to which there is a uniquely creative way of thinking.

Is There a "Creative Way of Thinking"?

Despite the distinctive biological responses that characterize creative thought, we firmly believe that there is no such thing as an uncreative person. To be sure, the brains of some highly creative people may be "wired" in such a way that they can make unusual associations and come up with new ideas faster or more frequently than others. But we are not slaves to the biology of creativity—or to any other inherited characteristics. On the contrary, practically anyone can become more creative simply by learning to employ the Breakout mechanism.

How can you enhance your own creativity through the Breakout?

First, it's important to become more aware of the kinds of thinking patterns associated with greater creativity. With this understanding, you will be in a stronger position to move smoothly into one of those patterns and enjoy the benefits of more creative thinking after a Breakout. To put this another way, it's essential to learn in practical terms what exactly is involved in "thinking out of the box," to use a familiar but apt term, and how to identify such unconventional thought patterns in yourself.

A number of reports suggest that an essential factor in such creative thinking is a conceptual leap outside linear, analytical logic, into an offbeat realm of thought that has been described as "holistic," "asymmetric," "nonlinear," or "dialectical." A common philosophical challenge can provide us with an illustration as to how this process may work.

How Joe Went Nonlinear

A divinity school student, Joe, was working on a research paper on the intellectual history of the Reformation when he found himself facing a seemingly intractable problem of logic—how to reconcile God's absolute sovereignty with human responsibility and free will. Although he had no illusions about his ability to solve completely this classic theological mystery, he did at least want to settle the issue to his own satisfaction.

Joe immediately recognized that an easy linear solution to the problem was that one principle might be right and the other wrong. But that simple solution didn't satisfy him, so he began to look for a way to reconcile the two positions.

Joe read various theological treatises and struggled with the concept for days, but couldn't seem to find a way out of the dead-end logic demanded by each position. Then he took the fortunate step of taking an uncharacteristically long shower. After he had stood under the water for several minutes, he found that he was no longer thinking about theological dead ends. Instead, random thoughts and ideas began to bounce about in his mind—concerning the party he was planning to attend the next evening . . . the squash match he had scheduled for the following day . . . an outing in the woods he hoped to take to see the changing autumn leaves.

Seemingly out of nowhere, thoughts about the theological problem started to tumble back into his consciousness, but in no particular order. He almost seemed to be observing a conceptual jigsaw puzzle, with the main pieces floating about before him. In the midst of this experience, he found himself becoming convinced that those pieces would eventually fit together, but he felt no compulsion to push toward a solution. Instead, he remained relaxed and watched and waited—and then it happened.

With the water still pouring down around his head and his eyes still closed, Joe remembered a principle he had read about months before—a concept known as an antinomy. The term refers to two true principles that nevertheless seem to be in tension, conflict, or contradiction. What might happen, he wondered, if he applied this principle to his challenge?

As Joe continued to examine the concepts with his mind's eye, he realized that he had been trying to solve the theological problem within a *temporal* human framework. On its face, that approach seemed doomed to failure. So Joe moved beyond the usual human categories and tried to contemplate the contradiction from a transcendent, *timeless* vantage point. Immediately, he realized that *both* concepts might be true if they could somehow be reconciled according to a divine "logic" that transcended space-time—a kind of "extra-dimensional" logic that might remain beyond the reach of human reason.

In short, Joe had found a way to approach the problem from an entirely different perspective. In shifting from linear analysis to nonlinear creative thought, he was able to shift from his usual Western mind-set to a non-Western acceptance of philosophical mysteries and logical contradictions. In the end, Joe concluded that he had discovered a highly effective and provocative way to think more creatively, outside his normal Western "box."

From Analysis to Mystery

Researchers specializing in cognition have sometimes drawn a distinction between thinking based on Western, Aristotelian logic on the one hand, and Middle Eastern or Far Eastern holistic thinking on the other. In Western cultures, the preferred thinking strategy propels the thinker along a kind of "mental line," which may be described in various ways, as:

- Moving from a basic assumption to a reasonable conclusion; or
- Moving from a cause to an effect; or
- Moving from a specific problem to a specific solution; or
- Moving from a set of facts gathered from vigorous research to an inferred meaning based on those facts; or
- Moving from a scientific hypothesis, to an experiment based on the hypothesis, to a conclusion about the validity of the original hypothesis; or
- Moving from an abstract principle to practical applications of that principle.

In following these linear thought patterns, Westerners have made great progress in technology, science, and other scholarship and research that depends primarily on systematic, logical analysis. In fact, rigorous linear thinking—especially the kind that moves from hypothesis to experiment to established theory to application—is a foundation of the scientific method. But in their success, Western scientists and intellectuals have often placed an unnecessary limit on creative faculties. At some point, maximum creativity requires the analytical thinker to *step outside* the framework of analysis and explore the issue from an entirely new perspective.

Non-Western cultures can provide us with models of this kind of thinking. For example, studies comparing European Americans to East Asians, which have been conducted by Dr. Richard Nisbett of the University of Michigan, suggest that those from these differing cultures think differently (see "How Culture Molds Habits of Thought," *New York Times*, August 8, 2000, D1, D4).

In responding to conflicting arguments, for instance, Americans tend to argue strenuously against weaker positions in an effort to eliminate all contradictions. East Asians, in contrast, often accept or incorporate weaker positions and modify their original viewpoints.

This East Asian way of thinking is similar to what Joe, in the illustration above, experienced during his Breakout. When he broke his linear thought patterns in the shower, the idea about the antinomy principle came to him. This principle encourages nonlinear thinking by saying that two seemingly contradictory theological positions can be accepted as true, without necessarily being reconciled logically.

The East Asian mind-set is also suggestive of the dialectic approach to truth advocated by the nineteenth-century German philosopher Hegel, who believed that reality could be understood only in its totality, or in a holistic sense. Or as he said, "the truth is the whole." More specifically, Hegel taught that to find real truth in politics, religion, logic, or other fields of human endeavor, contradictory positions—which he called the thesis and the antithesis—should be merged into a "synthesis," or a solution that was superior to either of the two original positions.

It may be argued that with Hegel's dialectic, a synthesis could be reached by the same kind of analysis and linear thinking that produced the contradictory thesis and antithesis. The Breakout Principle takes a quite different approach: namely, that the synthesis must be reached *not* by linear logic, but by *cutting off* linear thinking and allowing the whole brain—or the brain in a "coherent" state—to come up with a solution.

How might such holistic or nonlinear dialectical thinking work in practice?

One way is to focus on parts of a problem that are often overlooked by Western analytic thinkers. Richard Nisbett and another University of Michigan researcher, Takahiko Masuda, asked Japanese and American subjects to look at an underwater scene and describe what they saw. The Japanese began by describing the background or context of the scene, such as the physical appearance of the lake or pond bottom. Americans, however, were more likely to focus on the largest fish, and the direction of the action as the fish moved about (*NYT*, D4).

To put this another way, the Americans were more interested in the most obvious or attention-getting elements in what they observed. The Asians, in contrast, were more inclined to look at the entire context, including how different parts of what they observed fit into the whole.

The Cultural Promise of the Breakout

The above research provides us with strong evidence that the biochemical and physiological changes that occur during a Breakout have the power to cause a radical shift in the *cultural* thought patterns of Americans, Europeans, and other products of Western civilization and education. Specifically, a Breakout appears to move Westerners from an analytic to a holistic or dialectic mode, which tends to produce an increase in "oddball," "out-of-the-box," creative ideas and insights. Or to put this another way, Westerners begin to "think Eastern."

But are products of Western culture the only people who can benefit creatively from such a shift in thought patterns?

In fact, though evidence is scant at this point, we anticipate that many holistic "Eastern" thinkers will become more creative if they shift periodically to the analytic, linear thought patterns of the West. In other words, *anyone* who hopes to become more creative requires a greater coherence of the brain's hemispheres, and one way to achieve this coherence is to encourage your brain to work through both linear and nonlinear channels. The biological basis for all creativity adds further support to this conclusion.

In the end, then, the Breakout Principle should prove to be a common, cross-cultural phenomenon. In every culture, every Breakout should require a severing of familiar and uncreative thought patterns, whatever those patterns might be. This breaking of prior patterns will then enable individuals *of any culture* to move on to more innovative thinking.

Just the Beginning of Creativity

Experiencing a Breakout that culminates in a peak experience of creativity may be just the first step in transforming yourself into a more creative person. After you get the "feel" of enhanced creativity after your first few Breakouts, you may very well find that it becomes relatively easy to trigger "mini-Breakouts" that enable you to shift back and forth between different mind-sets.

At first, you will almost certainly find that you must consciously rely on one of the basic Breakout triggering mechanisms—such as repetitive activity, immersion in your belief system, or an altruistic focus. But after those initial Breakouts, things will get easier. I've encountered a number of creative people who move effortlessly, and even unconsciously, from an analytic to a dialectic mind-set when they encounter a mental roadblock. Then, after the breakthrough idea or insight comes to them, they automatically shift back to an analytical thinking mode.

One staff writer for a technical magazine reported that he

would often forge ahead fairly easily for several pages as he fleshed out a subtheme that explained some aspect of his main theme. But when he was ready to shift to another subtheme, he was sometimes stumped. He found he was unable to figure out a smooth way to make the transition to the new subtopic and relate it to his main theme.

To break the mental barrier, he would simply stand up and walk away from his computer to an entirely different part of his office. Then he would wander around, eyes half-closed, for a few minutes and concentrate on breathing regularly. Sometimes, he found he could make his mind go blank by humming one note softly as he exhaled. In less than five minutes of this routine, a new transition would usually come to him, along with a way of relating his new subtopic to the main topic.

What had happened in this situation? You might call the writer's technique a "mini-Breakout" because it had elements of a classic, full-blown Breakout. For example, he triggered the experiences with repetitive walking and breathing. Also, he broke prior mental patterns by causing his mind to wander and go blank for a few moments.

Mild writer's block was also the focus of a January 1998 study in the *Canadian Family Physician* (92–97). There, the researcher identified writer's block as a distinctly uncomfortable inability to write, which can interfere with professional productivity. One successful treatment was to lessen anxiety by engaging in brainstorming or role-playing—activities that can also break prior, negative mental patterns.

Such solutions may seem less dramatic than some other Breakouts we have described. But remember, your ultimate goal is to exploit the same biology that drives every Breakout—and if you're a blocked writer, it doesn't really matter how you achieve this end.

Clearly, the Breakout mechanism has the potential to enhance creativity in a number of ways. But how can *you* incorporate these principles into your thinking? How can *you* become more creative?

To answer these questions, let's consider three scenarios, which should provide some guidelines. They illustrate a number of specific and quite different ways that a Breakout may help anyone think and approach problems more creatively.

Three Creative Scenarios

The following three scenarios, which involve creative breakthroughs in different fields, should suggest the potential when a person triggers a Breakout who then moves into a peak of creativity. But this is by no means an exhaustive list, nor is it meant to provide hard-and-fast rules or techniques that will make you more creative. Rather, these illustrations are intended mainly to help you understand just how broad the creative Breakout can be—and how you might improve your performance in your occupational field or other area of interest.

Scenario #1: The Broadway Actor

Patrick Stewart, the renowned English stage actor, who became a household word in the United States after starring as Captain Picard in *Star Trek: The Next Generation,* was momentarily stumped. He wanted to return to live theater, but a number of obstacles stood in the way.

For one thing, how could he find time to rehearse with his demanding television schedule? The obvious answer was to do a one-man show, which would give him great flexibility and eliminate the need to depend on the schedules of other actors.

But what show should he choose? He riffled through a variety of books and epic poems and finally found himself focusing on Charles Dickens's *A Christmas Carol*. His inner movement, from indecision to firm commitment about the direction he should take, comes across clearly in Stewart's first-person account "Walking onto a Bare Stage (and into Scrooge's Skin)," published in the *New York Times* on December 23, 2001 (AR3).

He said that he had read the story for the first time while on location for a movie in the north of England. "Held on standby in a small hotel on a wet day, I took the thinnest volume from the residents' lounge bookshelves and read *A Christmas Carol* in one sitting," he related.

During that reading, a deep, life-changing insight came upon him.

"Oh, yes, I saw what C.D. [Charles Dickens] was doing," he wrote. "I saw all the narrative and journalistic tricks at work. I felt him pulling at my heartstrings and tweaking my emotions, but with my actor's cynicism firmly in place, I read on and on and finally closed the book, blinded by tears. A power I had not identified had been at work on me all the time. The potency of redemption, the headiness of liberated joy, the relief of the eleventh-hour reprieve was overwhelming."

In the terms we have been using in this book, Stewart moved from hard work, research, and analytic thought to a kind of abandon to Dickens's art when he read *A Christmas Carol*. As a result, he was overcome by the emotional impact of the classic tale. Still, all questions about the use of Dickens's work onstage hadn't been answered.

"But could this be communicated by an actor alone on a stage?" Stewart asked in his *Times* piece.

What ensued was further struggle: "I read and reread the story . . . cutting and pasting as I went, it still troubled me. I felt there was a hidden force in the book, the power that had made me weep, and I didn't know if I could expose it. That I might fail . . . frightened me."

As he labored, he sought a way to "release" the "hidden power" of the story, but that required inspired editing for the stage production. "Oh, the agony of what to leave out," he said.

Finally, he was ready to present a preliminary version of his work in 1988 at the Wadsworth Theater on the UCLA campus. It was an uncharacteristically chilly December night in southern California, and Stewart recalled, "I could see my breath in the air as I growled, 'Bah, humbug.'"

Yet the response of a small audience was gratifying and encouraged him to move ahead with his preparations. At Christmastime in 1991, Patrick Stewart walked out on a Broadway stage to perform his version of Scrooge—to great applause and acclaim.

An interesting feature of Stewart's description of his work on *A Christmas Carol* is the extent to which his creative experience parallels what we have been discussing about creativity. He worked hard, struggling with the material, until an emotional insight overwhelmed him. Then Stewart went back to work, and the cycle began again. Once more, analytical preparation was the starting point, from which he ascended to new heights of creativity on the stage.

But creativity is by no means limited to the arts, as the next scenario demonstrates.

Scenario #2: The Scientist

As a scientist myself, I am well aware of how important flashes of creative insight can be in moving a research project forward. First of all, it's important to exercise a degree of creativity simply to state the main purpose of an experiment. At various points in conducting a study, we inevitably encounter conceptual obstructions, which we often have to surmount by applying nonlinear thought patterns. Finally, arriving at conclusions about the results of a study may require the greatest surge of creativity. All along the way, conclusions about creative Breakouts can help open mental doors and smooth the way to a successful end.

This movement from preparatory struggle, through a Breakout, and into a creative mind-set is basically the same for scientists as for those in other fields. Observe the way the creative experience in science is described by Sir John Eccles, winner of the 1963 Nobel Prize in physiology/medicine:

> When I am searching for a good new idea, I fill up my mind with the knowledge on the problem and my critical evaluation of the attempted solutions of that problem. Then I await the outcome of the mental tension so created. Maybe I take a walk, as Einstein often did, or I listen to music. This procedure is called an incubation period. I don't struggle with my mind under tension, but hope that a good creative idea will burst forth, and often it does. It sometimes is useful to write the problem and ideas in words. It is clear that much of the creative process is done subconsciously. But if a good idea suddenly bursts forth, one is then involved in intense mental concentration, which may be quite prolonged—as in the story about Isaac Newton, in his trancelike state in his rooms

in Trinity College. (*Evolution of the Brain: Creation of the Self* [New York: Routledge, 1989], 233)

In this description, Eccles provides us with a series of enlightening observations. First of all, in describing his creative process, he makes it clear that he moves along the classic Breakout channels in coming up with new scientific ideas. To summarize, he does his research to "fill up my mind with the knowledge on the problem" and possible solutions.

This first phase creates "mental tension," he says. But instead of fighting the tension, he backs off to "await the outcome." He may take a walk, thus providing the physical repetition that can trigger a Breakout. Or he may listen to music. In either case, he engages in activities that break prior stressful thought patterns.

His reference to this backing-off phase as an "incubation period," where the work of creativity is occurring subconsciously, is an especially appropriate and informative metaphor. In fact, as we know from our research, a mental "birth" is precisely what happens as the overall brain calms down, certain attention and executive-control centers fire up, and EEG coherence within the brain increases.

With the groundwork in place, his new creative idea appears in a flash. Or in the terms we have been using, the Breakout produces a peak experience of creativity.

Finally, Eccles shows that he understands that his experience is not an isolated personal phenomenon. He refers to Newton's trances and Einstein's walks, which led to great new scientific insights. According to one account, Einstein also invoked his imagination to picture himself "surfing on a beam of light, or being pulled along in an accelerating elevator through empty space"—a mental exercise that gave him "apparently simple insights that would lead him to remake physics" (from Jim Holt's review of *Einstein in Love* by Dennis Overbye, *New York Times Book Review,* October 8, 2000, 12).

Scenario #3: The Musician

Similar descriptions of the creative process can be found in the world of music. First of all, in a number of the medical studies cited above, researchers found that distinctive brain waves are involved in musical creativity, as well as other creative thought.

Also, other studies have suggested that music can have a particularly soothing effect on the brain—and any influence that soothes tends to break thought patterns that arise from stress and tension. For example, a report in the September 25, 2001, issue of the *Proceedings of the National Academy of Sciences* found that music can stimulate parts of the brain associated with positive, happy, or even euphoric emotions. The researchers found that food and sex also switch on many of the brain structures activated by music.

One business executive illustrates these soothing, antistress powers of music. He found that when he confronted a difficult conceptual problem and was unable to go to the gym and work out the mental difficulty on a treadmill, he could often experience a creative Breakout by closing the door to his office and turning on some Bach or Mozart. One of the Brandenburg Concertos, or repetitive rondos such as those found in Mozart's compositions, had the power to switch his mind from his business problems to focus exclusively on the melodies he was hearing. In part, the power seems to have lain in the pleasant familiarity of the pieces, which he had heard scores of times; and in part, the power lay in the measured, steady, and repetitive nature of the music. Often, after this executive had listened to the Bach or Mozart for only five minutes or so, a new idea would come to mind and enable him to move ahead with his planning.

In another example, a woman had founded a successful non-profit math workshop for teenagers who were interested in pursuing their interests outside of regular high school classes. But she found that she could easily become confused and tense as a result of the many loose ends she had to deal with: the dozens of students, who were at different levels in their math abilities; regular workshops that required massive publicity efforts and other planning; and grant proposals to keep the whole operation going. At the same time, she had to perform her regular duties at work and try to be a good mother and spouse.

Periodically, when she felt she was going to "go crazy" in the midst of all this stress, she found solace in sitting down at her piano and playing some simple music she had learned years before. Some of it was popular show tunes; other pieces were classical compositions; and others were gospel songs. Taking simple, short "music breaks" in her hectic daily schedule helped her calm down and order her thoughts within minutes. With this new mind-set, she was able to return to her professional or nonprofit work with greater energy, and often with new ideas and insights.

In a radical version of what I have called the release stage of the Breakout sequence, the romantic folk-rock singer and composer Leonard Cohen actually withdrew for five years to a mountaintop monastery above Los Angeles. While there, he immersed himself in menial chores and did his best to avoid mental distractions.

As a result of this lengthy retreat, he emerged with musical compositions that have been described as having greater clarity and moving toward a spiritual unity. His compositions, which he calls *Ten New Songs,* "combine the earthy details of country music . . . with an almost biblical oracularity," according to one reviewer.

Also, according to the reviewer, who sees elements of the Far East in Cohen's efforts, the new work "evokes that hardest to grasp Zen idea: the oneness of mind and body, earth and heaven, now and then." But the reviewer also observes that for "those uninclined to seek Eastern wisdom in Mr. Cohen's music, that sense of serenity can be seen as the wisdom of aging, a singular mind's reflections turned by time toward commonalities. Mr. Cohen himself would probably take this view" (*New York Times,* October 28, 2001, AR 29–30).

Obviously, it is difficult, if not impossible, to capture in ordinary words everything that happens in the creative mind. Cohen's reviewer, and the rest of us as well, inevitably bump up against the limits of language in trying to convey what happens when the musician, the novelist, the poet, the scientist, or the business executive experiences a new, transformational insight.

But the biology behind the Breakout, and the practical understanding we can derive from that biology, at least move us a few steps closer to understanding the creative process. Most important of all, what we now know about the Breakout can help all of us access the science of the process in our daily lives—and pull those inner triggers that will make us more creative and enhance our overall performance.

Now, let's turn to a related topic—productivity. Productivity on the job or in volunteer activities often relies heavily on the individual creative impulse. But productivity in an organizational setting also involves being able to work together and stimulate creativity in others.

8

The Third Peak— Productivity

In many respects, the third peak experience—productivity— represents an extension of personal creativity into an organizational setting. In other words, to become *more productive,* it's often necessary to first become *more creative*—that is, to find innovative ways to do an efficient job. The kind of organizational creativity that can ultimately lead to higher productivity on the job presents us with three special Breakout Principle issues.

- First, productivity in an organization usually depends heavily on that form of *creative collaboration* that was introduced in the first and second chapters as the Breakout Network. (*Note:* You'll recall that the term *Breakout Network* refers to a combination of two or more people—whether in a business, volunteer organization, family setting, or other group—who work together to trigger both individual and joint Breakouts that benefit all participants.)

- Second, despite the presence of more than one person in a Breakout Network, maximum creativity and increased productivity in the organization depend on the ability of *individual participants* to trigger their own personal Breakouts.

- Third, the Breakout Network, like the individual Breakout, is rooted in its own special biology and science.

The Science Behind the Breakout Network

The science behind the Breakout Network begins with the same mind-body phenomena that are associated with the individual Breakout. You already know that the sine qua non for triggering an individual Breakout is to engage in some activity or thought process that effectively *breaks prior thought and emotional patterns*.

The same principle holds true when Breakouts occur in an organizational setting. To maximize your creativity in a discussion group or other idea-generating session, you try to trigger one or more personal Breakouts by relying on one of the mechanisms or activities described in Chapters 2 and 5.

But an increasing body of research evidence suggests another, broader Breakout dynamic may occur in the right kind of group setting.

The quest for a "living company"

For example, the London Business School's A. de Geus, writing in the *Harvard Business Review* (75 [1997]: 51–59), described

148

what he calls "living companies"—or organizations that have unusual staying power in the world economy. Instead of ending after about twenty years, which is the life of the average corporation, these living companies may continue for hundreds of years. As an illustration, de Geus cites the Swedish company Stora, which is more than seven hundred years old.

The author argues that many companies "die young" because their politics and practices are based too much on ordinary—and by implication, linear—economic thinking. But those that have a long life have a different focus, according to de Geus.

While weaker companies emphasize production of goods and services and the generation of profits, the companies with greater staying power recognize that the organization is actually a *community of human beings*. As a result, they approach their company like "careful gardeners," who encourage growth and renewal, but without endangering the employee "plants" they are nurturing.

As a consequence of this personal orientation, the executives and their employees are better able to work together to ensure their collective survival in an unpredictable world. To this end, they pursue more effective strategies of adaptation, renewal, and innovation, including the ability to make dramatic organizational changes when necessary. In their development, these long-lived companies typically create opportunities for employees to learn from one another—through such vehicles that we have described as the Breakout Network.

A successful Breakout Network is also dependent upon what other researchers have called a "participative culture," with employees from all parts of the organization contributing to the success of the entire corporation (see *Organization Dynamics* 13 [1984]: 4–22; and *Journal of Business Strategy*, 1989, 38–42).

Again, the Breakout Network represents a powerful vehicle to marshal the creative contributions of workers from every type of background and thinking style.

Of course, the mental and creative stimulation that can be generated in well-organized small groups isn't limited to commercial companies. In a 1999 report published by scientists at the Department of Neurology at the University of Chile, a group of older participants, averaging 66.6 years of age, showed significant increases in thought stimulation after participating in a study that featured sixteen special workshops.

Specifically, the project required the seniors to attend ninety-minute workshops, twice a week over two months. During the sessions, they were exposed to a number of cognitive strategies, including group memory activities and pantomime plays that motivated them to think more creatively (*Review of Medicine in Chile* 127 [1999]: 319–22).

Synchronize—don't homogenize!

Although an effective Breakout Network requires that very different people be pulled together in one forum so that they can interact, the Network should *not* be designed so that the participants are all encouraged to become the same, like products of a corporate cookie cutter. Instead, each person should keep his own identity as his ideas interact and clash with others.

Business researcher M. Sawhney, writing in the *Harvard Business Review* in 2001, described this principle with an imperative that he used as the title of his article: "Don't homogenize, synchronize" (100–108, 145). Centering on the business need to be sensitive to the needs of the customer, Sawhney argued in favor of making an organization "permeable to information." Among other things, this means that while a company should synchronize its databases, workers should be encouraged to retain their individual strengths and outlooks. Only through such diversity in the workforce can an organization expect to move closer to its customers, sustain product innovation, and improve overall operational efficiency and productivity.

When an organization establishes interactive groups based on the above objectives—that is, *when the organization forms a "living company," which is based on a "participative culture" with diverse but "synchronized" worker interactions*—it is well on the way to establishing a potent Breakout Network. Furthermore, such groups can become a significant new source of creativity and productivity for *any* organization—including commercial corporations, nonprofit organizations, and ad hoc associations with various missions and purposes.

But these considerations represent just the first step in designing a true Breakout Network. The fundamental principle underlying a Breakout Network—as is also the case with the individual Breakout—is that it should be designed to foster an *atmosphere that encourages the breaking of unproductive thought patterns in individual participants.*

Sometimes, all that is required to achieve this severing of previous thought "tapes" is to toss around new ideas in a comfortable setting with trusted colleagues—preferably those who think differently from the way you do. Such interaction, which will at least expose you to ideas that have been generated outside your own mind, may on occasion be enough to sever your own prior patterns, or those of other participants.

The final result may be a *personal Breakout in a group setting,* which in turn leads to a personal peak experience of creativity or other significant insight that has the power to change the direction of the group. In other words, the individual who has undergone such a Breakout will usually first share his or her innovative breakthrough with the group. Then, together, they will be able to shape and fine-tune the new concept into a usable application, which will result in greater productivity for the organization.

But more often, a relaxed discussion among old friends won't be enough to get the creative juices flowing freely in an organizational setting. A stronger creativity-stimulating impulse is required. In many successful Breakout Networks, this impulse may arise out of a dynamic that we call the Grating Paradox.

What Is the Grating Paradox?

Harvard researchers D. Leonard and S. Straus—reporting in a 1997 article in the *Harvard Business Review* provocatively entitled "Putting your company's whole brain to work" (110–21)—introduced a group process of innovation that they called creative abrasion.

The authors recognized that in the contemporary business environment, it was absolutely necessary to innovate, or the company was likely to fall behind the competition. But not all organizations are set up to take advantage of a socially based creative impulse.

A common problem that the researchers encountered in observing a number of organizations during their investigation was that many companies had failed to transform conflict into a constructive "grating" process. In other words, the companies might put different people with divergent thinking styles together on the same team. But instead of "grating" or "sharpening" one another to produce creative solutions, the relationships deteriorated into a noxious blend of bad feelings and pitched battles.

In effect, the Harvard Business School researchers uncovered a powerful paradox, which we have incorporated in the Breakout Network as the Grating Paradox. In brief, the paradox can be stated this way:

In an organization, intense but cordial disagreement is necessary to produce innovation, enhanced productivity, worker satisfaction—and lasting agreement.

Because of the inevitable conflicts that will arise in such a Breakout Network group, it is essential to emphasize the "cordiality" qualification in the above definition. This caveat becomes especially important when the members are highly accomplished in their respective fields and probably possess an extra measure of self-confidence, if not arrogance.

As such participants "bump" up against one another, feelings simply cannot be allowed to career out of control. Consequently, the organizers must establish a structure where disputes do not become personal. Wildly different worldviews and personalities must be placed in contact so that they can continue to "grate" against one another, but at the same time, they must be juxtaposed so that they don't produce destructive conflict. The ultimate goal of the Breakout Network—coming up with new ideas that will enhance productivity—must always take precedence over any individual's desire to dominate or dictate.

What Do Other Experts Say About the Grating Paradox?

Researchers in other fields and venues have also arrived at conclusions that back up the Grating Paradox.

For example, an article by Becca Orchard of Becca Orchard

and Associates in Duluth, Georgia, emphasized that conflict and disagreement are a fact of life in business. But the author recommended *optimizing* differences rather than minimizing them as a means to promote greater creativity (*AAOHN Journal* 46 [1998]: 302–12, 313–14). Those organizations that succeed in managing and using such differences will be in a much stronger position to increase mutual respect among workers and also to find better solutions to problems, such as those involving productivity.

To increase productivity, many experts focus on molding and training middle management. R. M. Kanter, writing in the *Harvard Business Review,* notes that productivity depends on the design of new products, the institution of new structures to accommodate change, and the installation of new equipment (60 [1982]: 95–105). Such advances depend largely on the level of innovation generated at the middle management level, Kanter says.

She found that the most innovative managers are visionary, comfortable with the idea of change and persistent in pursuing new concepts. Furthermore, her research revealed that innovation flourishes in organizations where the areas of responsibility and expertise of various individuals overlap, workers interact across functional lines, and information flows freely.

These grating-related principles are not limited to the field of business. In medicine, for instance, researchers increasingly emphasize the importance of capitalizing on cross-disciplinary discussion groups, which include participants who can interact with thinkers outside their own narrow fields (*Cultural Medicine and Psychiatry* 22 [1998]: 55–92).

In a similar fashion, Japanese cancer researchers have criticized the use of traditional scientific paradigms, which are often rooted in an assumption that human biology is based on linear thinking and simplistic cause-and-effect relationships. This linear approach has "outlived its usefulness," they said. Instead, it has now become necessary to integrate medical findings into a broader, more complex framework that may not fit neatly into conventional scientific thought patterns (*Japanese Journal of Clinical Oncology* 30 [2000]: 529–33).

Such conclusions are particularly interesting to me because my sometimes "nonlinear" research observations have been assailed throughout my entire career as "unscientific," even though those observations have subsequently been confirmed by newer technology that follows the "linear" rules of science.

Clearly, designing an effective Breakout Network that promotes "creative abrasion" without fostering acrimony requires considerable education of participants, advance planning, and rule setting—or part of what we have described as the hardworking struggle phase of the Breakout. So what are some of the practical parameters to keep in mind when your organization decides to make use of the Grating Paradox—and move toward forming an effective Breakout Network?

From the Grating Paradox to a Breakout Network

For the Grating Paradox to work effectively in a Breakout Network, the group must be of a manageable size—ideally from four to six people. Of course, there will always be exceptions. Two or three people have sometimes operated effectively as a Network group. But usually such a small group works only when every person is unusually creative and compatible, or when they have a history of "playing off" one another to good effect.

As many as seven or eight participants can also sometimes

interact effectively, so long as they know one another fairly well and feel comfortable talking freely in one another's presence. A group of more than eight usually becomes unwieldy or less effective. Typically, in such a large group, two or three assertive or highly articulate individuals dominate the discussion.

More than a numbers game

But Breakout Networks involve more than a numbers game. Each participant must recognize that the others have been chosen not because everyone is the same or naturally compatible, but for the *opposite* reason—i.e., because as many participants as possible are *quite different* from one another and may even be prone to intense disagreements.

This Network "rule" may seem counterproductive for effective discussions. However, a group composed of people who think along the same lines is simply not as likely to come up with as many innovative ideas as one composed of dissimilar individuals who see the world through radically different eyes, but who can nevertheless speculate and muse together.

Furthermore, the rules of an effective Network require each participant to show respect for the others or the creative dynamic won't work. The fastest way to shut down free discussion is to belittle or make fun of someone else's idea or suggestion. Those experienced in working with the Grating Paradox in groups insist that each participant must:

- Respect other fields of expertise and educational backgrounds.
- Respect other thinking styles—and recognize the importance of having participants with both linear and nonlinear thinking patterns.

- Never disparage or ridicule the contributions of others.
- Firmly commit to the principle that *no ideas are bad ideas*.
- Assume that one person's viewpoint will probably not prevail—at least not without "massaging" and adjustments from others.
- Recognize that a seemingly irrelevant or offbeat idea will often be as valuable, or even *more* valuable, than an idea expressed through an elegant sequence of reasoning or linear logic.
- Assume that it will probably require some time—hours, days, or even weeks—to arrive at the best solution. *One reason:* Group interaction becomes most productive when the participants begin to feel more comfortable with and trusting of one another.
- Understand how the biology of the Breakout works— and how this phenomenon can be triggered. *Corollary:* It is advisable for each participant to be instructed in the Breakout process individually before joining a Breakout Network. Such training will make each person more alert to the great potential for innovation in every participant as the discussion proceeds.

In a sense, the Breakout Network is a projection onto a broader, group scale of the individual holistic or dialectical thinking process described in the previous chapter. We have seen that individuals with an Asian mind-set may tackle problems first by relying on nonlinear thinking, which may involve accepting concepts that might at first seem contradictory. Furthermore, Western-style thinkers—who operate mostly by relying on linear logic and analysis—have found that triggering a Breakout often causes them to leap out of their previous, linear thought patterns into a holistic Eastern mind-set.

In this fresh-thinking mode, they have often discovered more creative ways to solve the problems they were facing. The advantages of applying such dialectical thinking to organizations or to societies can be seen in Sternberg's *American Psychology* article cited in the references for the previous chapter.

Organizations that transfer divergent thinking modes successfully to their small groups will benefit from the creative collision of both holistic-dialectical thought patterns and analytical-linear patterns. The result is that the Breakout Network capitalizes on the powerful Grating Paradox, and the principle of creative abrasion described by Leonard and Straus in their *Harvard Business Review* article.

Grating works for any organization

The Grating Paradox works for practically any type of organization, including those involved in scientific projects. You may remember that the studies we have done at Harvard Medical School in recent years often involved participants from widely divergent fields—such as cardiology, neuroscience, biochemistry, or psychiatry. By assembling a multidisciplinary team for certain projects—and by being certain that all members are sufficiently compatible to be able to resolve their inevitable conflicts and disagreements—we are much more likely to come up with a better final result.

As you move to establish a Breakout Network in your organization, a question that often arises is how, if at all, does the Network differ from traditional brainstorming? In fact, there are some similarities—but also some decisive differences.

What About Brainstorming?

Some have suggested a link between the Breakout Network and old-fashioned group brainstorming sessions, and there are some similarities. For example, both the Breakout Network and effective brainstorming require that each participant come into the group session prepared with facts, figures, and plenty of personal analysis. Also, in both types of groups, it's important to define the problem to be solved, and to set a strict time limit on each session.

To achieve these goals, it will almost always be necessary to appoint a group facilitator in both the Breakout Network and a regular brainstorming session. But the facilitator should not make the mistake of slipping into the role of dominant leader. This guide should fulfill only certain limited functions, such as:

- Be sure that everyone understands the basic issue to be explored (one central issue is almost always preferable to multiple issues).
- Make administrative preparations, including extra pads of paper, pens, display boards, and computer facilities.
- Keep track of the agreed-upon time limit for discussion.

Depending on the nature of the issue under discussion, a Breakout Network or a brainstorming session may run from a minimum of about forty-five minutes to a maximum of about two hours. Anything longer than two hours typically causes participants to lose focus or become physically or mentally fatigued.

Finally, in both types of groups, the facilitator or another designated "recorder" should jot down new ideas. Failing to keep a record will cause good ideas to be forgotten and perhaps lost forever.

But there are also major differences between the Breakout Network and garden-variety brainstorming.

Beyond brainstorming

A fundamental distinction is that ordinary brainstorming sessions tend to be staged with the organizers giving little prior thought to the *individual mind-sets of group members*. In other words, the participants' *thinking styles* are not usually included as part of the planning equation.

In contrast, an effective Breakout Network requires that organizers pay close attention to the creative and thinking styles of each participant. Both linear and holistic thinkers must be included in the mix, so that they will be able to "grate" against one another—with minimal personal conflict—as they knock ideas back and forth. (*Note:* This grating process is the group version of the struggle phase that typically precedes a Breakout.)

Also, participants should be instructed about the nature of the two main thinking styles—linear and nonlinear—so that they will know more about what to expect as they begin to interact.

In addition to including those with different thinking styles, a Breakout Network group should draw in participants with divergent educational and training backgrounds. If an organization includes legal professionals, blue-collar workers, and salespeople, representatives of as many of these backgrounds as possible should be in a discussion group.

But perhaps the most important difference is that a Breakout Network is based on a well-researched biological phenomenon—the Breakout Principle, with all its distinctive brain and biochemical transformations. These same biological changes will occur in individuals in a group setting when the Breakout Network has been properly designed. But they are not as likely to occur in an ordinary brainstorming session.

In fact, as we will see in the next section, ordinary group brainstorming may not be as effective in producing creative ideas as would "individual brainstorming," which has all the prerequisites to produce a Breakout. Such individual brainstorming includes situations where several people, operating in isolation from one another (such as on private computers), mull over the same problem or issue. Then they transmit their thoughts and insights to a central location, where all contributions are processed and, if possible, merged.

To sum up, all Network members should be aware not only of different thinking styles but also of the biological events that may occur as the discussion proceeds. With this knowledge, they will become more alert as a group to the possible onset of Breakout experiences and the appearance of fresh ideas about productivity and other issues, both in themselves and in other participants. Because of the importance of this biological dynamic, all Network participants should be trained in how to trigger their own personal Breakouts.

Now, with this broad base of research in mind, let's return to the practical challenge of setting up a workable system that will maximize the organizational creativity that improves productivity. We have already discussed the optimum size and constituency of the group. But two fundamental questions remain:

When you begin to design or participate in a Breakout Network, how, exactly, can you cause Breakouts to occur during a discussion? What is the secret to triggering a Breakout on the *organizational* level, when you're deeply embroiled verbally with other people?

Some Suggestions for Triggering Breakouts in Groups

Any practical strategy that has the power to trigger creative Breakouts in a Network must be built on the basic principles we have been discussing. The most important include:

- The *severing of prior patterns of thought and emotion*—which is also the fundamental prerequisite for any individual Breakout.
- The *Grating Paradox*—which assumes an ongoing but civilized clash of ideas and thinking styles.

A number of effective group strategies based on these criteria have emerged in our research and are reflected in the following list. These suggestions are not intended to be exhaustive or prescriptive, merely suggestive, as you design your own Breakout Network.

Strategy #1: A Relaxation-Response Break

When your work or volunteer team loses its creative or productive edge, you might consider trying an approach that Harvard colleague Dr. Ruanne K. Peters and I tested in the corporate offices of a manufacturing firm (*American Journal of Public Health* 67 [1977]: 946–53; see also my earlier article on combating stress in a corporate environment in *Harvard Business Review* 52 [1974]: 49–60).

Dr. Peters divided 126 volunteers into three groups and told them that over a twelve-week period she was going to test the effectiveness of daily relaxation breaks against the harmful effects of stress. Groups A and B were given differing instructions, while group C, a control group, received no instructions.

Groups A and B were asked to take two fifteen-minute relaxation breaks each day, one in the morning and the other in the afternoon or evening. They had to take the breaks on their own time—either before or after work, or during the usual company coffee-break time. The A group was taught how to elicit the relaxation response. The B group was told just to sit quietly during their relaxation time.

At the end of the study, the A group, who had utilized the relaxation-response technique, showed significant improvement in health symptoms, illness days, sociability and satisfaction, and job performance. Job performance included evaluation of the participants' levels of physical energy, strength of concentration, ability to handle problems, and overall efficiency.

The B group, which had simply been told to sit quietly, also did well on these measurements, though not as well as group A. The C group, which had received no instructions, did the worst.

This result provides research confirmation of what we would expect to occur in a well-designed Breakout Network. That is, engaging in an activity that breaks prior emotional and thought patterns is likely to raise performance levels, productivity, and overall job satisfaction.

Strategy #2: Laughing

One of the most effective ways to break prior thought patterns in a group is through humor. A joke, diverting story, or a few minutes of banter can often distract Network participants from unproductive ideas and emotions and set the stage for further progress.

Katherine Hudson, writing in the July–August 2001 *Harvard Business Review* (45–48, 51–53), reported that injecting some fun into a traditional Midwestern company's serious culture helped increase performance and sales. By encouraging both formal programs featuring humor and also spontaneous joking, she found that the company reaped a number of benefits, including:

- A stronger company esprit de corps.
- Greater camaraderie on company teams.
- Increased innovation.
- More efficient communication of basic corporate messages and policies.
- Increased productivity as a result of reduced stress.
- Doubling of sales, and tripling of net income and market capitalization over seven years.

The lesson for Breakout Network groups: Be prepared to punctuate your discussions with humor! It's not necessary that a "joke time" be institutionalized. But each group organizer and facilitator should make it clear that the discussions are supposed to be enjoyable—an observation that will almost always automatically open the door to spontaneous humor.

Strategy #3: Teaching

It's been said that the best way to learn a subject is to teach it. For purposes of the Breakout Network, shifting to teaching mode can also be a powerful means of breaking your prior thought patterns and moving into a new creative space.

Noel M. Tichy of the University of Michigan Business School reported in the April 2001 issue of the *Harvard Business Review* (63–70, 166) on a "boot camp" for new corporate recruits in one major corporation. In two three-month sessions, top executives were assigned to teach new employees about new products and to interact with them on innovative ideas that the new people had been asked to develop.

These sessions were so successful in generating and fine-tuning new ideas that the teaching strategy became the company's main research-and-development engine. The organization's technical experts became mentors for the new recruits, and the seasoned executives and other experts found that they could learn a great deal from the fresh-thinking recruits.

An important lesson from this illustration is that changing roles in a Breakout Network can often help you slip through mental bottlenecks. For example, you might change facilitators from time to time. Or when the group seems stymied, you might suggest that each person switch conceptual positions by arguing as vigorously as possible for the opposite viewpoint.

Strategy #4: Corporate Athletics

Sometimes, just sitting or interacting in one enclosed office space can become an obstacle to creative thought. To break out of this mold, the entire group might take a walk or go on an outing.

Because discussions in organizations often tend to be sedentary, with everyone sitting in a familiar seat, some form of moving about should usually be programmed into the agenda. You'll recall that getting a little exercise, especially repetitive activity, can be sufficient many times to break prior trains of thought and trigger a Breakout. Or if the participants are particularly athletic, even more vigorous activity may be helpful.

In the January 2001 *Harvard Business Review,* J. Loehr and T. Schwartz recommended the development of "corporate athletes"—employees who were capable of sustained high performance on the job. The authors suggested that following a model that they called the "performance pyramid" could develop such top achievers.

The foundation of this pyramid, they said, was physical well-being, on which emotional health, mental acuity, and spiritual purpose could be developed. They suggested rigorous exercise as an essential component to develop a sense of emotional balance, which could clear the way for peak mental performance.

In many ways, this "corporate athlete" concept represents an extension into the organizational realm of some of the personal Breakout triggers we have already explored, such as repetitive walking and jogging. Undoubtedly, interspersing more vigorous activity with sedentary discussions will be likely to stimulate your mind to think in more innovative directions.

Strategy #5: Fresh Graphics

Some groups have discovered that their creativity was stifled because they were using overly familiar, boring, or confusing graphics to illustrate points in their discussions. The obvious solution is to look for new ways to illustrate your points. For example, if you've been using PowerPoint, you might switch to a dry-erase board. Or if dry-erase isn't working, you might have each person draw a diagram, then shuffle the diagrams around so that everyone is looking at someone else's creation.

A report in the September–October 1999 *Harvard Business Review* (87–94, 184) suggested the use of "organigraphs" instead of organizational charts to stimulate discussion about how the company's functions and key players might be reorganized. An organigraph, the authors explained, is not a chart but looks more like a map, which provides an overview of the company's functions and the ways people operate at work.

Perhaps the most important use of organigraphs in promoting productivity is that by showing the operation of the company from an entirely new perspective, it might help managers develop a better understanding of where the company's main strengths and expertise lie. With such insights, the managers could make better decisions about what new part of the world should be a target of expansion, or what untapped area of business, such as the Internet, might hold significant promise.

A lesson about the senses

An important lesson from research into graphic aids is that in designing your Breakout Network you should take into account *all of the senses*—and especially the visual. Seeing something in a fresh way will often break those old mental tapes and usher in an entirely new—and highly productive—thought pattern.

But don't forget the other senses. When the main focus in an organization is to generate new ideas that have the potential to provide significant increases in productivity, highly unusual techniques may be in order. For example, smelling a pleasant aroma, such as baked bread, can trigger all sorts of new, positive associations in many people. Similarly, fresh and pleasant sounds, tastes, and tactile sensations can often reverse negative patterns of discussion and get the creative juices flowing again.

A related issue is "synesthesia," or the triggering of responses in one sense when a completely different sense is stimulated. For example, some people may see certain colors when they hear certain music tones. Evidence suggests that many people beyond those identified as real "synesthetes" may respond with another sense when they are exposed to stimuli associated with an entirely different sense.

One group, for instance, consistently chose light colors when they heard high musical notes, but dark colors when they heard low notes (see *American Journal of Psychology* 109 [1996]: 219–38). In other experiments, subjects associated sneezes with bright colors and coughs with dark colors. Also, sunlight was regarded as "loud" and moonlight as "soft" (see *Journal of Experimental Psychology, Human Perception, and Performance* 8 [1982]: 177–93; and *Journal of Neuropsychiatry and Clinical Neuroscience* 11 [1999]: 58–65).

Many times, these studies are discussed in terms of metaphors, which explain a perception or experience in one area of life in terms of those from a different area. In using some of these concepts as part of Breakout Network strategy, you might display visual aids to the group, such as paintings or colored panels, or expose them to music. Then ask them to record any thoughts or ideas. The sensory stimulation may well cause them to think in new, more creative terms about the issue at hand.

Strategy #6: Storytelling

Another powerful strategy that can stimulate creativity in groups is storytelling. Assume, for instance, that your discussion on a topic has grown stale. To add a little zest, you might push the participants to start explaining their points with specific illustrations or analogies.

Typical prompts that a group facilitator or other participants might use to spark storytelling—and a return to creativity—include:

- Give me an example of that!
- Can you illustrate that point?
- Can you think of a similar situation—an analogy of some sort—to help us understand better?

Once members of a Network get used to providing examples and stories to back up their points, the group will usually find that their ability to think flexibly and "out of the box" increases.

A September 2001 article in *Medical Education* (862–66), for instance, demonstrated how interest and memory in students could be enhanced through the use of stories as a vehicle in teaching medical management. Among other things, the authors found that using stories could provide a framework for what they call "web" or "net" thinking—i.e., nonlinear thinking. When the participants moved into a more dialectical mind-set, they often discovered that it was easier to establish links among objective and subjective details in complex case management scenarios.

Strategy #7: Linear Swordplay

Another effective technique for breaking past, unproductive patterns in a Network discussion is for one of the participants to interrupt with a completely new linear argument or suggestion. In effect, the new logical concept "slices" through the discussion in what we call linear swordplay.

Robin's "magic three"

In one such discussion, scientists in a commercial corporation were trying to solve an Internet problem. As they moved forward in a classic linear progression, the participants systematically eliminated contradictory or weaker arguments. At the end of their discussion, however, they had no answer that their company could implement on the Internet. Though they had come up with a very logical answer, they were still far from a satisfactory solution.

To get the discussion moving again, one of the participants, whom we'll call Robin, broke in with a rather disruptive observation.

"There have to be at least *three* answers," she said.

After a brief silence, someone asked, "What do you mean? We already have the best answer."

"But we all agree that it's *not* the best—it's not quite right," Robin said. "I've always found there are always at least three reasonable answers for any problem like this. So let's find the other two."

Finally, the group saw where she was heading. If they could come up with at least two more reasonable solutions—both of which could be derived by employing linear logic—one of those might be better than the one they now had. Or by combining two of the answers, they might find a superior result.

To act on Robin's suggestion, the participants had to put aside their prior line of thought—i.e., break the old mental pattern of the group—and embark together on an entirely new track. Finally, they came up with not just two, but three additional possible solutions. Then they began to merge the old idea and the new concepts and found a number of *combinations,* which provided them with a variety of more creative and satisfying solutions than the first solution alone.

In effect, Robin and her colleagues had used a dialectical model to "push" or "bump" conflicting concepts against one another as thesis and antithesis. Eventually, one of the combined solutions—in effect, a synthesis—provided the best possible answer and gave them a promising strategy for using the Internet more productively in their business.

Slashing with the thesaurus

Similarly, when a discussion in one of his client companies runs into a creative wall, a leading management consultant sometimes pulls out a copy of the extended contents page of an old thesaurus, which, he says, "summarizes all human knowledge."

The detailed contents—or "synopsis of categories"—in a classic Roget's thesaurus, for instance, divides human knowledge into broad "classes," such as "abstract relations," "space," "physics," and "sensation." These, in turn, are broken down into subcategories.

"Sensation" is divided into such topics as "sensation in general," "touch," "taste," and so on. Finally, the subcategories are subdivided into specific topics. Under "taste," for instance, you find "savoriness," "unsavoriness," "insipidness," "sweetness," "sourness," "pungency," and "tobacco."

The consultant frequently finds that simply exposing discussion participants to additional words and concepts in the general area of the topic under discussion can help them break through mental blocks. The fresh terms stir up the interaction and help the members come up with a more complete, holistic train of ideas.

Strategy #8: Electronic Brainstorming

Finally, a series of studies—conducted by researchers from Japan, Canada, and Texas—have shown that, many times, putting people face-to-face in groups results in less creativity than keeping them in separate locations, where they free-associate without worrying about how others will respond to their ideas.

A useful vehicle for this approach is what has been called electronic brainstorming, in which participants in front of computers contribute ideas via keyboard.

Researchers from the Graduate School of Humanities and Sciences, Ochanomizu University, in Tokyo, divided one hundred undergraduate women into groups of four, with three groups using computers to brainstorm and a fourth, nonelectronic control group. The study found that the three electronic groups did better than the controls in generating ideas (*Shinrigaku Kenkyu* 72 [2001]: 19–28).

Similarly, researchers at the School of Business, Queen's University, Ontario, noted that brainstorming groups have consistently produced fewer ideas than an equivalent number of individuals working by themselves. To explore this issue further, they compared groups using electronic aids with those interacting traditionally, in a nonelectronic group setting. Among other things, they found that the electronic groups were more productive than the nonelectronic groups (*Journal of Applied Psychology* 76 [1991]: 137–42).

The Group as a Creative Organism

Sometimes, a well-constructed Breakout Network, which may begin by using one or more of the above strategies, can actually develop to the point that the group functions as a single, creative organism. The thinking of all participants may interact in such a way that the contributions of the members finally merge automatically into a productive consensus.

In effect, the members move into a "group zone," which involves an almost mystical interplay of different individuals' thought patterns. This group zone experience is reminiscent of the free-flowing mental patterns that characterize individual athletes who sometimes operate in a near subconscious or even mystical state as they compete at the peak of their performing ability.

When such a pervasive creative impulse takes over, the Network discussion *in itself* may be enough to sever past thought patterns. In other words, devising separate triggering strategies may not be necessary. The group dynamic may be sufficiently powerful to trigger a personal Breakout in you, in another participant, or in several participants simultaneously.

It is difficult, if not impossible, to separate this kind of organic "group thought" process into its component parts, at least with current scientific methodology. Hooking up participants in a Breakout Network to brain-mapping fMRI machines, EEGs, or the like without destroying the creative group interaction may not be feasible.

But what we *can* do is examine more closely several case studies that illustrate how creative impulses have been harnessed in different organizations. These real-life examples suggest the broad range in which a Breakout Network may be able to operate.

The Broad Range of the Breakout Network

To stimulate your thinking about the possibilities of the Breakout Network, consider these "short takes" of situations in several different organizations. In each, a flash of creativity has resulted in significantly enhanced productivity.

The software translator

During an airplane trip a number of years ago from San Diego to San Francisco, I found myself in a long ticket line. As I waited, I noticed that the man in front of me was carrying a box but no luggage. To break the boredom, I asked, "Where are you going?"

"Nowhere," he replied. "I'm just mailing this box."

"It's too bad you have to wait so long just to mail a box."

"I have a deadline I have to meet. I work as a language translator—and I came up with a special computer program. It translates English into Chinese, and Chinese into English. I have to send it by the safest, quickest route to my partner, and this seemed the best way."

Fascinated, I asked him to tell me more about how he had come up with the idea for his program.

"Frankly, I was stumped," he continued. "I reached a point where I just couldn't figure out my next step. I was really hitting a wall. But then I went out to browse in a local bookstore, and I picked up a book, *The Relaxation Response*. The author, a guy named Benson, describes a technique that helped my mind work in new directions."

He went on to explain that he began to understand more fully why the two languages are so different. Some of his thinking overlapped with points that have been made previously in this

174

book—that English is linear, whereas Chinese is more holistic. English builds letters to syllables to words to sentences. But Chinese looks at the whole picture first.

"Anyhow, I followed the steps Benson suggested," he continued. "I sat down and closed my eyes, repeated one of my favorite Chinese phrases, and pretty soon, I stopped worrying about my mental block. Funny thing, though, just after I stopped worrying and started relaxing, the idea came to me about how to finish this translation program. It was a real breakthrough."

Needless to say, I got a kick out of the look on his face when I told him that I was the Benson who had written the book. But in some ways, I was even more intrigued about his discovery that the relaxation response could trigger creativity—and lay the groundwork for a significant increase in his business productivity.

This encounter was important to me on at least two levels. First of all, at that time I was in a relatively early stage of formulating some of the Breakout concepts described in this book. This fortuitous meeting with the software programmer helped nudge me further along in my thinking.

Second, and just as important for our current purposes, his experience suggested how individuals in various types of organizations could break prior thought patterns by relying on relatively simple activities and techniques. His Breakout—and I definitely think that is what occurred inside him—apparently arose from a combination of sources, including walking around the bookstore, reading a new book, and then applying the relaxation-response technique he learned from his reading.

The same sort of inner transformation could easily happen with any member of a Breakout Network who follows a similar line of activity. So organizers and facilitators of such groups should be alert to any activities or techniques—such as reading a provocative section from a book or engaging in some group relaxation-response exercise—that could trigger a Breakout in one or more Breakout Network participants.

The power to change corporate culture

Groups that possess the power to effect change in an organization are likely to take their role as idea generators much more seriously. So it would be wise to set up your Breakout Networks in such a way that their ideas and suggestions are funneled directly to upper management.

Upper management should, in turn, understand that it's important to take the Network-generated ideas seriously and, whenever possible, implement them. Finally, when a decision is made on an idea, it is essential to provide the Network group with feedback to explain the rationale for accepting or not accepting their contributions.

Carol Bernick, president of the Alberto-Culver Company of Melrose Park, Illinois, described how similar organizational dynamics worked for her in a June 2001 *Harvard Business Review* article (53–58, 60–61, 146). In an effort to remake the corporate culture and increase productivity, Bernick began to publicize the values and behaviors that she regarded as important for company improvement.

Also, to generate new ideas and foster higher productivity, she created the role of "growth development leader" (GDL). These GDLs were assigned as mentors to about a dozen people and were given real power to make changes. In particular, they could vote on issues that had to be addressed by the business as a whole. When the GDL groups and others achieved certain goals, the successes would be celebrated through awards for leadership and innovation.

As a result of these changes in the corporate culture, over a seven-year period the company cut employee turnover in half, experienced an 83 percent sales growth, and enjoyed a 336 percent rise in pretax profits.

The moonshine shop

According to Whack's Buzzword Compliant Dictionary on the Internet, a *moonshine shop* is a "place where ideas are distilled and turned into working models in short order." As a prime example, the dictionary cites the moonshine shop program at Boeing—which was featured in the *Wall Street Journal* on September 5, 2001. There, the moonshine shop refers to a team that works outside the company's usual channels of operation to develop cheaper, faster ways to build airplanes.

In some respects, the Boeing moonshine shops seem almost a prototype for an effective Breakout Network. In one project conducted by the shops, a team was pulled together from divergent sectors of the company to find an efficient way to move bulky airplane seats from the factory floor up several stories to the level of the plane. Then, the chairs had to be inserted through the narrow door of the aircraft. Usually, the seats were moved via an overhead crane, but this created a bottleneck that slowed assembly to a snail's pace.

The moonshine team, led by a mechanic who was given authority to operate outside normal production channels, came up with an unorthodox but highly effective solution. The team abandoned the crane and installed a farmer's hay elevator, which was equipped with a metal-studded conveyor belt. With this, workers could move the seats relatively fast and steadily up to the plane door, and productivity in the factory increased significantly.

In another breakthrough, a Boeing moonshine team member

devised a mobile pneumatic machine the size of a hundred-pound go-cart, which could push a seventy-five-ton 757 airliner. The cart was so powerful that it replaced the old twenty-thousand-pound tugging devices that had previously been used. Boeing even sought a patent for its use in multiple ways throughout the industry (*WSJ*, A16).

The moonshine shops at Boeing have provoked some grumbling among traditionalists, including union representatives who argued that the shops make unauthorized use of nonunion workers, according to the *Wall Street Journal* report. Also, the moonshine shops ran into some bureaucratic resistance from those who were suspicious of any innovation that threatened to change the usual way of doing business. But for the most part, the success of the shops overcame the opposition—as you might expect from any Breakout Network that increases productivity and makes a business more profitable.

The power of smell

The Green Mountain Coffee Roasters organization has been touted by Forbes.com as "one of the smartest small companies in America" (see *Forbes* magazine, October 29, 2001, www.forbes.com). But the founder, Robert Stiller, was definitely not a conventional linear thinker—at least not while he was enrolled at Syracuse University, where he was unable to maintain a C average.

On the other hand, Stiller was a creative type par excellence. After finally getting a degree from Parsons College in Fairfield, Iowa, he and a partner built a successful rolling-paper company, which reached annual sales of $11 million. They sold it in 1980, with each partner receiving $3.1 million.

But Stiller still had to figure out what to do with the rest of his life. As he relaxed, enjoying the taste and aroma of a gourmet coffee at a ski condo in Sugarbush, Vermont, he was struck by the idea that he should investigate the restaurant that sold these great beans.

After visiting the restaurant and dreaming of the possibilities with a partner, he bought the organization and eventually became the sole proprietor. The company rose to number 16 on the *Forbes* list of the 200 Best Small Companies, with Stiller's stake rising to $89 million.

A suggestive element in Stiller's experience is that if you're stuck mentally, a change of scene—along with a pleasant aroma, such as fine-roasted coffee—may enhance your creativity. As we saw previously with synesthesia, stimulating the senses, such as exposing yourself to new sights and smells, can help sever prior thought patterns and open the portals of the mind to innovation.

The Buck Rogers idea

The founder of FedEx, Fred Smith, is always alert to a "Buck Rogers idea," or a dramatic, unconventional concept that can change the way he does business (Associated Press, December 2, 2001).

Though he received only an average grade for his efforts, he came up with just such a transforming idea on an economics paper he wrote as a Yale undergraduate. His idea was that as companies relied more heavily on technology and computerization, they would need to keep their equipment operating, but without relying on a huge inventory of hardware parts.

The challenge was how to get the parts overnight to companies. Eventually, refusing to discard the basic idea, Smith decided that special airplane transport was the answer. The result—the FedEx company—has grown into a global organization with 215,000 workers who transport 5 million shipments per day.

Such breakthroughs in productivity—which suggest the presence of principles that underlie the Breakout Network—may also occur in a group context, as executives at a computer-chip maker discovered.

Linear swordplay in Silicon Valley

Executives at Nividia, a Silicon Valley computer-chip maker, found that they were producing an extraordinarily high percentage of flawed units of a new graphics chip—about 30 percent of the total. (The industry average was about 5 percent.)

With such an exorbitant rate of mistakes, the executives knew they couldn't ship the chips to major customers, such as Dell. They began to fear for the very existence of their company. A tense top-level meeting ensued—reminiscent of the struggle phase that precedes the Breakout.

Finally, when most possibilities seemed exhausted, one of the company founders, the vice president of hardware engineering, slashed into the discussion with a radical concept—an example of what we have called linear swordplay. He suggested that every one of the chips be tested by hand.

At first, the company president rejected the idea on the grounds that the monumental amount of work required "would kill us off," according to the *FSB* report. But the executives continued to work through the idea, until finally they realized that despite the onerous work, the idea could save the company.

In fact, that's exactly what happened. All the top specialists pitched in to test the hundreds of thousands of chips, at a rate of about five minutes per chip—and succeeded to the point that the new chip became a big hit in the industry (see *FSB*, September 2001, 61–63).

Toward Organizational Agility:
The Ultimate Goal of the Breakout Network

Perhaps the most important impact of interactive, creativity-generating Breakout Networks throughout an organization is to make the company more "agile," to use a word favored by some business management theorists (see *Harvard Business Review,* November–December 1997, 126–39).

Network-type small groups tend to pull more workers, with a wider variety of backgrounds and mind-sets, into the creative process. This expanded participation increases the possibility that the organization will become more productive and open to positive transformation.

A Breakout Network will be most successful—and will foster the greatest productivity in the parent organization—when each of the participants knows how to trigger creativity. The "agility" of the group depends heavily on the ability of each member to break prior unproductive patterns of thought and help all participants move into a more creative collective mind-set. Organizational productivity can usually be traced back to the creativity and productivity of each individual.

The Breakout Principle, then, has broad application not only to enhancing the creative life of the mind, but also to the more active life of the workplace. And for those who want to engage in intense physical activity—and maximize their performance in the realm of sports and physical exercise—the Breakout offers the possibility of a peak of athleticism, including a portal to the fabled "zone."

The Fourth Peak—
Athleticism

The high school baseball player who had been batting over .500 for the first six games of the season suddenly went into a slump. In eight straight at-bats, he struck out. He tried a variety of different swinging techniques and stances, but nothing seemed to work. The more he thought about his problem, analyzed it, and tried to apply the correct technique, the worse the situation seemed to get.

Then a family friend who understood the Breakout Principle came up with an idea. He had been watching the young man's batting movements closely for his last four at-bats, and he thought he had identified the problem. To be sure about his analysis, he videotaped the batting movements the next time the player came to bat. Sure enough, he confirmed his suspicions.

The batter, in trying to hit home runs, had fallen into the fallacy of "uppercutting" the ball as it passed over the plate. Specifically, as the ball left the pitcher's hand, the player would immediately lower his hands and his bat, instead of moving them slightly backward and upward in a classic "cock-the-trigger" motion. (*Note:* This baseball trigger has nothing to do with the Breakout trigger!) As a result of these mechanical problems, his hands began the swing toward the ball in a down-to-up motion, instead of the preferred up-to-down attack. The result was that he constantly missed the baseball by swinging underneath it.

To correct the problem, the friend explained to the player the mistake that he was making and ascertained that the young man understood the problem conceptually. Then the adviser had the batter practice the correct swing in front of a mirror without a ball; after that, they moved to a batting cage. Finally, with the preparation or struggle phase completed and the next game about to begin, the adviser told the batter to "forget everything" when he stepped up to the plate.

"Just swing!" the adviser said. "Breathe easily and regularly as you step into the batter's box. Stay loose. Focus only on the ball—from the time it rests in the pitcher's hand, to the time it leaves the pitcher's fingers, and finally to its movement in the air and as it spins toward the plate. But don't think about anything else. As you watch, if you sense it's a hittable toss, swing at it— but again, *without thinking about what you're doing!* In your mind, there should be nothing but that ball. As you shift toward it and begin your swing, you become one with it."

The batter took this advice, and as he positioned himself next to the plate, breathed with conscious regularity, and focused only on the ball in the pitcher's hand, he was overcome by a strange sense of quiet. The noise of the crowd receded. He and the ball were all that existed. He was highly alert, but paradoxically, he was also totally relaxed. He felt he had somehow *merged* with the ball, even though it was still in the pitcher's hand and he was in the batter's box. On the second pitch, he rapped a sharp single to left field.

Soon, this player was hitting everything that crossed the plate. He was "in the zone," as some athletes refer to this high-performance mind-set, where it seems the player can do no wrong. Gradually, he learned to evoke this inner state at will. As a result, he continued to keep a relaxed, loose body and a clear mind every time he came up to bat. He also moved back up toward his phenomenal .500 hitting average.

What had happened here from the standpoint of the Breakout Principle?

First, the batter "struggled" by identifying and analyzing his mistakes and working hard to correct them. He also practiced his technique diligently in the batting cage. But when he stepped up to the plate, he left his preparation mentality behind. He relied on regular breathing and a single-minded focus on the ball to break all prior thought patterns, all anxieties and analysis. In other words, he went through the release stage and pulled the Breakout trigger. With his thinking faculties suspended, his visual senses and raw motor skills took over. Finally, he achieved what we call a "peak experience of athleticism"—a transformed state of mind that resulted in a solid hit to left field.

This type of experience has occurred many times on the base-ball field and in other sports settings, and other athletes and observers have described similar outward manifestations of the phenomenon—though without an understanding of the underlying biology. In popular thought, this superior mind-body state has even sometimes been regarded reverently or in awe, as a serendipitous quality that is mostly enjoyed by great professional athletes.

The Groove

George F. Will, in his bestseller *Men at Work: The Craft of Baseball* (New York: HarperCollins, 1990), said that a "delicate mental equipoise" is necessary for good hitting (209). Citing the great hitter from the San Diego Padres, Tony Gwynn, as a prime example, Will wrote that Gwynn believed that a batter must first do prodigious work studying videotape, using batting machines, and relying on other practice techniques. But when he stepped up to the plate, he left behind the preparation and relied instead only on his ability to see the ball and his muscle memory—that is, the physical reactions that he had developed during those hours and hours of hard practice.

When a hitter is batting poorly, often because he has allowed his mind to get in the way of a fluid, nonthinking response to the ball, he begins to "struggle"—as Will and many baseball professionals call this negative state (211). In our terms, the hitter in this position reverts back to the struggle phase of the Breakout Principle, where he thinks, analyzes, and worries, but hasn't yet made his move to release these prior thought patterns and pull the Breakout trigger. The stress hormones, including epinephrine and norepinephrine, course wildly through the body and prevent the possibility of peak performance.

Will noted, with considerable insight into what we now know as the Breakout Principle, that when "batters are hot they say they are 'in a groove.' . . . A groove is something especially smooth, a path that guides movement effortlessly. To be in a groove is to have all one's 'mechanics' flowing together. 'Mechanics' that flow? No, to be in a groove is not to be mechanical, it is to be animal, with the grace that only something living can have" (209–10).

Later, George Will sums up the hitting groove—or what some

might call the zone—with a couple of telling observations. The first comes from Tony Gwynn, who believed that successful hitting came down to five words: "See the ball and react." A second description comes from Branch Rickey: "Full head, empty bat" (210). In these and similar reports, a common insight is that something distinctive—a "visual factor"—connects the human eye to peak athletic performance.

The Visual Factor

Many scientific studies—often related to ball-and-bat sports such as baseball and cricket—support the common assumption that the visual sense plays an essential role in superior sports accomplishments. For example, in professional baseball, even the slower-moving curveballs may take less than half a second to travel from the hand of the pitcher to the batter at home plate—a split second that allows little time for mental evaluation or decision.

In cricket, some scientific observers have said that laboratory measures of visual reaction time suggest the performance of the batter is "impossible" because there is too little time to respond to the unpredictable, moving ball (*Perception* 16 [1987]: 49–59). The explanation offered in this Oxford study is that with the best athletes, the muscle motor system responds more quickly to visual perception. Obviously, there is no time to "think" in such fast-moving encounters.

Other studies of cricket players have shown that when the ball leaves the "bowler's" hand, the top batsman monitors the movement of the ball with predictive saccades, or fast eye movements. He continues to follow it for about one-tenth to one-fifth of a second after it bounces off the ground, and then makes contact (*Natural Neuroscience* 3 [2000]: 1340–45; see also *Perception* 21 [1992]: 91–115). Obviously, such quick responses would be impossible if other parts of the brain were engaged.

What seems to be happening in such situations is that peak performance begins with the athlete's seeing the ball, or using the eyes in some other way, such as to monitor movements on the playing field. Then, motor memories that the athlete has embedded through earlier training about the trajectory and movements of the ball are transmitted *directly* from the eye to the player's muscle motor system, without passing through the analytical part of the brain.

(*Note:* It has been suggested that a similar phenomenon may occur among those who are experts at nonathletic physical activities, such as playing a musical instrument or touch typing. Playing sixteenth notes on a piano or violin, for instance, allows no time for thinking about striking or fingering individual notes or chords. The same is true when typing at high speeds. The eye may see the notes to be played or the words to be typed on a sheet of paper, but the message bypasses the analytical thinking faculties and moves directly to the motor memories and finally the fingers.)

At *all* top levels of sports achievement—including but not limited to various forms of skiing, contact sports, and fast-moving-ball sports—athletes, coaches, and expert observers consistently say that the best performances involve "instinct," "letting your body do the work," or "getting your mind out of the way." The essential combination is *visual perception plus muscle reaction*—without allowing thought or mental reflection to get in the way. When the athlete begins to think consciously about physical mechanics or movements, his or her performance usually deteriorates.

What are the implications of these findings for the Breakout Principle?

On one level, such descriptions of peak athletic performance may suggest that the athlete should eliminate any deep thinking, and in a sense, that's true. But the kind of deep thinking to avoid is *not* the profound, nonlinear sense of unity and well-being that often accompanies the Breakout. Rather, the anxieties and worries that are by-products of excessive linear analysis must be excluded.

Paradoxically, there is also evidence that we can learn more about our most profound inner experiences in sports not only by turning away from analytical intelligence but also by affirming the simple, "primitive" responses that often characterize the animal world.

"Become an Animal!"

Ally, an executive secretary in her late forties, had started jogging as part of a shape-up program designed to tone up her legs and get rid of some middle-aged body fat that had begun to accumulate around her hips and waist. Unexpectedly, she became so enthusiastic about the program that after a few months she decided she would enter a competitive five-kilometer run that was being held in a park near her home. In training for the run, however, she discovered inner mental barriers that she had never realized existed.

In particular, Ally found that when she faced the daunting prospect of running up two of the hills on the course, she always lost heart and walked the last few hundred yards to the top. No matter how hard she ran in training or worked out on weight equipment to strengthen her legs, she couldn't seem to keep running the final uphill stretch.

To counterbalance her dissatisfaction with herself, she decided to take her sedentary dog, Harry, on one of her training runs. "I figured that Harry was in worse shape than I was, so we could commiserate together," she said.

But she was surprised. As the two began to ascend one of the two challenging hills, Harry kept on going at the same pace that he had used on level ground. Ally became so mesmerized by his steady loping gait—and his apparent unawareness that the ground underneath him was now slanted upward—that she herself lost any sense that she was running, much less struggling up a steep grade. Before she realized what had happened, she was at the top of the hill and was starting the descent.

After this experience, Ally took Harry with her on every training run. After watching his behavior closely, she developed her own strategy, which she eventually found that she could employ even when Harry wasn't around.

She encapsulated the basic concept as a command to herself: "Become an animal!" When she confronted a difficult hill, she would imagine that she could see Harry loping easily just in front of her. Then she would fantasize that she and Harry had somehow merged—that she had changed from a running human into a running dog.

In a way, Ally had incorporated the same principle that writer George Will had observed among the top professional baseball batters. By using her powers of visualization and imagination, she found a way to bypass her analytical thinking, which was telling her that the hills were too steep and reminding her that she had never been able to run them without slowing to a walk.

With those limiting thought patterns out of the way, Ally could let her body take over. She not only shaved more than a minute off her 5K course time, but she also discovered that she had been selling herself short. She was capable of a much higher level of sports achievement than she had thought possible, but she would never have realized that improvement if she had failed to heed the lesson right there in front of her eyes, in the form of her loping dog, Harry.

What Ally learned about how to use her mental powers to enhance her physical performance has been summed up by some researchers in the term *mind-body fitness* (*Journal of Cardiovascular Nursing* 11 [1997]: 53–65). In brief, such fitness goes beyond conventional aerobic and strength training to combine physical activity with a focused—and even contemplative—internal mental state. Those who can achieve this powerful combination can improve their performance in any sport—including Olympic figure skating.

Nancy Kerrigan: A Case Study in "Mind-Body Fitness"

Nancy Kerrigan—the 1994 women's Olympic silver medalist in figure skating, and the 1992 bronze medalist—was always an excellent skater and a superb athlete. But to reach the top, she knew she had to improve her concentration and eliminate distracting negative thought patterns. So she decided to seek help at our Mind/Body Medical Institute in Boston before her Olympic bid in 1992 (see *Deaconess This Month* 3, 1). Much of the following account comes from this interview.

Before seeing us at the Deaconess Hospital, she was ranked fourth nationally and was a world-team alternate in women's figure skating. She said that she knew she needed to become more consistent and not let her mistakes "snowball" in competition. After a fall, she would often say to herself, "I stink."

With the help of Sue C. Jacobs, Ph.D., a scientist at the institute and an instructor at the Harvard Medical School, Kerrigan began to learn mind-body techniques designed to help her manage her stress better and ward off disruptions to her concentration. After using biofeedback techniques to evaluate Kerrigan's muscle tension and overall stress levels, Jacobs concentrated on helping the skater achieve a state where "her mind and body operate as one."

Among other things, Kerrigan learned how to employ the relaxation response through the kind of simple mental repetition that we have discussed as a means to trigger a Breakout. Also, she established preperformance rituals, such as visualizing her routine occurring exactly as it should, under optimal conditions.

The Special Role of Visualization

Visualization—imagining a picture or "mental movie" of an ideal performance—can become an important part of the struggle phase of athletic training. (Visualization can also be helpful in dealing with health problems. Specifically, if a person with a particular complaint, such as a headache or insomnia, learns to visualize what it is like to be free of the problem, that individual may begin to experience relief of the symptoms.)

The most effective visualization technique requires a two-step process:

Step #1: Elicit the relaxation response.

During preparation for competition, the athlete should elicit the relaxation response through one of the proven methods, such as progressive muscular relaxation, which is the sequential tensing and relaxing of each of the body's main muscle groups over about five to ten minutes.

A common approach is to concentrate first on the feet by tensing and then relaxing the foot muscles. Then, move on to tensing and relaxing the legs; the trunk, including the abdominal muscles; the arms and shoulders; and finally the neck.

Instead of this technique, the athlete might focus on breathing for the preliminary five-to-ten-minute period. Or she might repeat a sound, word, prayer, or phrase for a similar length of time. The instructions for eliciting the relaxation response through such mental repetition have already been described in Chapter 5 as the first triggering mechanism for a Breakout.

Eliciting the relaxation response before visualization prepares the mind to receive mental images of an ideal performance. The objective is to implant the visualization firmly in the mind and motor memory of the muscles. This preparation will then set the stage for the main Breakout, which will occur during competition and may culminate in a peak athletic performance.

Step #2: Form a detailed mental image of a perfect performance or other desired physical act.

This second step of visualization involves some mental work, which is part of the struggle phase before the main Breakout. But the initial opening of the mind and then the use of the imagination to picture an ideal performance reaches well beyond vague notions of positive thinking. Scientific evidence suggests that mental activity such as visualization *can actually strengthen muscles physically!*

At the November 11, 2001, annual meeting of the Society for Neuroscience, the Cleveland Clinic Foundation's Lerner Research Institute reported that a muscle can be strengthened merely by *thinking* about exercising it. A group of thirty healthy young adults were tested using a mental-workout regimen over twelve weeks. For fifteen minutes a day, five days a week, they were asked to imagine that they were doing fifty repetitions of exercise for their little finger and elbow flexor.

When the visualizers were compared with a control group at the end of the twelve weeks, the researchers found that the pinkie strength increased by 35 percent, and elbow flexor strength increased by 13.4 percent. In conducting its research, the Lerner Research Institute uses sophisticated measuring techniques, such as the fMRI (see *Washington Post,* December 18, 2001, HE03, www.washingtonpost.com; the Franklin Institute Online, "The Human Brain—Imagine Increased Muscle Strength!" sln.fi.edu/brain/exercise/neuromuscular.html; and www.lerner.ccf.org).

Athletes such as Nancy Kerrigan who use some form of this two-step visualization procedure fix a firm mental picture of a perfect performance in the mind *and the muscles* prior to competition. With this preparation, they put themselves in a stronger position to enjoy a peak performance when the games begin.

From the Mind to the Ice

As Nancy Kerrigan moved on with her Olympic hopes, the Harvard scientist Jacobs acknowledged that the precise contribution of the mind-body training was hard to quantify. But Jacobs said, "We helped her meet more of her potential by decreasing her stress and changing her thinking in a way that would help her to maximize her performance."

At the 1992 Olympics, which followed immediately after the mind-body training, Kerrigan surpassed her previous rankings and went on to win the bronze medal. Then, unbelievable stress and pressure cascaded down upon her in the historic and tragic incident in the 1994 Olympic trials, where she was clubbed on the knee by an attacker supporting rival skater Tonya Harding. Despite this setback and the pressure of Harding's continued presence as a teammate and a competitor at the Olympics, Kerrigan made the U.S. team and won the silver medal in the 1994 games. She was edged out for the gold by Oksana Baiul of Ukraine in a razor-thin 5–4 vote of the judges.

In an interview with *Boston Globe Magazine*, Kerrigan described her inner experience in 1994 this way: "I was focused, but it was not normal. That one competition was totally different. Jerry [Jerry Solomon, her agent] said he's only seen one or two other athletes focus like that, but not for that long—it was six weeks [between the attack and the Olympic competition]. It is amazing for me to look back, because I'm not sure how I could have done that. I guess I just sort of went on autopilot" (www.boston.com/globe/magazine/1998/2–1/interview).

Kerrigan is frequently cited in the news media as a phenomenon of sports psychology. She certainly provides us with a premier illustration of how the mind has biologically been designed to control and direct the body to triumph over even the most onerous outside pressures. Furthermore, the power of the Breakout Principle is evident throughout the descriptions of her inner strength and her subsequent athletic triumph over unbelievable odds.

But we must remember that her tremendous achievement was rooted in a simple secret, summed up this way by Scott Hamilton, the 1984 male figure-skating gold medalist, in an NBC-TV interview during the 2002 Salt Lake City Olympics:

"Skate stupid!" Hamilton said, referring to a quip from an earlier gold medalist, Dick Button.

In other words, after you have done extensive preparation and begin the competition, get your analytical mind out of the way! Let your body and intuitive responses take over. The same basic advice applies to those who participate in any athletic event.

Clearly, the Breakout Principle—with its characteristic four-stage sequence of (1) struggle, (2) release/trigger, (3) Breakout/peak performance, and (4) return to an enhanced "new-normal" level of activity—has broad application to top-level performers. But the benefits are not by any means limited to the elite athlete.

What About the Average Athlete?

The weekend athlete will never rise to the level of a Nancy Kerrigan, but it is possible for practically anyone—including both elite athletes and those with average skills—to experience regular Breakouts that greatly improve athletic performance. Lisa, a social tennis player, provides some insight on this point.

Lisa's Serve

Lisa, a pediatrician, had always enjoyed her weekly game of doubles, with participants drawn from a pool of about ten friends. But she was on the verge of dropping out of the group because she felt she was always the weakest player.

She was particularly disturbed because she regularly choked when the pressure was on her, and she felt she rarely lived up to her athletic potential. Her main difficulty was that she became excessively nervous at crucial points, both when she was serving and when she was rallying with her ground strokes for a game or a set point.

She mentioned her problem to a friend who was familiar with the operation of the Breakout Principle, and he suggested, "You have to figure out a way to break prior patterns of anxious thought. Then your natural responses will take over and do the job for you."

Easier said than done, Lisa thought. But with her friend's help, she settled upon some simple techniques that enabled her to implement his advice and benefit from a Breakout. First of all, when it was her turn to serve at a decisive moment—and she felt the old anxiety paralyzing her—she would literally turn her back on the others for a moment and take several deep breaths. Simultaneously, she would quietly hum a favorite popular song. Then, still humming, she would slowly turn back to the court and take her position at the baseline.

As she tossed the ball into the air, she would focus only on the song and the precise point on the ball where she wanted to make contact. The inner melody and concentration on the ball enabled her to place the worries about her performance on a back shelf in her mind. Her motor memory, that is, the natural service motion she had developed from years of practice, would take over—and the serve would go exactly where it was supposed to go. From then on, Lisa never dreaded having to serve at a crucial time during a match. And she can't remember the last time she double-faulted under pressure.

Lisa's ground strokes required a somewhat different approach. When she was practicing before the competition started, she could almost always hit smooth, solid forehands and backhands. But once points were being counted, she found herself tightening up and hitting crucial shots into the net or over the baseline. No matter how hard she tried, she couldn't seem to rally during a match with the same ease and effectiveness that she did in practice.

Then during one rally, she forgot to think about what she "should" be doing. Almost by accident, she became engaged in an exciting exchange and hit several forcing shots, capped by a clean winning forehand. Immediately afterward, the truth dawned on her: "I wasn't thinking during that point at all. I was just focusing on the ball and reacting." She had used her visual focus to sever prior anxious thought patterns and, as a result, had entered a peak performance experience. The challenge for Lisa was to try to replicate this state regularly.

Finally, she discovered the secret. If she did three things— "concentrate on breathing regularly during a rally; never take my eyes off the ball; and decide I don't care what happens so long as I have fun"—she usually forgot about her nervousness. In terms of the basic triggering mechanisms for a Breakout, she employed a repetitive activity (regular breathing); filled her mind with a single visual image (the moving tennis ball); and "totally abandoned" herself to the fun of the experience.

Lisa also discovered that many times, regardless of whether she was experiencing a Breakout, she would start making mechanical mistakes in her serve or ground strokes. For example, she might begin to toss her ball for the serve too far forward, which would make it go into the net. Or she would start to stand up too straight on her ground strokes, rather than bending her knees, a mistake that caused the forehand or backhand to hit the net.

As a result, she found it helpful to move in and out of a Breakout during a match. When she noticed such a problem, she would resort to a linear-thinking, midcourse analysis to correct her stroke. Then she would return to her visual focus on the ball or to a repetitive mental pattern to trigger a Breakout, which would allow her to benefit from a nonlinear, holistic application of what she had learned during her analysis.

What Lisa and other weekend players have discovered in making use of the Breakout Principle is a variation on the zone that many expert athletes seek—that inner state that is an athlete's mental Holy Grail.

What Is the Zone—and How Can You Enter It?

The zone in sports competition is generally described as a temporary state of superior performance where the athlete, who has prepared and trained extensively for a particular event or game, enters into an almost mystical state of consciousness or reality. In the midst of a zone experience, the player may sense that he can "do no wrong." Or she may feel she is operating without effort—on "autopilot," as Nancy Kerrigan put it. Or she may be able to anticipate exactly what an opponent is going to do. Or the athlete may feel that time is slowing down, or that his senses—especially the visual sense—have been sharpened to an almost superhuman edge.

In 2001, when Jennifer Capriati rose to the number one spot in the world in women's professional tennis, she provided AP reporter Hal Bock with a succinct description of being in the zone: "It's pretty hard to explain. It's making shots that you don't even know that you're going to make and you just make. They just go in. It's like nothing can go wrong. It's a pretty cool feeling. It's like a rush" (Associated Press, September 4, 2001).

Although Capriati identified several characteristics of a peak performance of athleticism, she also revealed how difficult it is to put such an experience into words. The inner experience can become so profound that human language simply can't convey the full picture. On the other hand, certain descriptions of the athletic zone suggest a strong link to scientific concepts we have already discussed.

Marshall Faulk, the great running back for the St. Louis Rams, has been credited with the uncanny ability to see and react to another team's defensive movements in milliseconds (*New York Times*, February 1, 2002, A1, A26). Normal sensory perception wouldn't allow the average person to understand the defense's strategy and anticipate open spots on the field, as twenty-two players simultaneously run about and collide with one another.

An assistant coach likened Faulk's performance to that of a person with "two sets of eyes." Rams coach Mike Martz has speculated that Faulk has the ability to slow the action down in his mind—a capacity that has often been associated with being "in the zone."

Scientific research has added considerable credibility to these observations. A study in the *Journal of Sports Medicine and Physical Fitness* evaluated mental strategies used by the most successful starting players for each position on a college football team (29 [1989]: 209–12). The researchers, relying on observation of eye-movement patterns and the descriptions of each player, determined that both offensive and defensive stars relied heavily on their vision. Also, the visual sense dominated the athletes' creativity and decision-making on the field much more than the sense of hearing.

Descriptions by various athletes of zonelike experiences strongly suggest that the athletic zone is another variation on the Breakout/peak experience phenomenon we have been discussing elsewhere in this book. We hypothesize that when a player moves into the zone, an overall quieting of the brain occurs; yet at the same time, certain areas of the brain, such as the attention centers and executive-control and focus functions, become active. In addition, we predict that distinctive biochemical changes occur, such as the increased release of nitric oxide and neurotransmitters, including endorphins and dopamine.

Entering the zone in athletic competition requires triggering a Breakout through mechanisms similar to those that lead to peaks of creativity, productivity, and self-awareness. But some mechanisms seem more useful or powerful than others for opening portals to peak performance in athletic competition.

Athletic Portals to the Zone

You can access the peak experience of athleticism—including entry into the zone—through a wide range of activities and techniques, some of which we have touched upon in the above discussion. So far, some of the common strategies we have explored include:

- *Visual focus.* Here, your eye picks up the movement of a ball or interactions on the playing field and transmits this information directly to the body's motor responses.

  Such total, focused concentration cuts out the "thinking brain" and increases the odds that you will perform better. The visual focus portal works particularly well in fast-moving sports, such as baseball hitting or basketball play, where there is no time for any mental activity other than taking a quick "snapshot" with your eyes.
- *Total abandon to the game.* When you forget worrying about the mechanics of movement and just give yourself completely over to the exhilaration and enjoyment of the experience, you are more likely to perform at a high level.
- *Pattern-breaking mental, physical, or vocal activities.* The idea here is to focus your mind on a simple activity—such as humming by the tennis player Lisa—

200

that will effectively cut off your awareness of past
mental and emotional patterns. With such a change in
mental direction, a Breakout is more likely to occur—
and a window may be opened to the zone.

In addition to the above portals, other routes to peak athletic achievement may be better suited for certain "slower" athletic events. For example, endurance activities such as distance running or cycling lend themselves to various types of mental repetition, which can trigger a Breakout.

The Mental Repetition Portal

There is compelling evidence that utilizing relaxation-response techniques during or immediately before exercise—or merely allowing your mind to become absorbed in repetitive body movements, such as the steady leg action of aerobic sports like running and bicycling—can trigger a Breakout and open the door to various peak experiences. (*Note:* The term *aerobic* sports—including endurance activities such as walking, jogging, distance bicycling, swimming, or cross-country skiing—refers to activities in which the athlete achieves a balance between the intake and the use of oxygen. In contrast, *anaerobic* sports, such as sprinting and fast basketball play, require the use of more oxygen during the activity than the body is able to take in. As a result, after a relatively short period of anaerobic activity, the athlete tends to become "out of breath.")

A study that I conducted a number of years ago with colleagues at the Harvard Medical School explored how eliciting the relaxation response during a light but steady aerobic workout on a stationary bicycle might enhance the efficiency with which an exerciser's body processed oxygen (*Journal of Human Stress,* June 1978, 38–42).

Previous studies had established that oxygen consumption ($\dot{V}O_2$)—the measurement of metabolic rate—decreases when a person is eliciting the relaxation response at rest. In other words, the body processes oxygen more efficiently. But we didn't know what would happen if the relaxation response occurred during exercise.

Also, we had heard anecdotal reports from long-distance runners who claimed they used "secret" mental techniques to improve their performance. So we wondered, if those special techniques did indeed exist, could they somehow be related to the elicitation of the relaxation response? And if so, could we suggest ways that they might be made more generally available for every athlete?

The participants in the study were instructed in the mental technique of eliciting the relaxation response at rest by repeating silently the word *one.* Then they were asked to exercise on stationary bikes at a steady-state heart rate between about ninety-five and one hundred beats per minute. At the same time that their heart rates were being monitored, their exhaled gases were collected in a bag through a rubber mouthpiece and measured for oxygen consumption.

The research subjects exercised for three ten-minute periods. During the first and third sessions, which served as control periods, they simply pedaled without any conversation. During the second period, they also pedaled silently, but in addition, they practiced the technique that elicited the relaxation response, specifically, repeating the word *one* as they exhaled; also, when distracting thoughts entered the mind, they gently ignored them and returned to their repetition.

After evaluating the results, we found that oxygen consumption decreased by 4 percent during the second period, when the participants elicited the relaxation response. In other words, *the aerobic efficiency of these exercisers improved significantly:* They performed the same work, but they utilized less oxygen.

A study that I coauthored with researchers from the University of Massachusetts Medical School lent some support to the hypothesis that exercise *plus* a cognitive strategy—such as eliciting the relaxation response—is more effective than exercise alone in promoting feelings of well-being from exercise (*Medical Science, Sports and Exercise* 27 [1995]: 765–75).

In addition, a number of studies have shown that combining relaxation-response training with exercise can produce significant physical benefits. A Norwegian study concluded that meditation training may reduce the blood lactate concentration in runners after one of their standard exercise sessions (*British Journal of Sports Medicine* 34 [2000]: 268–72). (The buildup of lactate can interfere with optimal physical performance.) Furthermore, the use of meditation techniques by runners can also reduce the tendency of a strenuous physical workout to suppress the immune system (*British Journal of Sports Medicine* 29 [1995]: 255–57).

A variety of other studies also indicate that the relaxing, mood-elevating powers of repetitive aerobic exercise *by itself* can benefit specific groups, such as women of different ages and students with high levels of test anxiety (see *Journal of Psychosomatic Research* 35 [1991]: 437–49; *Perception and Motor Skills* 69 [1989]: 35–41; and *Perception and Motor Skills* 76 [1993]: 795–801). Another study involving 154 schoolchildren from the fourth, fifth, and sixth grades reported that aerobic running enhanced the cardiorespiratory health and the school creativity of the participants (*Health and Psychology* 5 [1986]: 197–207).

Summing up the power of repetition

In light of such findings, it seems clear that rhythmic aerobic exercise by itself—or such exercise linked to a specific relaxation-response technique—can provide a potent athletic and mental combination.

Many of these studies also suggest that the benefits of the relaxation response can be triggered by means other than traditional meditation, which involves sitting quietly with eyes closed. For example, the participants in our 1978 Harvard study described above were in motion and they had their eyes open.

Furthermore, we have determined through our research that repetition of a meaningful word or phrase isn't always necessary to evoke relaxation-response benefits. In other words, the relaxation response—and a Breakout—can be triggered simply by focusing on the repetitive motion of bicycle pedaling, or on the cadence of repetitive footfalls and breathing during running (see my testimony before the U.S. Senate Appropriations Subcommittee on Labor/HHS & Education, March 28, 2000, 5–6).

One Australian study established that the release of endorphins and other mood-elevating bodily secretions, which accompanies traditional meditation, also occurs in workouts by elite distance runners—without the use of special meditation techniques (*Biology and Psychology* 40 [1995]: 251–65). For more on mood elevation that occurs during aerobic exercise alone, see my coauthored investigation in *Medical Science, Sports, and Exercise* 27 (1995): 765–75 (see also the *Journal of Psychosomatic Research* 35 [1991]: 437–49).

Even if you choose not to combine your athletic activity with a mental device, you should select some other focus, such as the movement of your legs, a ball that is in play, or your regular breathing. Otherwise, you are likely to become distracted or confused by the action on the field or court; anxiety or mental confusion will invade your consciousness; and your performance will suffer.

Ironically, not every athlete has been happy to hear about the directions that our research has been taking. At a presentation that I made to a group including seasoned marathoners, some of the competitive distance runners actually became angry with me for revealing the "secret" of their superior performance.

In our discussion, they admitted that they used repetitive techniques, including a focus on breathing and on regular foot motion, to achieve a "high" state where they use their oxygen more efficiently. But they would clearly have preferred me to keep quiet about the specifics of our research.

What about the runner's high?

Finally, our 1978 study, along with later research, raises the possibility that the reduction in oxygen expenditure—which occurs when the relaxation response is combined with aerobic exercise—may contribute to the "runner's high" reported by elite distance runners.

Among other things, we have learned that when distance runners concentrate on their breathing or cadence, the high typically occurs relatively early—in the first or second mile of the run. In contrast, when the athlete runs *without* this mental-focus technique, the high usually appears later, during the fourth or fifth mile. (Again, see my testimony on March 28, 2000, before the U.S. Senate Appropriations Subcommittee on Labor/HHS & Education.)

Other research, some of which we have referred to above, has shown that the increased output of such neurotransmitters as endorphins, as well as other mood-elevating hormones, is also associated with the high experience. Similar mental states—which, as we have seen, may sometimes be referred to as a "zone," "flow," or "groove" experience—have been reported by cyclists, basketball players, and other athletes.

The Breakout connection

As you can see, the Breakout Principle in many ways represents a culminating concept that ties together previous research relating to a variety of seemingly mysterious phenomena, such as the "zone," changes in time perception, visual focus, and increases in aerobic capacity. We suggest that the Breakout Principle may be the ultimate nondrug answer for athletes who want to optimize their performance.

Those athletes who learn to move past the struggle-preparation phase of training—and to pull the inner trigger that severs past thought patterns and produces a Breakout—will be much more likely to rise to the peak of athleticism that we have been discussing in this chapter. You may not win an Olympic gold medal after learning to trigger such a Breakout, but you will be more likely to maximize your own athletic potential—and that may well be sufficient to win quite a few tennis matches, golf outings, fun runs, or pickup basketball games.

In moving toward this goal, however, aspiring athletes should be aware of studies that have shown the importance of creating a finely balanced competitive edge of optimum anxiety just *before* the action begins.

The Optimum-Anxiety Portal

To lay the groundwork for a Breakout and peak performance during athletic competition, it's important for the athlete to carefully manage stress levels not only after the action starts, but also just *before* the event. If anxiety gets out of hand before the game or performance, unnecessary energy will be wasted. Also, distracting thoughts may become so overwhelming that it becomes impossible to get into the flow of the game, eliminate prior thought patterns, and undergo a Breakout.

Know your IZOF!

A number of studies on the link between preperformance anxiety and athletic performance have explored what researchers call the individual zone of optimal functioning, or IZOF. This concept refers to the ideal emotional range just before play begins, where the athlete's nervousness is intense enough to produce an effective competitive edge and alertness but not so intense as to impair performance. A "meta-analysis," or in-depth comparative evaluation, of nineteen studies of skilled athletes showed that the performance of those who were within their optimal anxiety zone was significantly better than the performance of athletes outside their zone (see *Journal of Sports Science* 17 [1999]: 873–87).

How can you tell what your personal IZOF may be? The scientific literature suggests several guidelines, most of which require a subjective self-evaluation by the athlete:

- Recall how anxious you felt just before your best performance of the season—and in your mind, try to replicate that feeling (*Scandinavian Journal of Medical Science and Sports* 7 [1997]: 253–58).
- If you are unsure of your best zone or balance, lean toward slightly higher anxiety rather than low anxiety. Some researchers have found that even if an athlete is

very nervous before competition, he can still perform at his best (253–58).

- Don't expect your IZOF to be the same as that of any of your teammates or competitors. Every athlete responds differently to precompetition anxiety, so it's essential for each individual to experiment and determine what level of anxiety suits him or her best (*Medical Science, Sports, and Exercise* 28 [1996]: 378–85; and *British Journal of Sports Medicine* 28 [1994]: 47–51).

These insights are an extension into the athletic arena of the Yerkes-Dodson Law, which was introduced in Chapter 2. You will recall that business executives and others under stress do well initially when the pressure is on. But when stress increases beyond a certain point—represented by the top of the Yerkes-Dodson bell curve—productivity and quality of performance decline precipitously.

In the end, you must experiment and determine from experience what level of precompetition stress suits you best. Then you can apply various relaxation-response techniques to maintain your nervous energy in an optimal range just before you perform.

What strategy should you use to manage precompetition anxiety?

A simple elicitation of the relaxation response through a mental repetition technique works for many athletes. Others have relied on a wide, highly creative range of such strategies. A 1993 study of U.S. Olympic wrestlers, for instance, showed that the team members coped with stress with such strategies as mental focusing, prayer, concentration on goals, following a set precompetition routine, visualization, or putting the event into perspective (*Research Questions in Exercise and Sports* 64 [1993]: 83–93).

Practices of other elite athletes reflect similar strategies. Professional and well-trained amateur-tournament tennis players will often maintain their focus between points during a match by staring at the strings of their rackets. Athletes in individual Olympic events, such as track and field, skiing, or swimming, can frequently be seen with heads bowed and eyes closed—deep in a relaxation exercise, meditation, or prayer. Figure skaters may isolate themselves in a corner of a training room and quietly trace and visualize movements they expect to make on the ice.

As you can see, many of these precompetition strategies coincide with the Breakout triggering mechanisms and techniques we discussed in Chapters 2 and 5—which further emphasizes how far-reaching and complex the Breakout Principle is. In this chapter alone, we have seen that it may be important to go through Breakout-related exercises at several points during the struggle-release-Breakout-peak-experience sequence. These include:

- The struggle phase, as the athlete prepares well in advance for the event with visualization exercises.
- The precompetition moments, when Breakout-related relaxation-response techniques can help keep stress in the preferred IZOF range.
- Finally, the main release and Breakout during competition, which can lead to the zone and a peak athletic performance.

But as complex and comprehensive as the athletic Breakout may be, the next two peaks—rejuvenation and transcendence— provide us with even more dramatic and far-reaching illustrations of this phenomenon.

The Fifth Peak—
Rejuvenation

The 1956 Olympic gold medalist for women's figure skating, Tenley Albright—my classmate and friend at the Harvard Medical School—and her brother Nile, a surgeon, invited me to attend in 2001 the first Hollis Albright Annual Symposium, which had been established in honor of their father.

I certainly wasn't expecting to discuss the Breakout Principle at this event. But during the reception, I had a fascinating conversation with a surgeon who had been one of her father's colleagues and had operated upon grossly psychotic patients back in the 1920s and 1930s.

Knowing that I was a specialist on mind-body issues, he told me that these patients, who had been cared for before the era of antipsychotic drugs, had consistently done better in recovering from surgery than mentally normal patients. The only explanation that he and his colleagues could come up with for the differ-ence was that the psychotic patients had clearly not worried about their surgery, whereas the normal patients had often been gripped by anxiety.

Unexpectedly, the disturbed mental condition of these patients had apparently worked in their favor, allowing them to keep their analytical faculties out of the way as they underwent surgery and began their recovery. They lacked the mental frame of mind that processes and magnifies stress. As a result, their natural healing power—the *vis medicatrix naturae* of Hippocrates—was able to take control of their minds and bodies and enhance their recovery from the wounds of surgery.

In more technical terms, their brain condition enabled them to escape the problems imposed by the normal brain's highly active neocortex, with its proclivities toward worry and linear thinking. Because the patients short-circuited ordinary anxiety, they also avoided the negative impact of the effects of the fight-or-flight response, including excessive production of the hor-mone norepinephrine.

In short, these patients seemed to have experienced a kind of Breakout—characterized by enhanced, faster recovery—as their diseased minds *automatically* blocked off stressful thought pat-terns. Fortunately, these and other wide-ranging physical and emotional benefits are available to those with normal mental capacities in the form of the "peak of rejuvenation."

What Is the "Peak of Rejuvenation"?

A peak of rejuvenation—which involves enhancements to per-sonal emotional and physical health—may accompany any of the other Breakout peaks. When you experience a breakthrough in creativity, productivity, or athleticism, you can often expect to feel more energetic and confident. Also, in many cases, physical complaints—such as backaches, headaches, angina pain, high blood pressure, or other stress-related conditions—will fade or disappear.

If you are particularly bothered by a health problem, you may seek a peak of rejuvenation as an *end in itself* to give you relief. Of course, before you use the Breakout Principle for health purposes, you should first consult with a physician lest you overlook a condition that is best treated with drugs or surgery. Still, various studies have shown that 60–90 percent of all visits to the doctor's office are stress-related, and that mind-body interventions, not requiring surgery or drugs, could produce partial or full cures.

To achieve these results, any Breakout trigger will work, but three of the most common and powerful are:

- Repetitive actions, mental exercises, or other activities that elicit the relaxation response—which helps free the body's natural healing capacities.
- Immersion in one's deep personal belief—which has an independent impact on improving health through the placebo effect or "remembered wellness."
- A combination of the two.

We will shortly be exploring each of these special rejuvenation triggers in more detail. But first, the following case of Larry should be helpful in illustrating just how powerful the third—the combination approach—can be.

No More Headaches

Larry, who frequently suffered from headaches and elevations in his self-monitored blood pressure when the stress in his office rose to unusually high levels, was on blood-pressure-lowering medication. He had also tried various prescribed drugs and over-the-counter medications to relieve his pain. But upon finding that he needed increased and more frequent dosages to manage the headaches—and thinking that perhaps he needed an additional prescription drug—he was referred to us for help.

After a discussion of his problem, a direct link became evident between Larry's headaches and two difficulties with his job. First, he became upset when his immediate boss responded poorly to stressful situations; second, Larry felt his stomach "tie up in knots" when a particular coworker became excessively confrontational during disagreements with him.

Typically, during and after one of these difficult personal clashes, Larry would become obsessed with replaying the encounter in his mind, as though he were hearing or seeing the same tape over and over. He wanted to forget the unpleasant interaction, but instead he often became obsessed with analyzing and dismantling the conversation to discover what had gone wrong—and what he might do to make things better the next time.

The answer to Larry's problem seemed clear. To begin with, he had to learn some basic stress-managing techniques to escape the repetitive mental tapes that were making his life miserable—and also harming his health. This skill would provide him relief of pain through the peak experience of rejuvenation. Just as important, he needed to develop a strategy for regularly inserting those peaks of rejuvenation into his daily work life.

I started by instructing him in basic techniques to elicit the relaxation response, which would enable him to move beyond the struggle phase in his relationship and open the door for a Breakout. Specifically, I suggested that he regularly elicit the relaxation response before breakfast every morning. He was asked to select a short word or phrase that reinforced his belief system.

Larry was an amateur gospel singer who regularly performed in his local African Methodist Episcopal congregation. So he picked *precious Lord,* from the title of the famous hymn by African-American gospel composer Thomas Dorsey. Larry was instructed to sit quietly with his eyes closed for about ten minutes and repeat this phrase silently as he exhaled.

We suggested that when he expected to encounter significant stress, he should also find a nice, comfortable chair in a secluded spot—if possible, in his own office—where he could have some privacy by closing the door. Usually, he incorporated this quiet time as part of his preliminary preparation for stressful meetings. Also, because ten minutes was about the length of a typical coffee break in his office, he substituted a short meditation period of just a minute or two in place of the caffeine time.

Almost immediately after incorporating this strategy in his daily schedule, Larry found that he could handle abrasive encounters with both his boss and coworker more calmly. Just as important, after only about two weeks of developing his ability to respond mentally and emotionally to these high-pressure interactions, he discovered that his mind was beginning to move in new directions in managing the relationships.

After one relaxation session at home, for instance, a series of new ideas occurred to him about constructive ways to deal with his boss and his coworker—and to redirect the pressure they

were placing on him. With the boss, he started trying to anticipate areas that might cause her to become upset.

She wasn't usually dissatisfied with his work, but rather, with
pressure or criticism being directed at her by her own superiors.
When she became irritated, she took out her frustration on who-
ever happened to be nearby, and more often than not, Larry
found that he bore the brunt of her reaction. So he got into the
habit of empathizing with her and then asking immediately,
"What can I do to help with this?" Invariably, his boss calmed
down and a more productive discussion ensued.

The coworker presented a somewhat different challenge, but
again, after only a few sessions, Larry was able to cope quite
effectively. Among other things, whenever this other employee
began to raise his voice during a disagreement, Larry just looked
at him thoughtfully and nodded without answering immediately.
Then, Larry would begin with a complimentary or agreeable
response, such as "That's an interesting point," and he would
ask for a more complete explanation before he ventured his
opinion. Usually, the coworker would calm down at this unexpected answer. If the man remained agitated, Larry would once
more come back with a soothing rejoinder of some sort.

How did this new interpersonal strategy affect Larry's health
complaints?

Within several weeks he discovered that his headaches had
disappeared. Furthermore, when his blood pressure was checked
about a month later, the measurements were close to normal. He
was able to reduce the dosage of his antihypertensive medication, with the prospect that if his blood pressure stayed reduced,
he might be able to eliminate the drug altogether.

Larry's experience with lowered blood pressure was entirely
consistent with studies we have conducted at the Mind/Body

Medical Institute and published in various medical journals. One such study, in which I participated with fellow researcher Eileen M. Stewart and other colleagues, showed that similar relaxation-response techniques could enable patients with hypertension to lower their blood pressure significantly over three years. Also, they ended up requiring lower drug doses or eliminated their medications entirely (*Journal of Cardiovascular Nursing* 1 [1987]: 1–14; see also *American Journal of Public Health* 67 [1977]: 954–59).

The successful elements in Larry's approach might have come straight out of a Breakout Principle manual. First, he was embroiled in a classic struggle scenario in his office, with an array of disturbing emotions and health-harming stressors. Then he *severed* the prior stressful emotions and thoughts by using a repetitive technique of prayer at home, and shorter meditation periods in his office.

As we know, such repetition can be quite effective in triggering a Breakout. Furthermore, the words he chose, *precious Lord,* came directly out of his deepest beliefs and personal religious practice. In effect, he reinforced the repetition with another Breakout trigger—an immersion in his personal belief system.

After the Breakout, Larry's stressful, anxious thought patterns were replaced by a more placid flow of new ideas. Holistic thinking replaced linear—or "circular-tape"—worry patterns. Most important of all, several of those new ideas that occurred after the Breakout were quite helpful in improving both of his problem relationships. Larry's short Breakouts in the quiet of his office—which he continued to pursue regularly—helped transform his work environment, not to mention his personal health.

In terms of the Breakout Principle, he moved first through the struggle phase to a severing of—or release from—prior struggle patterns, which automatically "pulled" the Breakout trigger. Then he entered the actual Breakout stage, with its attendant physiologic, biochemical, and neurological responses. Along with the Breakout came a series of peak experiences, with improvements both in his health (peaks of rejuvenation) and in his understanding of how to improve his work relationships. Finally, Larry returned to a "new-normal" level of operating on the job, which was more satisfying and productive—and healthier—than the level at which he had started.

The sequence of his improvement and healing can be expressed in a Breakout diagram:

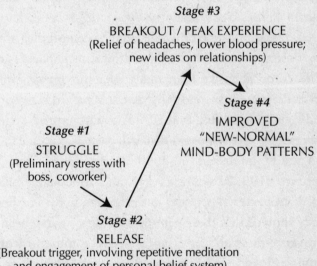

Stage #3
BREAKOUT / PEAK EXPERIENCE
(Relief of headaches, lower blood pressure;
new ideas on relationships)

Stage #4
IMPROVED
"NEW-NORMAL"
MIND-BODY PATTERNS

Stage #1
STRUGGLE
(Preliminary stress with
boss, coworker)

Stage #2
RELEASE
(Breakout trigger, involving repetitive meditation
and engagement of personal belief system)

Larry's experience is just one example of a broad-based phenomenon that we have been monitoring at the Harvard Medical School for more than three decades. To understand the medical factors behind his healing, let's consider first the way that he controlled the stress in his life and cleared the way for the natural powers of his body to go to work. Then, we'll turn to the healing effect of his personal beliefs.

The Natural Healing Power of Human Biology

It is important to keep in mind this basic principle, which underlies the discussion I had at the Hollis Albright Annual Symposium: When you sever past emotional and thought patterns, especially those related to stress, *you actually free the body to perform its natural healing functions*. The operation of *vis medicatrix naturae* depends on your ability to get your anxiety-prone analytical faculties out of the way.

Recent research, some of which I have been privileged to participate in, suggests that the body's self-healing capacities may be far more comprehensive than many of us in medical research have ever suspected. Increasingly, scientists are discovering that our body contains molecules that function as natural antibiotics, much as penicillin and related drugs do.

In a study published in 2000 in the *Journal of Neuroimmunology* (109, 228–35), French and American researchers identified antibacterial peptides in the human body. Furthermore, our study showed that these peptides—which, having been found in both vertebrates and invertebrates, are common throughout the animal kingdom—are released naturally during coronary bypass surgery. In other words, the body possesses its own protective antibiotic mechanisms, which go into play when tissue is damaged.

In another recent finding, German researchers reported in *Nature Immunology* on November 5, 2001, that human sweat contains an antibiotic that is effective in fighting several disease-causing bacteria, including skin infections such as impetigo (see http://immunol.nature.com). This natural antibiotic, which the scientists called dermcidin, joins a number of other antibacterial substances in the skin that assist in repairing skin injuries and wound healing.

Of course, serious injuries and infections require stronger responses than these natural antibacterial agents. That's why the watershed discovery of penicillin and other antibiotics through modern research has been vitally important. But along with other living creatures, we possess a vast arsenal of natural agents in our bodies, which are always working hard to heal and protect us.

In addition to freeing his body's natural healing functions through the Breakout, Larry also discovered an important second principle—namely, that the Breakout process could improve his health through the *active* agency of personal belief.

In Chapter 12, we will explore in some depth how a profound set of *intrinsic* personal beliefs—operating with use of the Breakout Principle—can transform your life in ways that reach far beyond your health. But because the belief system can have such a potent impact on physical well-being, it's important to consider here the medical potential of the type of belief that benefited Larry.

Can Belief Really Heal?

When you rely on your belief system to help produce a Breakout, you move into one of the most mysterious and controversial areas of modern medicine. Increasingly, scientific evidence—as well as ongoing individual reports that arrive in my offices regularly from around the world—shows that belief can play a decisive role in improved health. But not everyone is willing to accept this fact.

For a brief time in mid-2001, the public and a segment of the medical community were shaken by the news that the placebo effect—the healthful benefits produced by personal belief as part of an effective treatment or cure—might not even exist. The cause of the disturbance was a May 24, 2001, report in the *New England Journal of Medicine* entitled "Is the Placebo Powerless? An Analysis of Clinical Trials Comparing Placebo with No Treatment" (344, 1594–1602).

The Danish authors concluded that there was "little evidence in general that placebos had powerful clinical effects," though they conceded that there were "possible small benefits" in the alleviation of pain. They also claimed that no specific identifiable scientific mechanisms explain the placebo effect and concluded that the placebo effect doesn't exist. Finally, they said that apart from their use in clinical trials, there was "no justification" for the use of placebos. Unfortunately, the interpretations of this report and related research on the placebo effect have been misleading—for a number of reasons.

First of all, the term *placebo effect* is one of the most misunderstood and misused designations in modern medicine. Most medical terms have a precise meaning that knowledgeable researchers accept and recognize. But *placebo effect* is used in a wide variety of ways and sometimes becomes more a term of art than of hard science.

As mentioned in Chapter 3, when I have used the term in my journal articles and books, I usually renamed it *remembered wellness*. One reason I have switched terms has been the desire to avoid the misunderstandings associated with *placebo effect*. Also, the specific nature of the belief that is required to produce healing often includes a *memory* of what it was like to be "well."

This memory, wired into the brain as specific nerve-cell configurations, has specific bodily responses linked to it. These nerve cells can, in turn, be activated by the person's recollection. This is why in cases where the placebo effect—or remembered wellness— has been reported active, there are so many reports in the medical literature of beneficial health changes.

The placebo effect, or remembered wellness, encompasses three components that can have an impact on health and on Breakout-related phenomena. These include:

- The belief and expectation of the patient or individual receiving the medical or other benefit.
- The belief and expectation of the physician, instructor, or mentor who is working with the patient or beneficiary.
- The belief and expectation generated by the positive relationship between these two individuals.

In the critical *New England Journal of Medicine* article by the Danish researchers, the authors explicitly eliminated the third factor, saying, "We reviewed the effect of placebos but not the effect of the patient-provider relationship. We could not rule out a psychological therapeutic effect of this relationship" (1599). As a result, they placed themselves in the position of addressing a quite different phenomenon from the broader placebo effect that many researchers, including myself, have studied.

A study of Parkinson's disease by Canadian researchers

reported in *Science* in 2001 (293, 1164–66)—as also noted in Chapter 3—reported that the "placebo effect in PD [Parkinson's disease] is powerful and is mediated through activation of the damaged nigrostriatal dopamine system" (1164).

Furthermore, these investigators said, evidence suggested that the magnitude of the placebo response was similar to that of doses of the drugs levodopa or apomorphine, which are typically employed to treat Parkinson's. In fact, they noted, in some cases most of the benefits achieved in patients receiving the drug might actually come from the placebo effect!

That the Canadian team indicated a clear molecular mechanism was involved with the placebo effect (or remembered wellness) suggests just how foundational the biological interactions of the Breakout are. Remember, too, that my colleagues at Harvard and I believe that a separate molecular event, the secretion of nitric oxide, is fundamental to both the placebo effect and the relaxation response (Stefano et al., *Brain Research Reviews,* 2001). When the nitric oxide counteracts the stress hormone norepinephrine, natural healing in a wide gamut of illnesses becomes possible. In fact, nitric oxide is closely related to dopamine and natural opiates, such as endorphins, as well as to secretions that control the immune function.

Dr. Esther Sternberg of the National Institute of Mental Health summarized the situation quite well in a March 27, 2001, interview with CNN when she noted that mind-body research, which links belief to wellness, has "suddenly become mainstream" (www.cnn.com).

In other words, medical researchers now accept that belief—whether it occurs in the context of a "peak of rejuvenation," or "remembered wellness," or the "placebo effect"—can play a significant role in improving one's health. Further testimony to the power of belief in healing can be found in the growing list of diseases and conditions that can be helped or cured by deep personal convictions.

What Medical Conditions Can Be Improved by Belief?

The health problems and complaints that have been improved through belief—including the belief that triggers a peak of rejuvenation following a Breakout—include:

- chest pains associated with restricted blood flow to the heart (angina pectoris)
- impotency
- diabetes mellitus
- hypertension
- rheumatoid arthritis
- congestive heart failure
- constipation
- bronchial asthma
- cold sores (herpes simplex)
- duodenal ulcers
- postoperative swelling and pain
- nausea and vomiting as a result of pregnancy
- various forms of pain—including backaches, headaches, stomach pain, muscle pain, joint aches, and pains in the neck, legs, and arms
- fatigue
- dizziness
- weight loss
- coughing

- degeneration of the heart muscle
- drowsiness
- nervousness
- insomnia
- skin reactions to poisonous plants
- false pregnancy
- deafness
- a host of other complaints (see my *Timeless Healing*, 228–29)

In addition, a study we conducted at the Mind/Body Medical Institute involving the Christian Science religious group, which uses mind-body healing techniques, concluded that fewer Christian Scientists experienced illness or symptoms as compared to non–Christian Scientists (*Journal of Nervous and Mental Disease* 187 [1999]: 540–49).

In a particularly intriguing twist, there is also evidence that strong belief can affect a person's time of death. Many of us know of cases of desperately ill patients who remained alive beyond all expectations and enjoyed an anniversary, a special holiday, or a wedding. In a famous historical example of this phenomenon, America's founding fathers John Adams and Thomas Jefferson both died on July 4, 1826—the fiftieth anniversary of the signing of the Declaration of Independence.

Though weak, Adams was acutely aware of the date. When he was informed that it was the fourth, he responded, "It is a great day. It is a *good* day" (David McCullough, *John Adams* [New York: Simon & Schuster, 2001], 646).

Jefferson had been unconscious since July 2, but he reportedly woke up on the evening of July 3 and said, "This is the Fourth." When he was informed that the day would soon arrive, he went back to sleep. He died the next day, on the fourth (McCullough, 646; see also, Joseph Ellis, *American Sphinx: The Character of Thomas Jefferson* [New York: Random House, 1996], 280).

But belief can also have a decidedly *unhealthful* effect. This negative side of personal belief can be quite powerful—as a recent study on Chinese- and Japanese-Americans suggests.

The Power of Negative Belief

A study in the *British Medical Journal* (323 [2001]: 1443–46) explored the high incidence of death associated with the number four in Chinese and Japanese societies. *Four* is pronounced like *death* in these languages—perhaps an explanation for why an unusually high number of Chinese- and Japanese-Americans suffering from chronic heart disease seem to be "scared to death" on the fourth of every month (*Science* 295 [2002]: 267).

The researchers from the University of San Diego, after analyzing mortality figures for almost one hundred thousand Chinese- and Japanese-Americans who died from 1989–1998, concluded that cardiac mortality increases on psychologically stressful occasions. Such reports suggest that personal belief can have a significantly *negative* impact on human health, which is sometimes described as the nocebo effect.

What Is the Nocebo Effect?

Probably the best way to think of the nocebo effect is that it is the mirror image—the precise opposite—of the placebo effect. So if you take the three elements of the placebo effect, or what I have called remembered wellness, and reverse them, you end up with something like this:

- A belief or expectation in your own mind that something *unhealthy* will happen to you.
- A belief or expectation in the mind of your physician or mentor that a *disorder* will happen to you.
- A *negative* set of beliefs and expectations that permeates the relationship between the two of you.

Such negative beliefs will be as likely to produce an undesirable result in your health and well-being as your positive beliefs are to produce a desirable result. Your belief system can work for you or against you. You can use your positive beliefs to trigger a Breakout and experience a healing peak of rejuvenation. Or you can allow negative beliefs, through the nocebo effect, to creep into your life and undercut your health. So it's imperative to learn to identify negative beliefs when they appear and take steps to counter them effectively.

A Strategy to Counter Negative Belief

There is a direct link between out-of-control stress and negative beliefs. For example, you may fear that the aches, pains, and high blood pressure you are experiencing are inevitable because of the unrelieved deadline pressures at work. Or you may be convinced that the pressures you are facing at home or at work are beyond your control. Or you may believe that no matter what you try to do in a given situation, your efforts will backfire.

Or you may assume that your relationship with a particular boss or coworker is doomed to go downhill.

If you slip into such a negative mind-set, you will probably find yourself in a dead-end, no-win predicament and may open the door to health problems. But you won't be alone. According to ongoing Gallup surveys, the stress levels of Americans have changed little over the last few years. A poll published on January 3, 2002, reported that 42 percent of Americans say they frequently experience stress in their daily life, while just 20 percent say they never or rarely experience stress (www.gallup.com). These numbers were basically the same as those reported in a 1994 poll.

An impressive body of evidence indicates that uncontrolled stress—often produced by negative beliefs—can exacerbate health problems and may even be the primary cause of some diseases. In a 1996 report in the *Annals of Internal Medicine* (124, 673–80), a researcher from the College of Physicians and Surgeons of Columbia University in New York City explored the work on stress of Thomas Holmes, a physician publishing in the mid-1950s. The article concluded that Holmes, who argued for a link between stress and tuberculosis, may have been correct. This conclusion was based on recent research rooted in immunology and biostatistics, which has suggested that stress may lower the immune function and open the door to disease.

The Holmes case represents just one instance among many of how stress can cause or exacerbate disease. Fortunately, there are many effective responses in our society—via the Breakout—to the challenge of stress.

Using the Breakout to Combat Stress in Your Life

In discussing the case of Larry earlier in this chapter, we saw that the two most common and powerful Breakout trigger mechanisms to the peak of rejuvenation—including lower stress and better health—are (1) repetitive techniques that elicit the relaxation response and (2) deep personal belief.

But any of the other basic Breakout triggering mechanisms described in Chapter 5 can also help you experience health benefits. That is, you can sever prior, unhealthful thought patterns through such channels as "total abandon," some significant personal encounter, an absorbing altruistic activity, or some dominant visual or other perceptual focus.

Here is a sampling from the medical literature of how various Breakout triggering mechanisms have worked to alleviate stressful situations and responses.

The disability paradox

Some researchers have explored the apparent paradox in which those who are disabled—and who in the view of many "healthy" people seem to live an "undesirable daily existence"— nevertheless report having a good or excellent quality of life. The solution to the paradox, according to researchers from the University of Illinois at the Chicago School of Public Health, is that many disabled people have found a satisfactory balance in their inner life and have established and maintained a harmonious set of relationships (*Social Science and Medicine* 48 [1999]: 977–88).

Such findings provide support for our position that an effective antidote to stress is a Breakout based on a significant personal relationship.

Healing music

A visual, auditory, or other strong perceptual focus can also produce Breakouts that improve health. Many people have found that immersing themselves in music or art can be a highly effective way to break stress patterns.

In one New York City intensive care unit, piping Muzak to patients helped lower the mortality rate 8 percent below the national average, according to a *New York Times* report (February 13, 2001, D8).

Another study found that when lullabies were played in a neonatal nursery, the babies gained weight and were discharged sooner. Still another report in the *American Journal of Hospital Palliative Care* (13 [1996]: 43–49) concluded that music therapy was effective in reducing sensations of pain. A number of experts have suggested that the pain-reduction effect may result from the release in the body of endorphins and other neurotransmitters and hormones that act as natural drugs to provide physical and emotional relief. As a result of such investigations, there has been a surge in certified music therapists. According to one recent count, there were more than 3,300 throughout the United States (*NYT*, D8).

But music must be utilized in a nonlinear fashion to produce such healthful benefits. Music specialists, for instance, tend to *analyze* the music they hear, and as a result they often fail to break prior linear thought patterns. (You'll recall that a common feature of every Breakout is shifting from linear to holistic thought patterns.)

In one investigation involving university students, for instance, both trained music majors and non–music majors were asked to listen to music. The non–music majors, such as biology students, underwent physiological changes associated with relaxation. In contrast, the music majors, who listened more analytically, released chemicals and hormones more associated with stress (*Perception and Motor Skills* 74 [1992]: 1079–90; and *Perception and Motor Skills* 77 [1993]: 227–34).

Relationships and the workplace

Those suffering from chronic pain in the workplace have been able to reduce symptoms or cure the problem entirely by following the guidance of occupational health nurses to make changes in their family life (*AAOHN Journal* 45 [1997]: 451–58). The most effective strategies focus on the whole person, including personal beliefs and relationships, and not just on painful symptoms.

Eastern movement therapies: an effective mechanism to sever stressful thought patterns

A series of studies have established that an effective antidote to stress is the practice of such Eastern movement programs as tai chi, chi gong, and yoga. These movements have been valuable additions to strengthening and stretching programs used in rehabilitation clinics, both for ambulatory and nonambulatory patients (*Physical and Medical Rehabilitation Clinics of North America* 10 [1999]: 617–29; see also *Comprehensive Therapy* 25 [1999]: 283–93).

Such movement therapies are successful not only because they stretch and strengthen the body but also because they calm the brain, lower metabolism, and produce other changes consistent with what we have identified as the relaxation response. The operative Breakout triggering mechanisms include concentration on physical movement and breathing, which breaks the conscious connection with prior stressful thoughts and emotions. After these old patterns have been severed, the door is open for a more relaxed mental state, which in turn increases the potential for physical and emotional healing.

Putting a cap on anger

Contrary to some popular assumptions, medical studies suggest that it may be better for your health to avoid intense, open expressions of anger, rather than just to explode (*Circulation* 94 [1996]: 2090–95). In this study, researchers from the Harvard Medical School studied the relationship between coronary heart disease and the extent to which the patients in the Veterans Administration Normative Aging Study had trouble controlling their anger. The investigators determined that high levels of expressed anger might be a risk factor for coronary heart disease among older men.

A number of Breakout mechanisms are effective in breaking prior angry thought patterns. In fact, our research team has found that the relaxation response—one of the important trigger mechanisms—is associated with diminished anger and hostility.

The Ultimate Healing Combination: Mind Plus Medicine

Of course, none of this evidence for the power of the Breakout Principle to enhance human health is intended to detract from the tremendous strides made in modern medicine with prescription drugs or surgery. Rather, our call is for physicians and patients to put the two areas together—into what might be regarded as the "ultimate healing combination."

Obviously, the Western scientific breakthroughs have been impressive and are so numerous that they would require volumes to enumerate. Any such list would have to include antibiotics for bacterial infections, anesthesia for surgery, immunizations for diseases like polio, cataract removal and lens replacement, organ transplants, artificial heart valves, and pacemakers. And this doesn't scratch the surface. (For a more complete list and discussion of this issue, see my *Timeless Healing*, 229–31.)

But our tremendous success in developing drugs, surgery, and other medical techniques and procedures has sometimes blinded us to the natural healing capacities that we and our ancestors have always possessed. Modern medicine, then, should be employed whenever necessary. But at the same time, we should always remain alert to the possibility of linking Western scientific medicine to *vis medicatrix naturae*. An ideal way to stay alert is to keep the mind and consciousness agile and versatile with regular Breakouts, which can open the door to the peak of rejuvenation—and ultimately, perhaps, to a peak of transcendence.

The Sixth Peak—
Transcendence

The final peak experience that may follow a Breakout—the peak of transcendence—is perhaps the most exciting and important phenomenon of all. But this peak also presents us with many complexities, including an intriguing enigma, which might be stated this way:

> The most significant experiences that transform human lives often cannot be explained in human terms.

In other words, certain transforming events, which have the power to alter individuals, communities, or even civilizations, may also "transcend" our reasoning and measuring abilities. By common definition, that which is transcendent surpasses ordinary experience and may even reach into realms beyond the physical universe, which science cannot evaluate or measure. That is, transcendent phenomena and forces may be quite real, but they lie outside the range of our physical senses and analytical capacities.

Many scientists attempt to resolve this puzzle by arguing that even if we cannot currently understand certain events, such as mystical visions, answers to prayer, or dramatic creative insights, someday we *shall* understand—*completely*. They contend that at some future time *all* phenomena—every detail of the universe—will be reduced to measurable, space-time dimensions. All that is needed is an appropriate set of technological breakthroughs.

Other scientists—and many philosophers and theologians—are uncomfortable with this "scientific" answer. They feel that such a response is simply too pat, too reductionistic, or too shackled by current scientific assumptions. In short, these critics say, scientists who insist that ultimately everything may be explainable in space-time terms may not be sufficiently open-minded to be willing to examine other possibilities.

Those who question the classic Western scientific mind-set as the only means to truth acknowledge the ability of modern science to transport us to new medical and technological levels—including the most advanced antibiotics, surgical procedures, communications systems, and space-age weapons. But they point out that there may be definite limits to such scientific progress.

For example, we currently have access only to space-time scientific tools, which limit us to operating within the four dimensions of height, width, depth, and time. But what if there are *extra* dimensions beyond or even inside our cosmos, as many theoretical physicists and mathematicians suspect? In such a case, how can we, as four-dimensional creatures, hope to understand fully, much less make use of, a fifth, sixth, or eleventh dimension?

The answer to such questions may lie in a deeper *nonrational* (*not* irrational!) exploration of transcendence and a serious investigation of the possibility of realms of reality beyond the confines of our familiar space-time. Furthermore, in a twist that may be disturbing to traditional Western scientists, such research may, by definition, require us to use nonlinear, nonrational means to probe extradimensional regions that they have previously rejected out of hand as "spiritual" or "supernatural."

This is certainly not to suggest that if these new areas of research are opened more widely, modern science will have to be discarded or subordinated as a tool in the search for truth. We researchers in the Western scientific tradition *must* continue with our work if we hope to continue to broaden our understanding of the physical universe, including the human body. But at the same time, Western scientists will have to learn to respect the insights of philosophers, theologians, and nonlinear thinkers from other cultures. Furthermore, when appropriate, Western researchers should begin to use these experts as resources, and perhaps even to collaborate with them.

If Western scientists take this more inclusive tack to knowledge and reality, they may be stimulated, and even surprised, at the possibilities that open to them. Remember the words quoted earlier from Robert Jastrow, the founder of NASA's Goddard Institute for Space Studies. He concluded his *God and the Astronomers* with the comment that when the scientist exploring the mysteries of creation scales the highest peak of research, he will be "greeted by a band of theologians who have been sitting there for centuries."

But some other caveats about the relationships between science and spirituality are in order before we proceed further.

Science versus Spirituality

In raising the possibility that scientists may actually benefit by studying theological or religious investigations and insights, we want to make it clear that, for purposes of this book, we have no intention of pronouncing here on the validity of any religious tradition. Any judgment as to the truth of any religion lies beyond the tools of science and must be left to the conscience of each reader.

As will become evident in the following discussion, however, various scientific studies do demonstrate that common biological foundations underlie the profound spiritual experiences in various religious traditions. Each human body is equipped with similar neural networks, neurotransmitters, hormones, biochemistry, and other physiologic features that may serve as a physical platform to facilitate transcendent experiences.

In addition, the scientific evidence demonstrates that the two realms, science and spirituality, often interact, and the Breakout mechanism frequently serves as a bridge between the two. In fact, at the beginning of a transcendent or "spiritual" peak experience, the physiologic, biochemical, and neurological changes in the body and brain follow precisely the same patterns that occur with other peak experiences, including those involving significant creativity, productivity, and athleticism.

What About Transcendence for Nonreligious People?

Something akin to a peak of transcendence may be experienced by a nonreligious person, especially when the individual is searching for some profound insights about the meaning or future course of his or her life. This person will typically move through the Breakout sequence of struggle-release-Breakout/peak-new-normal state.

We have already seen in Chapter 6 that the nonspiritual individual may often link this kind of profound, life-changing experience to a "peak of self-awareness." Also, these individuals may assume that the source of their life-changing experience lies in their own brains and bodies, and not in a transcendent dimension.

Others may fall into a category somewhere between religious and nonreligious. For example, a number of people who affirm no particular belief in God have said that they have experienced transcendent insights when reflecting in the midst of a serene, beautiful natural setting. One woman, who described herself as "mildly agnostic," had become especially agitated in her high-pressure work environment. But on a short vacation in Maine, she experienced a profound quieting of her mind and body as she floated at sunset in a canoe on a deserted lake.

While silently contemplating a group of loons who were calling back and forth to one another, she realized rather abruptly that her career and job situation were really quite unimportant in the broad sweep of existence. As she reflected, her breathing became more regular and slowed considerably. She even sensed that if she continued in this state, she might somehow merge into the sky, the water, and the trees that hung over the nearby shore.

After this experience—which had all the earmarks of a peak of transcendence—her life changed. She immediately began looking for another job in a more relaxed environment. Also, she began to study Native American literature to try to understand the closeness she had felt to nature on that lake, and the power that the experience had exerted over her.

A Mysterious Source?

Because of the special nature of such peaks of transcendence, science has been unable to make any convincing case about the precise source of such "spiritual" experiences. From a purely *non*reductionistic point of view, there seems to be at least as much reason to assume that these special breakthroughs may originate from another dimension—such as God, a "higher power," or some cosmic sphere untouched by modern science—as from somewhere in the brain or body.

This conclusion would seem to conform to the views of the majority of Americans, according to recent Gallup polls. In a 1999 Gallup survey, 86 percent of Americans said they believed in God, and another 8 percent believed in a "universal spirit/higher power" (see www.christianitytoday.com/leaders/newsletter/2001). So if you are one of those 94 percent who accept the existence of God, a universal spirit, or a higher power, how exactly might the Breakout mechanism relate to your own peak of transcendence?

Linking the Breakout to Transcendence

In terms of the now familiar Breakout sequence, there will frequently be a *struggle* or *preparation stage*. This may involve such factors as a profound sense of discontent and stress about the meaning of life; ardent searching for "ultimate" answers; analytical study of scriptures or theological texts; or arduous, pleading prayer.

Saint Benedict put it well in his sixth-century *Rule* when he called prayer the "Work of God," a precept that has been restated by later divines from various religious traditions as "prayer is work" (see *The Rule of Saint Benedict in Latin and English,* ed. and trans. by Abbot Justin McCann [London: Burns Oates, 1952], 71, 117, 119).

During this initial stage, stress levels are often elevated, emotions may run high, and the linear, analytical areas of the brain may be hard at work. These subjective responses are accompanied by the now familiar physical changes, including increases in such stress hormones as epinephrine (adrenaline) and norepinephrine (noradrenaline).

Although there will often be an extended period of searching, discontent, or emotional anguish during the struggle stage that precedes a peak of transcendence, sometimes this preliminary phase may be unusually short. For example, a moving sight in nature or a decisive word by a respected mentor may cause a relatively brief period of inner questioning, dislocation, or feeling of estrangement. Then the special vision or insight may occur abruptly, as a kind of "divine surprise" or "experience of grace."

The early-twentieth-century Protestant mystic and devotional author Oswald Chambers seemed to be describing this variation when he said, "However much we may know God, the great lesson to learn is that at any minute He may break in. We are apt to overlook this element of surprise, yet God never works in any other way" (*My Utmost for His Highest* [New York: Dodd, Mead & Company, 1935], 25).

Regardless of how long this spiritual-struggle stage may take—or the exact moment when it strikes—the individual will usually *pull the Breakout trigger* by "backing off," "releasing," or "letting go" of past thought patterns. Then he may enter a "listening" mode, along with a state of inner calm or quiet.

The philosopher-psychologist William James—during his analysis of religious conversion in his classic *Varieties of Religious Experience*—actually seems to have anticipated the Breakout triggering mechanism. "In many cases relief persistently refuses to come until the person ceases to resist, or to make an effort in the direction he desires to go," he wrote (*Varieties* [New York: The Modern Library, 1902, 1929], 205).

At this "cease to resist" point the Breakout occurs and a *peak experience of transcendence* is likely to follow. The peak may be perceived as a state of ineffable inner peace, profound spiritual insight or understanding, mystical oneness, spiritual renewal, or conversion. Again, William James put it well: "When the new centre of personal energy has been subconsciously incubated so long as to be just ready to open into flower, 'hands off' is the only word for us, it must burst forth unaided!" (*Varieties,* 207).

We have marshaled evidence that suggests that during the Breakout process, the inner events reported by James have a biological foundation. As demonstrated by our brain-mapping of Sikh meditators, we can expect an overall quieting of the brain, but at the same time an increase in activity in executive-control and attention centers.

Also, our extensive review of scientific studies suggests that the production of nitric oxide will increase in cells throughout the body. Other studies show that neurotransmitters associated with feelings of well-being, such as dopamine and endorphins, increase; overall bodily metabolism slows down; heart rate and blood pressure decrease; and breathing slows.

Finally, the previously cited studies from Slovenia show that as the Breakout proceeds—especially where the centers of creativity are involved—"coherence," or interaction between different areas of the brain, increases (*International Journal of Psychophysiology* 36 [2000]: 73–88; *Brain Topography* 12 [2000]: 229–40; see also *Brain Cognition* 40 [1999]: 479–99).

Those experiencing a genuine peak of transcendence will typically return to a *significantly changed or transformed daily life*—analogous to the new-normal state following a Breakout. The individual may describe this ongoing condition as being "permanently transformed," "enlightened," "centered," "renewed," "reborn," or "born-again."

In response to skeptics who challenged the idea of a real transformation after a religious conversion, William James called their views "shallow." He emphasized that his work at Harvard had demonstrated clearly that "all the more striking instances of conversion—all those, for instance, which I have quoted—*have* been permanent" (*Varieties*, 252).

What to Expect During a Peak of Transcendence

So what might you expect to sense or feel during a genuine peak of transcendence?

A search of the scientific and historical literature, along with interviews of those who report life-changing spiritual experiences, suggests some common, generic features, regardless of one's spiritual tradition or background.

Some of the possible feelings, sensations, or insights that occur during a genuine peak of transcendence include:

- *A sense of unity.* Conventional perceptions of space—
  and the barriers that separate the person from other

241

people, nature, or inanimate objects—may break down. The individual may describe this as a strong feeling of "oneness" with nature, other people, or God. Also, there may be a sense that the person's mind, body, and spirit have melded.

- *A sense of mystery.* A peak of transcendence is often characterized by a conviction that "something beyond" will always lie just outside the full comprehension of the human mind.

- *A new motivation.* A strong spiritual insight will often implant an inner drive to change one's life significantly in some way. More than one hundred years ago, William James reported that in a study of one hundred religious conversions among evangelical church members, more than half of whom were Methodists, only 6 percent relapsed significantly from their religious faith. In other words, the peak of transcendence experienced by these people remained a transforming, motivating principle in their lives (*Varieties*, 253).

- *An expanded or fluid sense of time.* Time may seem to stand still or move in slow motion. Or conversely, perceptions of time may speed up. As with the athletic "zone," a myriad of strong impressions may rush into the mind in split seconds to facilitate instantaneous action. Or they may remain there as indelible memories that serve as touchstones and motivators for later personal change.

- *A deep, lasting impression about the cosmos, about the overall meaning of life, about God, or about oneself.* Many who emerge from a peak of transcendence report

such insights as "I am not the center of the universe."
Or, "I possess some special importance in the universe."
Or, "Now I know for certain that God exists." Or, "I am
convinced now that prayer can heal."

Visualizing the Peak of Transcendence

The Breakout diagram that we have used to summarize peaks
of creativity, productivity, athleticism, and other transformational experiences can also be applied to the peak of transcendence. As you consider the accompanying visual depiction,
remember that the total experience cannot be captured in one,
linear graph. In fact, even the reference to "stages" in the
Breakout sequence falls short. In some instances—as we'll see
later in this chapter in the discussion of Moses as a model—the
main event may be preceded by other Breakouts that have
occurred during the struggle phase. Also, many of the components in this sequence—including the actual Breakout and the
accompanying peak experience—have holistic or nonlinear
qualities that probably couldn't be pictured or described ade-
quately even if we could create a moving, four-dimensional
hologram!

So when you study this diagram, use your imagination. In
your mind's eye, "lift" the lines off the page and try to understand the concepts in more than one or two dimensions. To the
best of your ability, flesh out the brief descriptions, such as "let
go" and "profound inner peace," with concrete memories or
knowledge from your own experience or study. By starting to
make the diagram your own in this way, you'll be in a stronger
position to prepare yourself for the kind of Breakout that can
lead to a peak experience of transcendence.

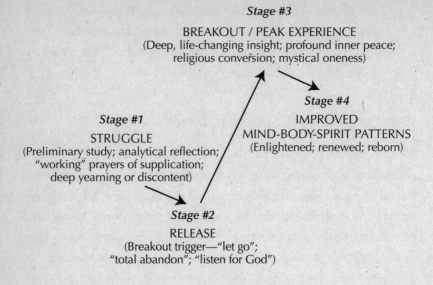

Stage #3

BREAKOUT / PEAK EXPERIENCE
(Deep, life-changing insight; profound inner peace;
religious conversion; mystical oneness)

Stage #4

IMPROVED
MIND-BODY-SPIRIT PATTERNS
(Enlightened; renewed; reborn)

Stage #1

STRUGGLE
(Preliminary study; analytical reflection;
"working" prayers of supplication;
deep yearning or discontent)

Stage #2

RELEASE
(Breakout trigger—"let go";
"total abandon"; "listen for God")

To understand better how the Breakout Principle may work in this complex realm of transcendence, it can be helpful first to test the concept against historical precedents. The calling of Moses by God in the biblical Book of Exodus provides an intriguing model of the stages that may occur in this type of experience.

Moses as Model

The process begins with Moses' struggles with the deity at the beginning of Exodus, chapter three, moves through his subsequent inner development in chapters three to fourteen, and culminates in a spiritual peak in chapter fifteen. We can only imagine the mind-body responses that may have occurred in the prophet's mind and body. But the many details in the account give us some justification to speculate.

At the beginning of Exodus, chapter three, Moses was apparently leading a tranquil, low-stress life as a shepherd. But everything changed when he saw the burning bush and heard the voice of Yahweh in the flames, calling him to confront the Pharaoh and lead the people of Israel out of bondage.

When God called "Moses, Moses?" in Exodus 3:4, the shepherd responded immediately "Here I am," or *hineni* in the Hebrew.

But far from providing an immediate sense of inner peace, this initial encounter with Yahweh raised Moses' stress levels significantly. According to the biblical record, the revelation launched a lengthy period of "struggle," characterized by fear and argument with God (3:6, 11ff). Such intense, contentious debate would typically provoke a classic fight-or-flight response. This state would involve a rush of epinephrine (adrenaline) and norepinephrine, accompanied by increases in heart rate, breathing rate, and blood pressure.

The stress continued to mount as the divine encounter proceeded. When God told Moses that He wanted him to lead the people of Israel out of Egypt—an undertaking that would require direct confrontations with the Pharaoh—Moses protested vigorously, to the point that God became angry with him (4:14). (*Note:* A contemporary analogue to this struggle stage of Moses' experience might be the individual who wrestles long and hard in prayer, asking for insight or guidance.)

Finally, Moses agreed to go along with God's plan, and he gained some support from his brother Aaron, who became his partner in the project. This temporary resolution might have reduced Moses' stress levels somewhat. But when the two men initially approached Pharaoh and asked for a short break for the Israelites so they could celebrate a feast in the wilderness,

Pharaoh not only rejected the request, he placed even more oppressive work burdens on them (5:1ff).

As a result, Moses returned to God with a frustrated prayer: "O Lord, why hast Thou brought harm to this people? Why didst Thou ever send me?" (5:22).

God revealed to Moses that He was causing Pharaoh to resist so that a greater divine purpose could be achieved—the permanent liberation of Israel from Egypt. But the news apparently wasn't what Moses wanted to hear. Instead he continued to protest about his speaking inadequacies and argued against the divine plan. Again, this "divine dispute" provides us with a suggestive picture of what may occur in any age, as the individual struggles in prayer to find the divine will and obey that will (see 6:12, 30).

The Exodus story then moves through the arguments, threats, and confrontations Moses endured as the ten plagues were inflicted on the Egyptians and their lands (Exodus, chapters 7–11). Despite the conflicts, Moses' faith and confidence in God seemed to grow during this period. Instead of being fearful and uncertain about the prospect of appearing before Pharaoh, for instance, he became quite bold and confrontational (10:29).

We can assume that even though the pressure on Moses mounted as events moved toward the final plague—the death of the firstborn—and the culminating Passover of the death angel (chapters 11–13), he was managing his stress much better. The adrenaline would still have been pumping in his system as he became angry with Pharaoh and otherwise strove to do God's will (11:8). But in this phase, his anxiety seemed to have been in a zone where he could perform and speak quite effectively. (An analogue to this state might be the precompetition "individual zone of optimal functioning," or IZOF, for elite athletes, discussed in some detail in Chapter 9.)

Finally, as this ancient drama moved to its climax, Pharaoh allowed the Israelites to leave Egypt, but then had a change of heart and chased them with his horses and chariots (14:1–9). The people of Israel practically dissolved in fear and once again criticized Moses for taking them to what seemed the brink of annihilation.

But by this time, Moses had become a changed man. He responded to the people confidently, "The Lord will fight for you while you keep silent" (14:14).

Then Moses stretched out his hand, the Red Sea parted, and the Israelites passed safely from one side to the other on the dry seabed. When they were safely across, the prophet lowered his hand, and the waters returned, engulfing the Egyptians.

Moses' experience finally culminated in what appears to be a classic peak of transcendence in chapter fifteen, as he led the people in an exuberant song of praise to God. We can only imagine the feelings that overwhelmed him as he sang:

> *Who is like Thee among the gods, O Lord?*
> *Who is like Thee, majestic in holiness,*
> *Awesome in praises, working wonders? (15:11)*

As for what was happening in his brain and body, it seems possible that the various Breakout responses were at work, just as they can operate in our own bodies today.

The parameters of this ancient Hebrew example are also echoed in the later Judeo-Christian tradition, including the New Testament and more recent conversion accounts. A number of special variations will be of particular interest to those readers who are among the approximately 90 million adult Americans identified as "born-again" Christians in national surveys by

Gallup and Barna Research (see Barna Research Online, "Born-Again Christians," February 26, 2002, www.barna.org; Princeton Religion Research Center, "Emerging Trends," Gallup polls from 1939 to 2001; and "What Do Americans Believe?" www.christianitytoday.com/leaders/newsletter/2001).

The Conversion Experience and the Breakout

The specific inner portal through which many Christians have experienced a peak of transcendence is the religious conversion popularly known as being born again. A closer look at this phenomenon suggests some remarkable similarities to the Breakout stages we have been discussing throughout this book. But before we attempt to apply the Breakout Principle, it's important to understand what segment of the population we are discussing.

The sociological definitions

In popular reports, such terms as *born again* and *evangelical* vary according to the understanding or definition of the particular writer or pollster. For example, Gallup's Princeton Religion Research Center has determined that almost half of all Americans, or 46 percent, are born-again Christians. The criteria he uses for the designation are that the individuals believe that the Bible is the actual word of God, have experienced a personal conversion, and try to evangelize nonbelievers (see above, www.christianitytoday.com, 2).

Similarly, Barna Research, which does extensive polling in the evangelical Christian community, determined in 2001 that 41 percent of Americans were "born-again Christians." On the other hand, Barna also established nine more restrictive criteria of belief to determine who should qualify as an "evangelical." As a result, he ended up with only 8 percent of adult Americans in this category. For our purposes, we'll stay with the broader *born-again* term, which in recent years has consistently included more than 40 percent of adult Americans.

In addition to these sociological considerations, it's also important to keep in mind the biblical and theological sources for the *born-again* terminology—because those in this segment of the population tend to define themselves and their spiritual experiences in a biblical context.

The biblical definitions—and their link to the Breakout Principle

The biblical roots of the terms *reborn* and *born again,* which have sometimes been overlooked in popular discussion, can be found in the third chapter of John's Gospel. There, Jesus says in his discourse with the religious leader Nicodemus that anyone who wants to "see the kingdom of God" must be "born again" or "born from above" (Greek: *gennethe anothen*). Another biblical phrase that Jesus uses to refer to this basic Christian peak experience is "born of the Spirit" (Greek: *gegennemenos ek tou pneumatos*; see John 3:3–8).

In this context, remember the analogy to the "spirit" that we suggested in Chapter 1. There, we compared the nitric oxide, which the scientific evidence shows may be released during the Breakout process, to the spiritual experiences often linked in the Bible to the Hebrew *ruah (ruwach)* and the Greek *pneuma*. These words, translated as "spirit," "breath," or "wind," are often associated with the divine presence that is the agent of personal transformation and conversion.

As used by contemporary evangelical Christians, the born-again experience can be summed up—and related to the Breakout—in this way:

The basic human condition is that everyone begins in a state of estrangement or alienation from God. That is, everyone is in a state of "sin" (see Psalm 14:3; Romans 3:9–10, 23). Or, in terms of the Breakout, everyone is enmeshed in an uncomfortable, alienated "struggle" that involves searching for the meaning of life. In his *Confessions,* Saint Augustine described this state with this classic observation: "Our hearts are restless till they rest in Thee" (New York: Sheed & Ward, 1942, 3).

The only way out of this struggle phase, which besets all humanity, is through the work and initiative of God—that is, by His "grace," which was expressed in ultimate form by the sacrifice of Jesus Christ on the cross (Romans 6:23). According to evangelicals, there is no way to work one's way into a relationship with God (see Ephesians 2:8–10). Rather, the individual must "let go" of self and allow God to take over one's heart or spirit. Or in biblical terms, the person must "receive" Christ or "believe on" Him (John 1:12).

Another expression of the born-again process—which provides a suggestive link to the Breakout Principle—is the command issued by Jesus to his disciples: "Repent and believe." In this context, the word *believe* implies more of a total sense of "releasing and receiving" than a limited intellectual conviction that arises from some analytical theological analysis (Mark 1:15). In terms of the Breakout, this "repent and believe" command might be restated as "struggle and release."

Finally, once an authentic conversion has occurred, the believer's life typically begins to undergo a radical change. Among other things, there is an expectation of an increasing display of "fruits of the Spirit," such as love, joy, and inner peace (see Galatians 5:22). Again, this final, ongoing spiritual transformation suggests the improved, new-normal state that typifies the final stage of the Breakout process.

Clearly, then—at least on the surface—there appear to be a number of strong similarities between the Breakout and the born-again phenomenon. First, the established sequence of the Breakout seems to conform closely to the theological and biblical descriptions of these conversions. In particular, the *sorrow-repentance-belief-salvation* sequence of the Bible is strongly reminiscent of the *struggle-release-Breakout/peak-improved-life* sequence of the Breakout Principle. (Of course, in making this comparison, we are *not* suggesting that the Breakout can explain the totality of the spiritual experience. Rather, the Breakout relates only to the biological platform on which the experience occurs.)

Furthermore, actual accounts of those who have reported religious conversions demonstrate that the born-again experience is not a recent or isolated phenomenon. Two dramatic and instructive illustrations from the past are the conversions of the nineteenth-century president of Oberlin College, Charles Finney, and the eighteenth-century founder of the Methodist movement, John Wesley.

The Spiritual Saga of Charles Finney

The Harvard philosopher William James frequently cited Charles Finney as a prime example of a deep religious experience that is quite similar to modern accounts of the born-again phenomenon. According to James, Finney, who was trained as a lawyer, began a diligent search for ultimate meaning in his life. "He then went into the woods, where he describes his struggles.

He could not pray, his heart was hardened in its pride" (*Varieties*, 204).

Eventually, this period of struggle reached a culmination—or what we have called the release point of the Breakout—when Finney reached an "ecstasy of happiness," according to James (*Varieties*, 249). In Finney's own words, as cited by William James, the experience reflects a classic peak of transcendence:

> All my feelings seemed to rise and flow out; and the utterance of my heart was, "I want to pour my whole soul out to God." The rising of my soul was so great that I rushed into the back room of the front office to pray. There was no fire and no light in the room; nevertheless it appeared to me as if it were perfectly light. (*Varieties*, 259)

Finney then dissolved in tears, as he

> received a mighty baptism of the Holy Ghost. . . . The Holy Spirit descended upon me in a manner that seemed to go through me, body and soul. I could feel the impression, like a wave of electricity, going through and through me. Indeed, it seemed to come in waves and waves of liquid love; for I could not express it in any other way. It seemed like the very breath of God. (*Varieties*, 250)

As described by Finney, this transforming event suggests the biological process we have been discussing throughout this book—including a complete severing of prior thought patterns, the onset of a Breakout, and a peak of transcendence. His reference to a "wave of electricity" shows just how dramatic and palpable this peak was for him.

Finney's "new-normal" post-Breakout life was also consistent with the Breakout Principle sequence. After his transforming experience, he became an itinerant revivalist, whose sermons led to the conversion of a number of highly educated people, some of whom became quite active in the antislavery movement. His converts included the prominent abolitionist Theodore Weld.

Finney himself went on to become president of Oberlin College, which became an agent of social change—admitting African-Americans and women along with white males, and also serving as a station on the Underground Railroad, which helped fugitive slaves escape to Canada. In the view of later historians, Finney's message of salvation became "the beginning of religious experience instead of its end. The emotional impulse . . . thus turned toward benevolent activity" (David M. Potter and Thomas G. Manning, *Nationalism and Sectionalism in America* [New York: Holt, Rinehart and Winston, 1949, 1961], 191; and Dwight Lowell Dumond, *Antislavery Origins of the Civil War in the United States* [Ann Arbor: University of Michigan Press, 1960], 23).

The changed lives evidenced by Finney and his converts illustrate quite well the final stage of the Breakout process, which involves the return of the individual to an improved new-normal life. Another striking historical account, which is similar to the born-again peak experience reported in our own day, comes from an even earlier source, the eighteenth-century founder of the Methodist movement, John Wesley.

John Wesley—a "Heart Strangely Warmed"

John Wesley, the eighteenth-century Anglican clergyman, spent the first part of his adult life trying to find God. In this search he "struggled" for many years over the meaning of his life and how he fit into the divine scheme of things.

Even before he had settled his own spiritual search, Wesley traveled from England to North America and worked as a missionary among the Native Americans in Georgia. But upon returning to England on January 29, 1738, he confessed in his *Journal* that throughout this American experience, he felt inner dislocation, estrangement, and doubt:

> It is now two years and almost four months since I left my native country in order to teach the Georgian Indians the nature of Christianity. But what have I learned myself in the meantime? Why (what I the least of all suspected), that I who went to America to convert others was never myself converted to God. (Percy Livingstone Parker, ed.; *The Journal of John Wesley* [Kent, England: STL Productions, n.d., 54)

Interestingly, Wesley, who was thirty-four years old at the time, attached an asterisk to the above statement and in a footnote included this qualification: "I am not sure of this."

Clearly, he was in a state of inner turmoil and spiritual confusion during this period. At different points in his *Journal* he described himself as generally "being sorrowful and very heavy"; "afraid" during a storm; and gripped by a "fear of death" (52, 53).

After his return to England, during February and March of 1738, Wesley spent considerable time discussing his deep spiritual discomfort and lack of faith with Peter Böhler, a German Moravian Christian whom he had met in London. They walked miles together; and Wesley also spent long, monotonous hours on horseback, all the while continuing to wrestle with whether it was possible to be saved through faith alone, apart from any personal effort or works (59–62).

In terms of the Breakout, he seemed to sense he needed to "release," "back off," or "let go" of his personal efforts and his limited, linear mode of thinking. The repetitious cadence of the walking and riding undoubtedly helped move him toward this release. But somehow, he couldn't bring himself to take the final step and let go completely of his rational doubts.

During this period, through Böhler's influence, John's brother Charles, who later became one of the greatest hymn writers of all time, was converted when it "pleased God to open his eyes" to the "one true living faith" (62). In other words, Charles experienced a peak of transcendence, and his life changed dramatically.

But John kept resisting. As a result, he wrote, "I had continual sorrow and heaviness in my heart" (63).

Finally, at five in the morning of May 24, 1738, John Wesley opened his Bible and began to meditate on two New Testament verses: "Ye should be partakers of the divine nature . . . Thou art not far from the kingdom of God." In the afternoon, he went to St. Paul's Cathedral and became immersed in an anthem: "Out of the deep have I called unto Thee, O Lord: Lord hear my voice" (63).

During this period of reading and meditation, Wesley began the final phase of releasing himself from his arduous spiritual search. He had done all he could do, humanly speaking, and now he was beginning to sense that he had to stop working, relax, and "let it happen." He was clearly moving into an inner phase where his prior thought patterns of doubt and confusion were being cut off, and an interior door was opening to something entirely new. All that remained—at least biologically speaking—was for a Breakout to occur.

That evening, John Wesley went to the meeting of a religious society at Aldersgate Street in London, where someone was reading Luther's preface to the Epistle to the Romans. As the reader's text covered "the change which God works in the heart through faith in Christ," Wesley said, "I felt my heart strangely warmed. I felt I did trust in Christ, Christ alone, for salvation; and an assurance was given to me that He had taken away my sins, even mine, and saved me from the law of sin and death" (64).

His account—including the famous "heart strangely warmed" description—provides us with yet another classic expression of the peak experience of transcendence that may follow a Breakout.

Immediately after this experience, Wesley stood and "testified openly to all there what I now first felt in my heart" (64). Plenty of doubts and questions followed this Aldersgate event, but John Wesley's life essentially changed from that point forward. His public confirmation launched a powerful, lifelong ministry, which ended in 1791, when he was in his eighty-seventh year. During his career, he had preached to thousands. The Methodist movement, which originated from his work, spread around the world in the form of the Methodist Church and related "Wesleyan" denominations. By any measure, he had decisively changed the face of Western religious history.

The experiences of Moses, Finney, and Wesley illustrate how a Breakout accompanied by a peak of transcendence can involve such a dramatic severing of past mental patterns that the entire future of the person's life may be changed. In addition, their stories serve as a good introduction to our final topic—the mind-set that scientific researchers call intrinsic belief.

12

The Power of Intrinsic Belief

A powerful mechanism for triggering any type of Breakout—and especially a peak of transcendence—is your personal belief system. For purposes of a Breakout, you can engage your most profound convictions in two primary ways:

- The use of *repetitive mental exercises* linked to your beliefs, such as repeating a meditative prayer or a belief-related phrase.
- *Nonrepetitive exposure to your beliefs,* such as becoming deeply absorbed in a meaningful book or poem; in a painting, piece of music, or philosophical concept; in a natural setting; or in the ambience of a worship center.

As you engage your deepest personal beliefs, the most important factor for initiating a Breakout remains the *breaking of prior patterns of thought.* When that happens, you will be more likely to experience a Breakout.

Such a deep personal belief also appears to be a *prerequisite* for experiencing a peak of transcendence. But exactly what kind of "deep personal belief" is required for such a life-transforming Breakout?

To answer this question, let's first try to put the concept of personal belief into a broader context. In Chapter 10, we explored how the placebo effect—or the type of belief that I have renamed remembered wellness—can benefit your health and in many cases keep you out of a doctor's office entirely. But even though the kind of belief that we will focus on now may include elements of the placebo effect or remembered wellness, it is far more comprehensive and reaches well beyond considerations of health.

In the previous chapter, we explored how the deep personal beliefs of Moses, Charles Finney, and John Wesley contributed to their peaks of transcendence and dramatically changed their lives. In these cases, as well as in situations involving beliefs in a variety of other traditions, the operative concept is what researchers have called *intrinsic belief,* as opposed to *extrinsic belief.*

Features of an Intrinsic Faith

The term *intrinsic belief* or *intrinsic faith* refers to a deeply felt set of convictions that influence the person's values and conduct of life. In contrast, an *extrinsic faith* may typically involve a general belief in God or a Higher Power, but the convictions are more abstract and intellectual than life-changing.

A 1991 research investigation that I coauthored with Jared

D. Kass of the Mind/Body Medical Institute and other colleagues reported that such convictions arise out of a "core spiritual experience." This special experience may enhance the individual's sense of life purpose, emotional satisfaction, health, and belief in God. Typically, an intrinsic faith involves the perception of a "highly internalized relationship between God and the person" (*Journal for the Scientific Study of Religion* 30 [1991]: 204).

In an effort to identify intrinsic belief, Kass, other colleagues, and I devised an "index of spiritual experience," a seven-item series of questions that we called the INSPIRIT scale. Usually, a high score on the scale is linked to a conviction that God exists and also to "feelings of closeness with God, including the perception that God dwells within" (205). Furthermore, higher scores are associated with a greater sense of life purpose and satisfaction, with health-promoting attitudes, and with decreased frequency of medical symptoms.

Because a profound belief system can be a powerful tool in triggering a Breakout, we have reproduced the INSPIRIT questionnaire and scoring questions below so that you can perform a preliminary test of your own system of beliefs (*Journal for the Scientific Study of Religion* 30 [1991]: 203–11).

Questionnaire on Spiritual and Religious Attitudes

The following questions concern your spiritual or religious beliefs and experiences. There are no right or wrong answers. For each question, circle the number of the answer that is most true for you.

1. How strongly religious (or spiritually oriented) do you consider yourself to be?
    1. Strong
    2. Somewhat strong
    3. Not very strong
    4. Not at all
    5. I don't know

2. About how often do you spend time on religious or spiritual practices?
    1. Several times per day to several times per week
    2. Once per week to several times per month
    3. Once per month to several times per year
    4. Once per year or less

3. How often have you felt as though you were very close to a powerful spiritual force that seemed to lift you outside yourself?
    1. Never
    2. Once or twice
    3. Several times
    4. Often
    5. I don't know

Please use *your definition* of God when answering the following questions.

4. Do you believe in God?
    1. Yes
    2. No
    3. I don't know

5. How close do you feel to God?
   1. Extremely close
   2. Somewhat close
   3. Not very close
   4. I don't believe in God
   5. I don't know

6. Have you ever had an experience that has convinced you that God exists?
   1. Yes
   2. No
   3. I don't know

7. Indicate whether you agree or disagree with this statement: "God dwells within you."
   1. Definitely disagree
   2. Tend to disagree
   3. Tend to agree
   4. Definitely agree

8. The following list describes spiritual experiences that some people have had. Please indicate if you have had any of these experiences and the extent to which each of them has affected your belief in God.

	Never Had This Experience	Had This Experience	
	Convinced Me of God's Existence	Strengthened Belief in God	Did Not Strengthen Belief in God

SPIRITUAL EXPERIENCE

A. An experience of God's energy or presence

| 1 | 2 | 3 | 4 |

B. An experience of a great spiritual figure (e.g., Jesus, Mary, Elijah, Buddha)

| 1 | 2 | 3 | 4 |

C. An experience of angels or guiding spirits

| 1 | 2 | 3 | 4 |

D. An experience of communication with someone who has died

| 1 | 2 | 3 | 4 |

E. Meeting or listening to a spiritual teacher or master

| 1 | 2 | 3 | 4 |

F. An overwhelming experience of love

| 1 | 2 | 3 | 4 |

G. An experience of profound inner peace

| 1 | 2 | 3 | 4 |

H. An experience of complete joy and ecstasy

| 1 | 2 | 3 | 4 |

I. A miraculous (or not normally occurring) event

| 1 | 2 | 3 | 4 |

J. A healing of your body or mind (or witnessed such a healing)

| 1 | 2 | 3 | 4 |

K. A feeling of unity with the earth and all living beings

| 1 | 2 | 3 | 4 |

		Had This Experience	
Never Had This Experience	*Convinced Me of God's Existence*	*Strengthened Belief in God*	*Did Not Strengthen Belief in God*

L. An experience with near death or life after death

1 2 3 4

M. Other (specify)___

1 2 3 4

9. Please describe your most significant spiritual experience as clearly and briefly as you can. If none, please indicate.

INSPIRIT QUESTIONNAIRE
SCORING INSTRUCTIONS

1. How strongly religious (or spiritually oriented) do you consider yourself to be?

   1. Strong = 4
   2. Somewhat strong = 3
   3. Not very strong = 2
   4. Not at all = 1
   5. I don't know = question recorded as missing

2. About how often do you spend time on religious or spiritual practices?
   1. Several times per day to several times per week = 4
   2. Once per week to several times per month = 3
   3. Once per month to several times per year = 2
   4. Once per year or less = 1

3. How often have you felt as though you were very close to a powerful spiritual force that seemed to lift you outside yourself?
   1. Never = 1
   2. Once or twice = 2
   3. Several times = 3
   4. Often = 4
   5. I don't know = question recorded as missing

4. Do you believe in God? = this question is not calculated in the scale.
   Note: Our research showed that a belief in God by itself was not associated with changes in psychological or physical health (207). Apparently, to have transforming power, the belief must be linked to other "intrinsic" belief factors, such as feeling close to God.

5. How close do you feel to God?
   1. Extremely close = 4
   2. Somewhat close = 3
   3. Not very close = 2
   4. I don't believe in God = 1
   5. I don't know = question recorded as missing

6. Have you ever had an experience that has convinced you that God exists?
   1. Yes = 4
   2. No = 1
   3. I don't know = question recorded as missing

7. Indicate whether you agree or disagree with this statement: "God dwells within you." (*Note:* "You" refers personally to the reader.)

    1. Definitely disagree = 1
    2. Tend to disagree = 2
    3. Tend to agree = 3
    4. Definitely agree = 4

8. List of spiritual experiences, A through M.
    If *any one* of A–M = 2, then score the question = 4
    If *any one* of A–M = 3 but none = 2, then score the question = 3
    If *any one* of A–M = 4 but none = 2 or 3, then score the question = 2
    If A–M = a combination of 1 and missing answers, then score the question = 1
    If *all* are *blank,* then question score = missing

9. Not scored.

Compute the mean (average) score of the seven scored items (questions 1–3, 5–8); this mean is the scale score. The subject must have answered at least six of the seven scored questions in order to receive a scale score.

Here's an illustration of how to calculate your score:

Assume that you answered seven of the seven scored questions and that your total raw score was 25. To get your mean (average) score, you would divide 7 (total number of scored questions) into 25. This would give you a mean scale score of

3.57. This result would put you in the upper range of those in our study who had a life-changing core spiritual experience.

In our study, which involved eighty-three adult outpatients, the mean score was 2.8. But 26 percent of the sample scored 3.5–4.0—a result that suggested strongly the impact of a core spiritual experience (206). The participants ranged in age from twenty-five to seventy-two and were mostly white female. Religious backgrounds included Catholic (37 percent), Protestant (23 percent), and Jewish (40 percent). Mean educational background was 16.1 years, or post–college graduate (204).

After taking this test, you will probably find that you fall into one of two categories. First of all, you may recognize that you don't really have a firm set of spiritually related beliefs. Most likely, you didn't have to calculate your INSPIRIT scale score to know that. If you are in this group—and you feel you would like to develop your spiritual side more fully—you might begin by revisiting the religious tradition of your youth. Or if another tradition has piqued your interest, you could start there. By immersing yourself in one tradition, you will be more likely to develop an intrinsic belief system of the type outlined in this chapter.

On the other hand, your scale score may show that you already have such an intrinsic faith. If that is the case, you may want to explore in more depth some practices related to the Breakout Principle that may help you deepen your spiritual awareness.

How Can the Breakout Enhance Your Intrinsic Beliefs?

Even though each person's belief system works a little differently, a proven method to incorporate the Breakout is to begin with an activity, exercise, or mental focus that breaks prior patterns of thought and emotion. By taking this initial, biologically based step, you will nudge open an inner door that may activate something new and exciting. Simultaneously, you will become more conscious of how your beliefs can begin to operate in a truly holistic sense in harmony with your body and mind.

(*Note:* In suggesting that you explore the connection between your beliefs and the Breakout, we are *not* in any way suggesting that the spiritual realm can be contained or explained by the Breakout mechanism. Nor are we implying that somehow the biochemical and physiologic phenomena of the Breakout are necessary for a deep spiritual life.)

What is clear, however, is that the well-established biology that underlies the Breakout trigger often serves as a physical portal or useful adjunct to spiritual experience. Possible physical analogues may include the *voice* as a vehicle for prayer or hymn-singing; *hands* raised in praise; the *quick bows* of Orthodox Jews during davening; and sacred *dance* in various traditions.

So it might be argued that just as these physical expressions may enhance spirituality, the Breakout mechanism is also a way to reach out through one's innate biology.

We have already considered a variety of situations—including the experiences of Moses, Finney, and Wesley—where intrinsic beliefs can trigger Breakouts that culminate in peaks of transcendence. These peaks, in turn, have the power to inject new personal meaning and completely change lives.

To demonstrate further the breadth of the Breakout phenomenon in the context of religious belief, it will be helpful to focus briefly on examples from other spiritual traditions. Then we'll examine how science continues to compile a body of research to support the power of intrinsic belief.

The Historical Testimony

For millennia, many deeply spiritual people have reported experiences that strongly resemble the biological event that we call the Breakout. Then they have ascended peaks of transcendence that appear to lie well beyond even our most advanced modern medical or scientific measurements.

Often, these practitioners appear to have passed through common types of physical portals—similar to those that we can identify through direct fMRI examinations and other medical tests. But after that, the specific manifestations of faith become as varied as the religions of the earth.

In the previous chapter, we saw how peaks of transcendence may occur in the Hebrew and Christian traditions. To illustrate further the far-ranging nature of the Breakout in this area, here are some additional "expressions" from entirely different spiritual traditions.

The Far Eastern Expression

Much of my research at the Harvard Medical School has focused on the impact on the body and the mind of Eastern meditation, especially the type practiced by Buddhists and Sikhs—who may display all the earmarks of what we have identified as an intrinsic system of belief.

In *Beyond the Relaxation Response* (New York: Berkley Books, 1985, 47–61), I described in some detail the tests I conducted on Tibetan Buddhist monks in the mountains of Dharmsala, India, in 1979. By practicing an advanced form of meditation, *gTum-mo* (fierce woman) yoga, they could raise their skin temperatures significantly—by up to fifteen degrees Fahrenheit in various parts of the body (see *Nature* 295 [1982]: 234–36). Other observers have documented that the Tibetan monks could maintain this remarkable increase for hours—or in some instances long enough to dry wet, icy sheets that were draped around their bodies in temperatures as low as forty degrees Fahrenheit.

The various heat-measuring devices we used included not only skin-temperature monitors but also rectal thermometers and a portable weather station. This apparatus established that the monks' skin temperatures increased independently of changes in air temperature. Also, their internal body temperature remained normal during the exercise.

In some instances, they also reported achieving some degree of the "bliss state," or the mystical happiness that this type of yoga is designed to produce. In this state, the monks believe that *prana*—"wind" or "air"—migrates from a "scattered consciousness" and merges in a focused internal column of heat. This heat then moves up and down a perceived central channel of the body. As this internal flow of heat intensifies, the person meditating may experience a "burning away" of the defilements of improper thinking and move toward a state of bliss (53–54).

Although we didn't do fMRI brain-mapping of the Tibetan monks during our study, the metabolic and respiratory tests that we conducted—and the subjective experiences the monks reported—are highly suggestive of the Breakout triggering mechanism. That is, during their preparatory meditation periods, subjects in these tests showed a marked decrease in breathing rate. While normal breathing averages about fifteen breaths per minute, one of the monks was actually recorded at only six breaths per minute. Also, their metabolic rate decreased by a phenomenal 64 percent, the greatest voluntary drop ever recorded from a resting state in normal subjects! (See *Behavioral Medicine* 16 [1990]: 90–95.)

In his classic novel *Siddhartha,* Hermann Hesse—the German novelist, poet, and 1946 winner of the Nobel Prize for literature—relied on his deep understanding of Eastern mysticism to communicate the possibilities of Buddhist meditative practice. In particular, a response by Siddhartha, a prototype for the Buddha, to a spiritual seeker suggests a strong link to the struggle and release of the Breakout:

> When someone is seeking . . . it happens quite easily that he only sees the thing that he is seeking; that he is unable to find anything, unable to absorb anything, because he is only thinking of the thing he is seeking, because he has a goal, because he is obsessed with his goal. Seeking means . . . to have a goal; but finding means . . . to be free, to be receptive, to have no goal. You, O worthy one, are perhaps indeed a seeker, for in striving towards your goal, you do not see many things that are under your nose. (New York: New Directions Paperbook, 1951, 1957, 141)

This snippet of dialogue shows first the limits of linear thinking and analysis by the "seeker." But according to Siddhartha, if the seeker lets go of his "striving" toward a specific goal, he will move into a "free . . . receptive" inner mode that will enable him to "find." In other words, the seeker must move from linear to nonlinear holistic thinking—and a proven way to do this is to trigger a Breakout.

In *How to Practice* (New York: Pocket Books, 2002), His Holiness the Dalai Lama, who is the leader of the Tibetan school of monks that our team tested, outlined in more detail certain meditative procedures that are quite similar to those we have identified with the Breakout process. For example, he emphasized that it is important to begin one's spiritual search with a struggle, or as he put it, "Analyze. Think, think, think. When you do, you will recognize that our ordinary way of life is almost meaningless" (37).

Then he suggested that those who engaged in meditation might pick any one of a variety of "objects" or focal points—such as breathing, a particular feeling, or "phenomena such as impermanence" (123). As meditation proceeds, the monk should observe several guidelines that conform closely to the release phase of the Breakout, including measures designed to break out of prior patterns of thought.

"When your mind is too intense and you experience excitement," the Dalai Lama wrote, "you need to loose it, like loosening the strings of a guitar a bit" (125). He advised that the "force behind developing concentrated meditation is mindfulness, which is the ability to stay with an object, not allowing distraction" (125).

This point conforms closely to the principles of repetition that evoke the relaxation response and may help trigger a Breakout. You will recall that to elicit the relaxation response, it is important to turn gently and passively away from distraction and return to the focus word or phrase.

Finally, in a comment that would fit nicely into our discussion of the peak of productivity in Chapter 8, the Dalai Lama suggested a technique of mental reflection designed to provide greater mental calm in the face of stress:

"Initially a problem can seem solid and intractable, until you investigate its true nature. To do this, work at understanding the range of suffering in your own life. . . . In the same way we have learned how to work with the nature of fire, we can learn how to work with suffering in our lives" (131–32).

In other words, the solution began with linear analysis. Then, he suggested moving to a more dialectical, holistic view of the problem: "Consider trouble from a broader perspective. . . . Reframe bad circumstances as forces assisting your spiritual development. . . . [With an enemy,] instead of stewing over that person's bad qualities, reflect on his or her attributes. . . . Reflect on the emptiness of inherent existence" (132–33).

Other biological responses that accompany such meditation are suggested in our studies at Harvard using fMRI brain-mapping techniques with Sikh meditators (see Chapter 4). The long-term goal of many Sikhs, whose monotheistic religion combines elements of the traditions of both Islam and Hinduism, is to become one with the deity by such practices as repeating "his name"—*sat nam*. We found during our investigation that when the Sikhs used these and related mantras, they experienced an overall calming of the brain, and also an increase in activity in certain neural areas, such as executive-control and attention centers (*NeuroReport* 11 [2000]: 1581–85).

Again, our purpose has mainly been to describe the scientifically measurable changes that occurred in the bodies of meditators. Then we have compared those changes with what we have learned about the Breakout Principle. But we have *not* attempted to evaluate the nature or validity of any specific spiritual experience.

The Catholic Expression

In our clinical work, I have also worked with many patients from other religious traditions, including Roman Catholicism. Typically, in engaging their intrinsic belief system during stress-lowering procedures, they will choose to focus on a prayer that is consistent with their belief system, such as "Lord Have Mercy," "Our Father," or "Hail Mary, Full of Grace."

Such practices have roots in a rich spiritual tradition that has given rise not only to soothing prayers for the laity but also mystical transports for some who have moved to the deepest levels of religious practice. A study by Benedict J. Groeschel, a Franciscan friar and pastoral psychologist from New York, provides a useful overview of the impact of prayer, contemplation, and meditation that arise out of a deep, intrinsic faith. He described how many well-known Catholic saints, including Teresa of Avila and John of the Cross—and also a number of relatively unknown believers—have relied on spiritual exercises to move through various peaks of transcendence to an ultimate sense of being in unity with the divine (*Spiritual Passages* [New York: Crossroad, 1986]).

In his study, Groeschel related one striking personal encounter he had with a Father Isidore Kennedy, who had been born in Ireland in 1897 and was seventy-three years old at the time of their meeting in California. Having contracted tuberculosis at a very young age, Father Isidore had come to terms with death at age eighteen and, as a result, viewed the "rest of his life as a gift from God" (188).

Father Isidore had devoted his existence to prayer and care for the poor. When Groeschel met him, he typically spent several hours every day "sitting quietly in the chapel in profound recollection."

After taking a seat behind the priest one day as he was saying his prayers, Groeschel saw that Father Isidore did not lean his back against the bench, and that he was "breathing at a very slow rate." He also appeared to be lost in his prayers, unaware of anything that was going on around him.

Because Groeschel had a deep interest in how people pray, he later pressed Father Isidore to disclose the "secret" of his prayer life. The priest replied, "Well, my secret, if you want to call it that, is not much. It is just sort of . . . an imagination that comes to me when things aren't just up to the mark. It's come to me since I got sick as a lad, and it comes now often in the day. Whenever I stop to think about it, it seems to me that I have spent my entire life sitting in the place of St. John at the Last Supper."

This report contains a number of features that relate to our discussion of the Breakout Principle. First of all, the slow rate of Father Isidore's breathing during prayer was a sign that his experience had decreased his metabolism. Also, that he was unaware of what was going on around him suggested that past thought patterns had been severed completely, so that he was lost in the present event. His additional disclosure of his "prayer secret"— his "imagination" that he was sitting in the place of Saint John at the Last Supper—shows that he had a focus for his meditation that was derived directly from his intrinsic Roman Catholic beliefs. Most likely, then, the distinctive physiological and neurological responses of the Breakout were in play and were moving him in his prayer sessions toward a peak experience of transcendence.

For hundreds of years, others adhering to this same Catholic meditative tradition have reported similar experiences. Here is a sampling from a variety of historical periods:

- *The fourteenth-century English Benedictine nun, Lady Julian of Norwich.* Lady Julian received a series of sixteen "shewings" or visions, which she meditated upon for twenty years. They were finally recorded as *The Revelations of Divine Love* (see key excerpts in *Enfolded in Love* [New York: Seabury Press, 1981]).

  Her insights, which came to her during meditation,

bear many of the marks of the classic peak of transcendence: "Nothing happens by chance, but by the far-sighted wisdom of God. . . . I am sure that no one can ask for mercy and grace with his whole heart unless mercy and grace have already been given to him. . . . The soul is immediately at one with God, when it is truly at peace in itself" (22, 23, 25).

- *The sixteenth-century Spanish mystic Saint Teresa of Avila.* In her *Interior Castle*, Teresa of Avila describes her inner journey of prayer and meditation through several "mansions" of spiritual experience (New York: Doubleday, 1944, 1961).

  These included a "seventh mansion," where there were "hardly any of the periods of aridity." Rather, in this state "the soul is almost always in tranquility." Also, there was no sense of the working, struggling, or interior disturbance that sometimes preceded this condition. Instead, "all the favours which the Lord grants the soul here . . . come quite independently of the acts of the soul itself, apart from that of its having committed itself wholly to God" (223).

- *Another sixteenth-century Spanish mystic, Saint John of the Cross.* In his *Dark Night of the Soul* (New York: Doubleday, 1959), John of the Cross described an advanced stage of contemplation this way:

  "This dark night is an inflowing of God into the soul, which purges it from its ignorances and imperfections, habitual, natural and spiritual, and which is called by contemplatives infused contemplation, or mystical theology. Herein God secretly teaches this soul and instructs it in perfection of love, without its doing anything, or understanding of what manner is this infused contemplation. . . . He prepared it for the union with God" (100).

John emphasized the necessary passive mental mode for his type of contemplation even more explicitly later:

"Because the receptive passion of the understanding can receive intelligence only in a detached and passive way (and this is impossible without its having been purged), therefore until this happens the soul feels the touch of intelligence less frequently than that of the passion of love" (141).

- *The seventeenth-century Carmelite friar Brother Lawrence of the Resurrection.* This humble Frenchman, who at various times was a soldier, footman, hermit, and kitchen worker, has captured the imagination and respect of Catholics, Protestants, and other religious adherents because of his intense search for deep spirituality while remaining in the role of a servant. Lawrence's approach to spirituality is contained in *The Practice of the Presence of God,* a collection of his letters and conversations recorded by the Abbé Joseph de Beaufort, who later became archbishop of Paris in 1695 (New York: Doubleday, 1977, 19).

Brother Lawrence suffered inner anguish for ten years as he felt his separation from God. Finally, he discovered the answer: "Having found different methods of going to God and different practices . . . I decided that they would serve more to hinder than to facilitate me in what I was seeking—which was nothing other than a means to be wholly God's" (87).

As a result of this insight, Lawrence said, "This made me decide to give all to attain all; so after having given all to God in satisfaction for my sins, I began to live as if there were no one in the world but Him and me" (87).

Part of Lawrence's "practice of the presence" involved a focus on the person and nature of God—and a method of ignoring distractions that foreshadowed the relaxation-response techniques. "I adored Him as often as I could," he said, "keeping my mind in His holy presence and recalling it as often as it wandered. I had no little difficulty in this exercise, but I kept on despite all difficulties and was not worried or distressed when I was involuntarily distracted" (87).

He pursued this meditative practice often throughout the day, including during breaks in his work:

"During our work and other activities . . . we should stop as often as we can, for a moment, to adore God from the bottom of our hearts, to savor Him, by stealth as it were, as He passes by. . . . What can be more agreeable to God than to withdraw thus many times a day from the things of man to retire into ourselves and adore Him interiorly . . . ?" (102).

- *The twentieth-century pastoral theologian Henri J. M. Nouwen.* In words remarkably similar to those of Brother Lawrence more than three hundred years before, Nouwen, who taught at Yale Divinity School and explored Catholic spirituality in many settings, described his meditative strategy this way:

"A word or sentence repeated frequently can help us to concentrate, to move to the center, to create an inner

stillness and thus to listen to the voice of God. When we
simply try to sit silently and wait for God to speak to us,
we find ourselves bombarded with endless conflicting
thoughts and ideas. But when we use a very simple
sentence . . . or a word such as *Lord* or *Jesus,* it is easier
to let the many distractions pass by without being
misled by them. Such a simple, easily repeated prayer
can slowly empty out our crowded interior life and
create the quiet space where we can dwell with God. It
can be like a ladder along which we can descend into
the heart and ascend to God. Our choice of words
depends on our needs and the circumstances of the
moment, but it is best to use words from the Scripture"
(*The Way of the Heart* [New York: Ballantine Books,
1981], 65).

Of course, many other spiritual traditions could be cited as
illustrations, such as the Muslim mysticism of the Sufis or Eastern Orthodox meditation, which encourages a focus on the icons
or images of Christ and the saints. But the main point for our
purposes is this: in each of these experiences we can detect common elements of the Breakout process.

There is always a preliminary struggle of some sort; then, a
point seems to arrive where the individual stops fighting and
"releases" prior patterns of action and thought. In every case,
this trigger is somehow connected to the person's intrinsic belief
system, such as by the repetition of a word or phrase that recalls
the personal faith. After this Breakout trigger has been pulled, a
peak experience and transformed life become possible.

Again, this is not to say that we can judge or evaluate any of
these experiences exclusively by medical and scientific measure-

ments. But there is little doubt that a common biological plat-form is in place.

It is also imperative to remember the "dark side" of faith—that is, that deep spiritual beliefs can be used for negative as well as for positive purposes. So here are a few caveats and guidelines that may prove helpful as you consider the implications of your own belief system.

Avoiding Potential Pitfalls of Strong Negative Belief

Powerful personal belief can not only produce remarkable benefits, but they may also pose serious dangers, such as emotional and physical illnesses that result from the nocebo effect—which we introduced in Chapter 10 in our discussion of the peak of rejuve-nation, or improved health. A mirror image of the placebo effect, the nocebo effect is based on a strong belief that bad things are going to happen. Such negative beliefs may do serious harm to individuals, or even societies in the form of "mass psychogenic ill-ness." Such mind-body sicknesses may be triggered by health fears, uncontrolled anxiety, or techniques that manipulate and foster negative beliefs, such as voodoo. Some of the techniques suggested for triggering a Breakout—such as repetitive exercises to elicit the relaxation response, or becoming immersed in a particular belief system—automatically open up the mind and may also expose the person to destructive philosophical beliefs and influences.

As a result of such dangers, experienced spiritual leaders and scientific researchers have suggested some guidelines for maxi-mizing the benefits of belief while minimizing or eliminating potential problems. Here are two that should help you keep your beliefs on a positive track:

Guideline #1: Secure a Responsible Mentor

Most major religious traditions insist that significant spiritual progress requires individual devotion to prayer, meditation, and one-on-one interaction with the deity. But spiritual literature frequently warns against seduction by cult leaders or abuse of trust by false prophets. One way often suggested to achieve such protection is to enlist the help of a spiritual guide or mentor—a more experienced participant in the tradition who is able to offer regular advice and midcourse corrections on the inner journey.

Benedict Groeschel, the Francisican friar who has written and lectured widely on Catholic spirituality, has said:

> Spiritual direction becomes a *sine qua non* if we are to avoid dangers while attempting to advance spiritually. A good director is a treasure. . . . When the dark recesses of our spirit become manifest, we especially need at least a friend to share our fears, and assure us that ours is not an uncommon experience. A person acting as a spiritual guide who is not open to the dark side of others is worse than no friend at all. (*Spiritual Passages*, 152)

Many years before, Saint Teresa of Avila, the sixteenth-century Spanish mystic, offered similar advice:

> Even though they be not in a religious Order, it would be a great thing for them to have someone to whom they could go, as many people do, so that they might not be following their own will in anything, for it is in this way that we usually do ourselves harm. . . . It is a great advantage for us to be

able to consult someone who knows us, so that we may learn to know ourselves. (*Interior Castle,* 68)

Similar advice comes from contemporary Protestant experts on spiritual growth. In his *Celebration of Discipline,* Richard Foster said:

Spiritual directorship has an exemplary history. Many of the first spiritual directors were the desert Fathers and were held in high regard for their ability to "discern spirits." . . . [The director] leads only by the force of his own personal holiness. He is not a superior or some ecclesiastically appointed authority. The relationship is of an advisor to a friend. Though the director has obviously advanced further into the inner depths, the two are together learning and growing in the realm of the Spirit. (159–60)

These and similar observations suggest not only that it is wise to secure a spiritual director for your journey of inner growth, but also that it is essential to choose *wisely* and be certain that the director continues to adhere to generally accepted scriptures and traditions. Many who have picked their spiritual mentors *un*wisely have fallen into cults or cultlike situations, where the director employs force of personality, rather than established standards of the particular faith, to assume control of those being guided.

Guideline #2: Be Aware That Any Spiritual Practice, Such as Prayer or Meditation, May Be Tainted by the Nocebo Effect

Another variation on the previous guideline is that serious doubt, a sense of unworthiness, or what might be described as "performance anxiety" may undercut the effectiveness of spiritual practices such as prayer. Such negative feelings, doubts, or beliefs may lead to counterintuitive results, including even the opposite result from what the individual expects.

Instead of operating out of positive intrinsic belief, the person may actually slip into the opposite mind-set—a kind of spiritual nocebo effect. Among other things, a mistaken understanding of the operation of prayer, God's will, or divine forgiveness may cause the individual to focus on failure, or on a sense that the worst is likely to happen. Such negative expectations may be so intense that they become self-fulfilling prophecies.

Fortunately, in most cases, as we attempt to explore peaks of transcendence, the positive results seem to outweigh the negative. But in the end, we can never know exactly what the ultimate event will look like after we pray, meditate, or practice other spiritual disciplines. The final result is always out of our hands.

As we try to plumb the depths of spirituality with our limited scientific tools, we must always hold out the possibility that something far beyond mere biology will ultimately enter the picture. That is, as we ascend a peak of transcendence, it may be that we will encounter another reality, a separate dimension of existence that simply can't be measured by human instruments or grasped by human reason.

The End . . . and the Beginning:

Realizing the Promise
of the Breakout Principle

At the beginning of this book we suggested that the Breakout mechanism might provide us with a kind of "ultimate self-help principle." In fact, the Breakout Principle *does* have the power to enhance many areas traditionally associated with self-improvement and personal transformation, such as creativity, productivity, athletic performance, health, and spirituality.

At the same time, however, much more is involved with the Breakout than just the facilitation of self-help programs. In his 1902 classic *Varieties of Religious Experience*, William James, quoting the early psychology-of-religion researcher Edwin Starbuck, suggested the existence of such a broad-based, interconnected phenomenon that his readers and listeners must have responded to him in some measure of wonder:

An athlete . . . sometimes awakens suddenly to an understanding of the fine points of the game and to a real enjoyment of it, just as the convert awakens to an appreciation of religion. If he keeps on engaging in the sport, there may come a day when all at once the game plays itself through him— when he loses himself in some great contest. In the same way, a musician may suddenly reach a point at which pleasure in the technique of the art entirely falls away, and in some moment of inspiration he becomes the instrument through which music flows. . . . So it is with the religious experience of these persons we are studying. (*Varieties,* 203, from Starbuck's *Psychology of Religion,* 385)

James and Starbuck displayed the amazingly early insight that widely divergent peak experiences, which by definition are individual and subjective, are also somehow connected by a common mechanism. With our emerging understanding of the biology behind the Breakout, we now see that an *objective reality*—a peculiar biochemistry, neurology, and physiology in the brain and the rest of the body—does indeed make up the physical platform on which these subjective events occur.

Furthermore, the Breakout mechanism appears to involve a peculiarly *human* phenomenon, which requires self-consciousness and understanding on the highest level. We know that lower animals respond to outside pressures and threats *automatically,* such as through the fight-or-flight response, which involves the unthinking release of epinephrine (adrenaline) and norepinephrine. As humans, we respond instinctively in the same way to stress.

But beyond this point the similarity ends. Current research suggests that animals lack the self-consciousness and advanced mental capacity to be able to understand their biological responses, to predict future consequences, and to devise a strategy to control their inner biology. Human beings, in contrast, can "step back" mentally and evaluate their current situation in terms of future results.

More than three decades ago, I began to explore how human consciousness and volition could elicit the relaxation response to counter the stress response. It has long been recognized that the ability to pursue a cognitive coping strategy represents a distinctively human capacity or skill, which requires a conscious decision. Now, we are beginning to see how this innate and unique human ability to influence our inner biology also works with the Breakout Principle.

The Breakout Promise . . .

To make the best use of this special human gift—the Breakout Principle—you will almost certainly find that you will first have to proceed through two basic steps:

- First, you must discover the nature and potential of the biology behind the Breakout, including the struggle-release/trigger-Breakout/peak-improved-normal sequence.
- Second, you have to become adept at "pulling" the Breakout trigger in a variety of circumstances in your life—and *in ways that work best for you.*

Comprehending and executing these two steps requires the application of your rational, thinking brain. But when you finally understand the process—and when you have prepared or "struggled" as much as needed—you then have to make a conscious decision to "back off" and let your "lower" brain and neurological functions take over. You sever past thought patterns by pulling the Breakout trigger, and that moves you into an entirely new, nonlinear, and holistic way of thinking, where great insights and performances are much more likely to occur. But this is only the beginning.

... and More

Many people we have encountered feel that the most exciting and life-changing Breakout experiences of all are those that lead to a peak of transcendence. Such an attitude is certainly understandable, because peaks of transcendence—as well as peaks of self-awareness, as we have defined them—touch upon those areas of life that deal with ultimate meaning and happiness.

If you hope to explore these realms fully, you will certainly find that a prerequisite will be the development of a potent, intrinsic personal belief system. Understanding the Breakout Principle can be a great help in such a philosophical quest, but make no mistake: Your fundamental philosophy of life comes first. The Breakout Principle is simply a biological mechanism that, if properly harnessed, can become an extremely useful tool in the service of your personal beliefs. But the beliefs themselves exist on a deeper plane.

Such life-transforming beliefs may begin in a sudden, blinding conversion or insight, but however they are launched, they typically develop and mature only over a lifetime of "spiritual work." Deep spirituality or philosophical awareness requires ongoing commitment, study, and discipline, including a willingness to set aside time regularly—preferably daily—to learn and cultivate those habits and inner attitudes associated with a profound philosophy of life.

As you rely on the Breakout Principle to help you explore these peaks of transcendence, you will almost certainly find yourself journeying beyond the boundaries of contemporary science. Science has definitely made our lives healthier and more comfortable in many ways. And science has much to contribute as we try to determine our ethical and social stance on difficult medical issues, such as those relating to genetic research. But ultimately, science cannot set adequate standards to judge the validity or potential of particular belief systems. That role must be reserved for responsible philosophers, theologians, and others who have been trained and who have vast experience in evaluating values and spirituality.

Finally, those who have effectively combined the Breakout Principle with their personal belief systems have often discovered that when they return to the concerns of their daily life, they enjoy an enhanced ability to trigger Breakouts in other areas—such as athletics, artistic creativity, or job productivity. Their deepest beliefs work hand in hand with the Breakout Principle to intensify their levels of personal motivation and commitment.

William James and Edwin Starbuck foresaw more than one hundred years ago that there may be similarities between peaks of transcendence and other peak experiences, such as those involving athletic prowess or musical expression. But those who believe they have been touched by something beyond space and time are often convinced that utilizing the common biological platform of the Breakout is just the beginning of the adventure.

In the end, the Breakout Principle can certainly help explain occurrences and feelings that may have escaped our understanding in the past. It can also enrich our daily lives by expanding our personal creative capacities and by moving us toward higher levels of achievement at work, in relationships, or in athletics.

But at the same time, as we explore these phenomena in greater depth, we should expect to be surprised. We should expect to be pointed in entirely new directions. And we *can* expect to experience insights that, in our analytical mind-set, we never anticipated or dreamed possible.

References

Basic References for All Chapters

Beary, J. F., and H. Benson. "A Simple Psychophysiologic Technique Which Elicits the Hypometabolic Changes of the Relaxation Response." *Psychosomatic Medicine* 36 (1974): 115–20.

Benson, H. *Beyond the Relaxation Response.* New York: Berkley Books, 1985.

———. *The Relaxation Response.* New York: Morrow, 1975.

———. *The Relaxation Response—Updated and Expanded.* 25th anniversary ed. New York: Avon, 2000.

———. *Timeless Healing: The Power and Biology of Belief.* New York: Scribner, 1996.

———. "Your Innate Asset for Combating Stress." *Harvard Business Review* 52 (1974): 49–60.

———. *Your Maximum Mind.* New York: Times Books, 1987.

Benson, H., and R. L. Allen. "How Much Stress Is Too Much?" *Harvard Business Review* 58 (1980): 86–92.

Benson, H., J. F. Beary, and M. P. Carol. "The Relaxation Response." *Psychiatry* 37 (1974): 37–46.

Benson, H., and R. Friedman. "Harnessing the Power of the Placebo Effect and Renaming It 'Remembered Wellness.'" *Annual Review of Medicine* 47 (1996): 193–99.

Benson, H., and D. P. McCallie Jr. "Angina Pectoris and the Placebo Effect." *New England Journal of Medicine* 300 (1979): 1424–29.

Benson, H., B. A. Rosner, B. R. Marzetta, and H. Klemchuk. "Decreased Blood Pressure in Borderline Hypertensive Subjects Who Practiced Meditation." *Journal of Chronic Diseases* 27 (1974): 163–69.

———. "Decreased Blood Pressure in Pharmacologically Treated Hypertensive Patients Who Regularly Elicited the Relaxation Response." *Lancet* (1974): 289–91.

Carrington, P., G. H. Collings Jr., H. Benson, H. Robinson, L. W. Wood, P. M. Lehrer, R. L. Woolfolk, and J. W. Cole. "The Use of Meditation-Relaxation Techniques for the Management of Stress in a Working Population." *Journal of Occupational Medicine* 22 (1980): 22–31.

Fuente-Fernández, R. de la, T. J. Ruth, V. Sossi, M. Schutzer, D. B. Calne, and A. J. Stoessl. "Expectation and Dopamine Release: Mechanism of the Placebo Effect in Parkinson's Disease." *Science* 293 (2001): 1164–66.

Hoffman, J. W., H. Benson, P. A. Arns, G. L. Stainbrook, L. Landsberg, J. B. Young, and A. Gill. "Reduced Sympathetic Nervous System Responsivity Associated with the Relaxation Response." *Science* 215 (1982): 190–92.

Lazar, S. W., G. Bush, R. L. Gollub, G. L. Fricchione, G. Khalsa, and H. Benson. "Functional Brain Mapping of the Relaxation Response and Meditation." *NeuroReport* 11 (2000): 1581–85.

New American Standard Bible. Cambridge study ed. Cambridge, U.K.: Cambridge University Press, 1977.

Peters, R. K., and H. Benson. "Time Out from Tension." *Harvard Business Review* 56 (1978): 120–24.

Peters, R. K., H. Benson, and D. Porter. "Daily Relaxation Response Breaks in a Working Population: 1. Health, Performance and Well-Being." *American Journal of Public Health* 67 (1977): 946–53.

Peters, R. K., H. Benson, and J. M. Peters. "Daily Relaxation Response Breaks in a Working Population: 2. Blood Pressure." *American Journal of Public Health* 67 (1977): 954–59.

Stefano, G. B., G. L. Fricchione, B. T. Slingsby, and H. Benson. "The Placebo Effect and the Relaxation Response: Neural Processes and Their Coupling to Constitutive Nitric Oxide." *Brain Research Reviews* 35 (2001): 1–19.

Wallace, R. K., H. Benson, and A. F. Wilson. "A Wakeful Hypometabolic Physiologic State." *American Journal of Physiology* 221 (1971): 795–99.

Other References by Chapter

Chapter 1: What Is a Breakout?

Adams, F. *The Genuine Works of Hippocrates.* London: Syndenham Society, 1849.

Berg, H., ed. "Abraham Maslow: Religious Aspects of Peak Experiences." http://www.uncwil.edu/people/bergh/p&r103/L31Rmaslow.htm.

Boeree, C. G. "Abraham Maslow." http://www.ship.edu/~cgboeree/maslow.html.

Castiglioni, A. *A History of Medicine.* Trans. E. B. Krimbhaar. New York: Alfred A. Knopf, 1941.

Kroenke, K., and A. D. Mangelsdorf. "Common Symptoms in Ambulatory Care: Incidence, Evaluation, Therapy and Outcome." *American Journal of Medicine* 86 (1989): 262–66.

Maslow, A. H. "Religions, Values, and Peak Experiences." *The Psychedelic Library.* http://mir.drugtext.org/druglibrary/shaffer/lsd/maslow.htm.

Matchan, L. "Look Who's Knitting." *Boston Globe,* January 31, 2002, H1, H4.

"Peak Experiences." http://indialink.com/Forum/Artsculture/messages/833.html.

Chapter 2: Anatomy of the Trigger

Bumiller, E. "The Overview: Prepare for Casualties, Bush Says, While Asking Support of Nation." *New York Times on the Web,* September 21, 2001.

Christianson, S. A. "Emotional stress and eyewitness memory: a critical review." *Psychological Bulletin* 112 (1992): 284–309.

Kumari, V., and P. J. Corr. "Menstrual cycle, arousal-induction, and intelligence test performance." *Psychological Reports* 78 (1996): 51–58.

Yerkes, R. M., and J. D. Dodson. "The Relation of Strength of Stimulus to Rapidity of Habit Formation." *Journal of Comparative Neurology and Psychology* 18 (1908): 459–82.

Chapter 3: The "Spirit" of Peak Experience

Christianson, S. A. "Emotional stress and eyewitness memory: a critical review." *Psychological Bulletin* 112 (1992): 284–309.

Cook, G. "Scientists Find Switch for Lights in Fireflies." *Boston Globe,* June 29, 2001, A1, A20.

"Diffusible GasNets Home Page—from Neuroscience to Control Systems." www.cogs.susx.ac.uk/users/toms/GasNets/home.html.

Eliot, T. S. *Four Quartets.* New York: New Directions, 1970.

Epstein, R. H. "Puff the Magic Gas." *Physician's Weekly* on-line, August 19, 1996.

Fountain, H. "Discovering the Tricks of Fireflies' Summertime Magic." *New York Times,* July 3, 2001, D4.

Fuente-Fernández, R. de la, T. J. Ruth, V. Sossi, M. Schutzer, D. B. Calne, and A. J. Stoessl. "Expectation and Dopamine Release: Mechanism of the Placebo Effect in Parkinson's Disease." *Science* 293 (2001): 1164–66.

Harte, J. L., G. H. Eifert, and R. Smith. "The effects of running and meditation on beta-endorphin, corticotropin-releasing hormone and cortisol in plasma, and on mood." *Biological Psychology* 40 (1995): 251–65.

Henry, J. L. "Circulating opioids: possible physiological roles in central nervous function." *Neuroscience and Biobehavioral Review* 6 (1982): 229–45.

Jastrow, R. *God and the Astronomers.* 2nd ed. New York: W. W. Norton, 1992/2000.

Jumari, V., and P. J. Corr. "Menstrual cycle, arousal-induction, and intelligence test performance." *Psychological Reports* 78 (1996): 51–58.

Lewis, C. S. *Miracles.* New York: Touchstone, 1976.

"Nitric Oxide Helps Networks Think Like Your Brain." *Business Week,* October 8, 2001, 99.

Prast, H., and A. Philippu. "Nitric oxide as modulator of neuronal function." *Progress in Neurobiology* 64 (2001): 51–68.

"President Bush's Address on Terrorism Before a Joint Meeting of Congress." *New York Times on the Web,* September 21, 2001.

"Sussex Scientists Use Toxic Gas to Give Robots New Powers." University of Sussex media release, December 21, 1998. www.sussex.ac.ik/press_office/media/media42.html.

Taylor, E. I. "The Connection Between Mind & Body." *Harvard Medical Alumni Bulletin,* winter 2000.

Ward, M. "Robot brains become more human." BBC News Online, September 13, 2001.

Chapter 4: Mapping the Creative Mind

Eccles, J. C. *Evolution of the Brain: Creation of the Self.* London: Routledge, 1989.

Newberg, A., E. D'Aquili, and V. Rause. *Why God Won't Go Away: Brain Science and the Biology of Belief.* New York: Ballantine Books, 2001.

Polkinghorne, J. *Quarks, Chaos & Christianity.* New York: Crossroad, 1994.

Chapter 5: The Ultimate Self-Help Principle

Stefano, G. B., G. L. Fricchione, B. T. Slingsby, and H. Benson. "The Placebo Effect and the Relaxation Response: Neural Processes and Their Coupling to Constitutive Nitric Oxide." *Brain Research Reviews* 35 (2001): 1–19.

Chapter 6: The First Peak—Self-Awareness

Goode, E. "Stress from Attacks Will Chase Some into the Depths of Their Minds, and Stay." *New York Times on the Web,* September 18, 2001.

Horton, M. J. "PTSD: When the Terror Won't Stop." CBS Health Watch by Medscape. http://aolsvc.health.cbshealthwatch.aol.com.

Kozinn, A. "George Harrison, 'Quiet Beatle' and Lead Guitarist, Dies at 58." *New York Times,* December 1, 2001, A1, A24.

Chapter 7: The Second Peak—Creativity

Atchley, R. A., M. Keeney, and C. Burgess. "Cerebral hemispheric mechanisms linking ambiguous word meaning retrieval and creativity." *Brain Cognition* 40 (1999): 479–99.

Carlsson, I., P. E. Wendt, and J. Risberg. "On the neurobiology of creativity. Differences in frontal activity between high and low creative subjects." *Neuropsychologia* 38 (2000): 873–85.

Eccles, J. C. *Evolution of the Brain: Creation of the Self.* London: Routledge, 1989.

Goode, E. "How Culture Molds Habits of Thought." *New York Times,* August 8, 2000, D1, D4.

"Goodness soaks." *Lexington* (Ky.) *Herald Leader,* published in the *Columbus Ledger-Enquirer,* March 13, 2001, D1, D2.

Holt, J. "Bodies in Motion." Review of *Einstein in Love* by Dennis Overbye. *New York Times Book Review,* October 8, 2000, 12.

Huston, P. "Resolving writer's block." *Canadian Family Physician* 44 (January 1998): 92–97.

Jausovec, N., and K. Jausovec. "Differences in resting EEG related to ability." *Brain Topography* 12 (2000): 229–40.

———. "EEG activity during the performance of complex mental problems." *International Journal of Psychophysiology* 36 (2000): 73–88.

King, S. *On Writing.* New York: Scribner, 2000.

Petsche, H. "Approaches to verbal, visual, and musical creativity by EEG coherence analysis." *International Journal of Psychophysiology* 24 (1996): 145–59.

Petsche, H., S. Kaplan, A. von Stein, and O. Fitz. "The possible meaning of the upper and lower alpha frequency ranges for cognitive and creative tasks." *International Journal of Psychophysiology* 26 (1997): 77–97.

Powers, A. "Down from the Mountain, Singing with More Serenity." *New York Times,* October 28, 2001, AR29–30.

Proceedings of the National Academy of Sciences, September 25, 2001.

Sternberg, R. J. "What is the common thread of creativity? Its dialectical relation to intelligence and wisdom." *American Psychology* 56 (2001): 360–62.

Stewart, P. "Walking onto a Bare Stage (and into Scrooge's Skin)." *New York Times,* December 23, 2001, AR3.

Chapter 8: The Third Peak—Productivity

Albrecht, G., S. Freeman, and N. Higginbotham. "Complexity and human health: the case for a transdisciplinary paradigm." *Cultural Medicine and Psychiatry* 22 (1998): 55–92.

Aleman, A., G. J. Rutten, M. M. Sitskoorn, G. Dautzenberg, and N. F. Ramsey. "Activation of striate cortex in the absence of visual stimulation: an fMRI study of synesthesia." *NeuroReport* 12 (2001): 2827–30.

Bangle, C. "The ultimate creativity machine. How BMW turns art into profit." *Harvard Business Review* 79 (2001): 47–55, 174.

Benson, H. "Your Innate Asset for Combating Stress." *Harvard Business Review* 52 (1974): 49–60.

Bernick, C. L. "When your culture needs a makeover." *Harvard Business Review* 79 (2001): 53–58, 60–61, 146.

Bettinger, C. "Use of corporate culture to trigger high performance." *Journal of Business Strategy* 10 (1989): 38–42.

Brust, J. C. "Music and the neurologist. A historical perspective." *Annals of New York Academy of Science* 930 (2001): 143–52.

Buzzword Compliant Dictionary. "Moonshine shop." www.buzzwhack.com.

Collis, D. J., and C. A. Montgomery. "Creating corporate advantage." *Harvard Business Review* 76 (1998): 70–83.

Cox, K. "Stories as case knowledge: case knowledge as stories." *Medical Education* 35 (2001): 862–66.

de Geus, A. "The living company." *Harvard Business Review* 75 (1997): 51–59.

Denison, D. R. "Bringing corporate culture to the bottom line." *Organizational Dynamics* 13 (1984): 4–22.

Donoso, A., P. Molina, P. Trujillo, C. Vasquez, and V. Diaz. "Cognitive stimulation workshops in old age: preliminary experience." *Review of Medicine in Chile* 127 (1999): 319–22.

Doody, M. F. "Broader range of skills distinguishes successful CFOs." *Healthcare Financial Management* 54 (2000): 52–57.

Dugosh, K. L., P. B. Paulus, E. J. Roland, and H. C. Yang. "Cognitive stimulation in brainstorming." *Journal of Personal and Social Psychology* 79 (2000): 722–35.

Dumaine, B. "The Man Who Came Back from the Dead Again and Again." *FSB,* September 2001, 61–63.

Everett, A. "Piercing the veil of the future. A review of the Delphi method of research." *Professional Nurse* 9 (1993): 181–85.

Gallupe, R. B., L. M. Bastianutti, and W. H. Cooper. "Unblocking brainstorms." *Journal of Applied Psychology* 76 (1991): 137–42.

Goodman, C. M. "The Delphi technique: a critique." *Journal of Advanced Nursing* 12 (1987): 729–34.

Hendricks, J. "Creativity over the life course—a call for a relational perspective." *International Journal of Aging and Human Development* 48 (1999): 85–111.

———. "The search for new solutions." *Gerontologist* 36 (1996): 141–44.

Hruskesky, W. J. "The temporal organization of life: the impact of multi-frequency nonlinear biologic time structure upon the host-cancer balance." *Japanese Journal of Clinical Oncology* 30 (2000): 529–33.

Hubbard, T. L. "Synesthesia-like mappings of lightness, pitch, and melodic interval." *American Journal of Psychology* 109 (1996): 219–38.

Hudson, K. M. "Transforming a conservative company—one laugh at a time." *Harvard Business Review* 79 (2001): 45–48, 51–53.

Kanter, R. M. "The middle manager as innovator." *Harvard Business Review* 60 (1982): 95–105.

Kroll, L. "Entrepreneur of the Year: Java Man." Forbes.com, October 29, 2001.

Leonard, D., and S. Straus. "Putting your company's whole brain to work." *Harvard Business Review* 75 (July–August 1997): 110–21.

Loehr, J., and T. Schwartz. "The making of a corporate athlete." *Harvard Business Review* 79 (2001): 120–28, 176.

Lunsford, J. L. "Lean Times: With Airbus on Its Tail, Boeing Is Rethinking How It Builds Planes." *Wall Street Journal,* September 5, 2001, A1, A16.

Marks, L. C. "Synesthetic perception and poetic metaphor." *Journal of Experimental Psychology, Human Perception, and Performance* 8 (1982): 15–23.

Marks, L. E. "Bright sneezes and dark coughs, loud sunlight and soft moonlight." *Journal of Experimental Psychology, Human Perception, and Performance* 8 (1982): 177–93.

McKenna, H. P. "The Delphi technique: a worthwhile research approach for nursing?" *Journal of Advanced Nursing* 19 (1994): 1221–25.

Miller, K. "FedEx's Smith in hunt for 'Buck Rogers ideas.'" Associated Press, December 2, 2001.

Mintzberg, H., and L. Van der Heyden. "Organigraphs: drawing how companies really work." *Harvard Business Review* 77 (1999): 87–94, 184.

Modell, A. H. "The synergy of memory, affects and metaphor." *Journal of Analytical Psychology* 42 (1997): 105–17.

Orchard, B. "Creating constructive outcomes in conflict." *AAOHN Journal* 46 (1998): 302–12, 313–14.

Pascale, R., M. Millemann, and L. Gioja. "Changing the way we change." *Harvard Business Review* 75 (1997): 126–39.

Peters, R. K., H. Benson, and D. Porter. "Daily Relaxation Response Breaks in a Working Population: I. Effects on Self-Reported Measures of Health, Performance, and Well-Being." *American Journal of Public Health* 67 (1977): 946–53.

Revonsuo, A. "Putting color back where it belongs." *Conscious Cognition* 10 (March 2001): 78–84.

Rizzo, J., and P. J. Eslinger. "Colored hearing synesthesia: an investigation of neural factors." *Neurology* 39 (1989): 781–84.

Sawhney, M. "Don't homogenize, synchronize." *Harvard Business Review* 79 (2001): 100–108, 145.

Scalzone, R., and G. Zontini. "The dream's navel between chaos and thought." *International Journal of Psychoanalysis* 82 (2001): 263–82.

Schlitz, K., K. Trocha, B. M. Wieringa, H. M. Emrich, S. Johannes, and T. F. Munte. "Neurophysiological aspects of synesthetic experience." *Journal of Neuropsychiatry and Clinical Neuroscience* 11 (1999): 58–65.

Tichy, N. M. "No ordinary boot camp." *Harvard Business Review* 79 (2001): 63–70, 166.

Tsukamoto, K., and A. Sakamoto. "The productivity of electronic brainstorming: a comparison of three systems with a control." *Shinrigaku Kenkyu* 72 (2001): 19–28.

Chapter 9: The Fourth Peak—Athleticism

Benson, H. Testimony before the United States Senate Appropriations Subcommittee on Labor/HHS & Education. Senator Arlen Specter, Chairman. March 28, 2000.

Benson, H., T. Dryer, and L. H. Hartley. "Decreased VO$_2$ Consumption during Exercise with Elicitation of the Relaxation Response." *Journal of Human Stress* 4 (1978): 38–42.

References

Blumenthal, J. S., R. S. Williams, T. L. Needels, and A. G. Wallace. "Psychological changes accompany aerobic exercise in healthy middle-aged adults." *Psychosomatic Medicine* 44 (1982): 529–36.

Bock, H. "Capriati plays the 'tough' points well." Associated Press, September 4, 2001.

Brown, D. R., Y. Wang, A. Ward, C. B. Ebbeling, L. Fortlage, E. Puleo, H. Benson, and J. M. Rippe. "Chronic psychological effects of exercise and exercise plus cognitive strategies." *Medical Science, Sports, and Exercise* 27 (1995): 765–75.

Christianson, S. A. "Emotional stress and eyewitness memory: a critical review." *Psychological Bulletin* 112 (1992): 284–309.

Cooper, A. "In the Zone: The Zen of Sports." Shambhala Sun Online. www.shambhalasun.com/archives.

Cramer, S. R., D. C. Nieman, and J. W. Lee. "The effects of moderate exercise training on psychological well-being and mood state in women." *Journal of Psychosomatic Research* 35 (1991): 437–49.

Daus, A. T., J. Wilson, and W. M. Freeman. "Predicting success in football." *Journal of Sports Medicine and Physical Fitness* 29 (1989): 209–12.

Dupcak, S. "Introduction to Sport Psychology." PennState on-line. www.personal.psy.edu/faculty.

Fitzgerald, B. "The BU Svengali behind the Olympic women's hockey team." B.U. Bridge, April 3, 1998. www.bu.edu/bridge/archive.

Goldola, J. C., and B. W. Tuckman. "Effects of a systematic program of exercise on selected measures of creativity." *Perception and Motor Skills* 60 (1985): 53–54.

Gould, E., R. C. Eklund, S. A. Jackson. "Coping strategies used by U.S. Olympic wrestlers." *Research Questions in Exercise and Sport* 64 (1993): 83–93.

Harte, J. L., G. H. Eifert, and R. Smith. "The effects of running and meditation on beta-endorphin, corticotropin-releasing hormone and cortisol in plasma, and on mood." *Biology and Psychology* 40 (1995): 251–65.

Hassmen, P., and N. Koivula. "Mood, physical working capacity and cognitive performance in the elderly as related to physical activity." *Aging* (Milano) 9 (1997): 136–42.

Horwitz, T. "A Coach for the Mind Games." *Wall Street Journal,* September 27, 2000, A8.

The Human Brain Exercise. "Where Mind Meets Body—the Neuromuscular Junction." The Franklin Institute Online. http://sln.fi.edu.

Joesting, J., and G. I. Whitehead III. "Comparison of women's studies students with female golf star athletes on the 16 PF." *Perception and Motor Skills* 42 (1976): 477–78.

Jokela, M., and Y. L. Hanin. "Does the individual zones of optimal functioning model discriminate between successful and less successful athletes? A meta-analysis." *Journal of Sports Science* 17 (1999): 873–87.

Keogh, F. "The Tonya Harding Affair." BBC Sport on-line, January 29, 2002.

Koch, J. "Nancy Kerrigan." *Boston Globe Magazine* on-line, 1998. www.boston.com/globe/magazine/1998/2.

Kushnir, L. H. "The Mind/Body Medical Institute makes its mark on the Olympics." *Deaconess This Month* 3 (1992): cover story.

La Forge, R. "Mind-body fitness: encouraging prospects for primary and secondary fitness." *Journal of Cardiovascular Nursing* 11 (1997): 53–65.

Land, M. F., and P. McLeod. "From eye movements to actions: how batsmen hit the ball." *Natural Neuroscience* 3 (2000): 1340–45.

Liggett, D. R., and S. Hamada. "Enhancing the visualization of gymnasts." *American Journal of Clinical Hypnosis* 35 (1993): 190–97.

Maroulakis, E., and Y. Zervas. "Effects of aerobic exercise on mood of adult women." *Perception and Motor Skills* 76 (1993): 795–801.

McBeath, M. K. "The rising fastball: baseball's impossible pitch." *Perception* 19 (1990): 545–52.

McLeod, P. "Visual reaction time and high-speed ball games." *Perception* 16 (1987): 49–59.

"Motion Detector." www.washingtonpost.com. December 18, 2001.

Murphy, T. J., R. R. Pagano, and G. A. Marlatt. "Lifestyle modification with heavy alcohol drinkers: effects of aerobic exercise and meditation." *Addictive Behavior* 11 (1986): 175–86.

Neural Control Laboratory, Lerner Research Institute, Cleveland Clinic Foundation. Cleveland, Ohio. www.lerner.ccf.org.

Olney, B. "Speedy Feet, but an Even Quicker Thinker." *New York Times*, February 1, 2002, A1, A26.

Osborne, K., E. Rudrud, and F. F. Zezoney. "Improved curveball hitting through the enhancement of visual cues." *Journal of Applied Behavioral Analysis* 23 (1990): 371–77.

Raglin, J. S., and M. J. Morris. "Precompetition anxiety in women volleyball players: a test of ZOF theory in a team sport." *British Journal of Sports Medicine* 28 (1994): 47–51.

Regan, D. "Visual factors in hitting and catching." *Journal of Sports Science* 15 (1997): 533–58.

———. "Visual judgements and misjudgements in cricket, and the art of flight." *Perception* 21 (1992): 91–115.

Selicki, F. A., and E. Segall. "The mind/body connection of the golf swing." *Clinical Sports Medicine* 15 (1996): 191–201.

References

"Skater attacked by another skater, A." ABC Sports Online. http://Espn.go.com/abcsports.

Solberg, E. E., F. Ingjer, A. Holen, J. Sundgot-Borgen, S. Nilsson, and I. Holme. "Stress reactivity to and recovery from a standardised exercise bout: a study of 31 runners practising relaxation techniques." *British Journal of Sports Medicine* 34 (2000): 268–72.

Solberg, E. E., R. Halvorsen, J. Sundgot-Borgen, F. Ingjer, and A. Holen. "Meditation: a modulator of the immune response to physical stress? A brief report." *British Journal of Sports Medicine* 29 (1995): 255–57.

Solomon, E. G., and A. K. Bumpus. "The running meditation response: an adjunct to psychotherapy." *American Journal of Psychotherapy* 32 (1978): 583–92.

Sugarman, K. "Peak Performance—Characteristics of Being in the Zone." www.psywww.com/sports/peak.htm.

Thelwell, R. C., and I. W. Maynard. "Anxiety-performance relationships in cricketers: testing the zone of optimal functioning hypothesis." *Perception and Motor Skills* 87 (1998): 675–89.

"Tonya Harding–Nancy Kerrigan Saga." Washingpost.com. 1998.

Topp, R. "Effect of relaxation or exercise on undergraduates' test anxiety." *Perception and Motor Skills* 69 (1989): 35–41.

Tsutsumi, T., B. M. Don, L. D. Zaichkowsky, K. Takenaka, K. Oka, and T. Ohno. "Comparison of high and moderate intensity of strength training on mood and anxiety in older adults." *Perception and Motor Skills* 87 (1998): 1003–11.

Tuckman, B. W., and J. S. Hinkle. "An experimental study of the physical and psychological effects of aerobic exercise on schoolchildren." *Health and Psychology* 5 (1986): 197–207.

Turner, P. E., and J. S. Raglin. "Variability in precompetition anxiety and performance in college track and field athletes." *Medical Science, Sports, and Exercise* 28 (1996): 378–85.

Warner, L., and M. E. McNeill. "Mental imagery and its potential for physical therapy." *Physical Therapy* 68 (1988): 516–21.

Will, G. F. *Men at Work: The Craft of Baseball.* New York: HarperCollins, 1990.

Wilson, G. S., and J. S. Raglin. "Optimal and predicted anxiety in 9–12-year-old track and field athletes." *Scandinavian Journal of Medical Science and Sports* 7 (1997): 253–58.

Yaffe, K., D, Barnes, M. Nevitt, L. Y. Lui, and K. Covinsky. "A prospective study of physical activity and cognitive decline in elderly women: women who walk." *Archives of Internal Medicine* 161 (2001): 1703–8.

Chapter 10: The Fifth Peak—Rejuvenation

Albrecht, G. L., and P. J. Devlieger. "The disability paradox: high quality of life against all odds." *Social Science and Medicine* 48 (1999): 977–88.

Archer, T. P., and C. V. Leier. "Placebo Treatment in Congestive Heart Failure." *Cardiology* 81 (1992): 125–33.

Basedow, H. *The Australian Aboriginal.* Adelaide: F. W. Preece, 1925. As quoted in W. B. Cannon. "'Voodoo' Death." *American Anthropologist* 44 (1942): 169–81.

Beecher, H. "The Powerful Placebo." *Journal of the American Medical Association* 159 (1955): 1602–6.

Benson, H. *The Mind/Body Effect.* New York: Simon & Schuster, 1979.

Benson, H., and J. A. Dusek. "Self-Reported Health, and Illness and the Use of Conventional and Unconventional Medicine and Mind/Body Healing by Christian Scientists and Others." *Journal of Nervous and Mental Disease* 187 (1999): 540–49.

Benson, H., and M. D. Epstein. "The Placebo Effect—a Neglected Asset in the Care of Patients." *Journal of the American Medical Association* 232 (1975): 1225–27.

Benson, H., and D. P. McCallie Jr. "Angina Pectoris and the Placebo Effect." *New England Journal of Medicine* 300 (1979): 1424–29.

Berlinger, N. T. "Music as Medicine and Minstrel as Therapist." *New York Times,* February 13, 2001, D8.

Cannon, W. B. "'Voodoo' Death." *American Anthropologist* 44 (1942): 169–81.

———. *The Way of an Investigator: A Scientist's Experiences in Medical Research.* New York: W. W. Norton, 1945.

Coronary Drug Project Research Group. "Influence of Adherence to Treatment and Response of Cholesterol on Mortality in the Coronary Drug Project." *New England Journal of Medicine* 303 (1980): 1038–41.

Egbert, L. D., G. E. Battit, C. E. Welch, and M. K. Bartlett. "Reduction of Postoperative Pain by Encouragement and Instruction of Patients." *New England Journal of Medicine* 270 (1964): 825–27.

Ellis, J. *American Sphinx: The Character of Thomas Jefferson.* New York: Random House, 1996.

Engel, G. "A Life Setting Conducive to Illness: The Giving-Up–Given-Up Complex." *Bulletin of the Menninger Clinic* 32 (1968): 355–65.

———. "Sudden and Rapid Death During Psychological Stress: Folklore or Folk Wisdom?" *Annals of Internal Medicine* 74 (1971): 771–82.

"Experts probe link between emotions and health." Cnn.com/health, March 27, 2001. www.cnn.com.

Farrell, S. J., A. D. Ross, and K. V. Sehgal. "Eastern movement therapies." *Physical and Medical Rehabilitation Clinics of North America* 10 (1999): 617–29.

Hart, B. G. "Chronic pain management in the workplace." *AAOHN Journal* 45 (1997): 451–58.

Hashish, I., H. K. Hai, W. Harvey, C. Feinmann, and M. Harris. "Reduction of Postoperative Pain and Swelling by Ultrasound Treatment: A Placebo Effect." *Pain* 33 (1988): 303–11.

Hippocrates. "Precepts." As quoted in J. Bartlett. *Familiar Quotations.* 14th ed. Ed. E. M. Beck. Boston: Little, Brown, 1968.

Horwitz, R. I., C. M. Viscoli, L. Berkman, R. M. Donaldson, S. M. Horwitz, C. J. Murray, D. F. Ransohoff, and J. Sindelar. "Treatment Adherence and Risk of Death After a Myocardial Infarction." *Lancet* 336 (1990): 542–45.

Hrobjartsson, A., and P. C. Gotzsche. "Is the Placebo Powerless?" *New England Journal of Medicine* 344 (2001): 1594–602.

"Human Sweat Contains Antibiotic." Associated Press, November 11, 2001.

Jones, J. M. "Little Change in Americans' Stress Levels over Last Eight Years." Gallup News Service, January 3, 2002. www.gallup.com.

Kannel, W. B., and P. D. Sorlie. "Remission of Clinical Angina Pectoris: The Framingham Study." *American Journal of Cardiology* 42 (1978): 119–23.

Kawachi, I., D. Sparrow, A. Spiro III, P. Vokonas, and S. T. Weiss. "A Prospective Study of Anger and Coronary Heart Disease: The Normative Aging Study." *Circulation* 94 (1996): 2090–95.

Lerner, B. H. "Can stress cause disease? Revisiting the tuberculosis research of Thomas Holmes, 1949–1961." *Annals of Internal Medicine* 124 (1996): 673–80.

McCullough, D. *John Adams.* New York: Simon & Schuster, 2001.

McKiney, C. H., F. C. Tims, A. M. Kumar, and M. Kumar. "The effect of selected classical music and spontaneous imagery on plasma beta-endorphin." *Journal of Behavioral Medicine* 20 (1997): 85–99.

Menninger von Lerchenthal, E. "Death from Psychic Causes." *Bulletin of the Menninger Clinic* 12 (1948): 31–36.

Murray, J. L., and G. E. Abraham. "Pseudocyesis: A Review." *Obstetrics and Gynecology* 51 (1978): 627–31.

Nakamura, H. "Effects of emotionality upon GSR and respiration rate and relationship between verbal reports and physiological responses." *Shinrigaku Kenkyu* 55 (1984): 47–50.

Nature Immunology, November 5, 2001. http://immunol.nature.com.

Neergaard, L. "Study: Stress Takes Toll on Brain." Associated Press, January 18, 2002.

O'Callaghan, C. C. "Pain, music creativity and music therapy in palliative care." *American Journal of Hospital Palliative Care* 13 (1996): 43–49.

Pandya, D. P., V. H. Vyas, and S. H. Vyas. "Mind-body therapy in the management and prevention of coronary disease." *Comprehensive Therapy* 25 (1999): 283–93.

Phillips, D. P., G. C. Liu, K. Kwok, J. R. Jarvinen, W. Zhang, and I. S. Abramson. "The Hound of the Baskervilles effect: natural experiment on the influence of psychological stress on timing of death." *British Medical Journal* 323 (2001): 1443–46.

Pogge, R. "The Toxic Placebo." *Medical Times* 91 (1963): 773–78.

Preston, R. A., G. J. Materson, D. J. Reda, and E. W. Williams. "Placebo-Associated Blood Pressure Response and Adverse Effects in the Treatment of Hypertension." *Archives of Internal Medicine* 160 (2000): 1449–54.

Roberts, A. H., D. G. Kewman, L. Mercier, and M. Hovell. "The Power of Nonspecific Effects in Healing: Implications for Psychosocial and Biological Treatments." *Clinical Psychology Review* 13 (1993): 375–91.

Saad, L. "Poll Analyses: Personal Impact on Americans' Lives." September 26, 2001. www.gallup.com.

Saul, L. J. "Sudden Death at Impasse." *Psychoanalytic Forum* 1 (1966): 88–89.

"Scared to Death by the Number Four." *Science* 295 (2002): 267.

Stuart, E., M. Caudill, J. Leserman, C. Dorrington, R. Friedman, and H. Benson. "Nonpharmacologic Treatment of Hypertension: A Multiple-Risk-Factor Approach." *Journal of Cardiovascular Nursing* 1 (1987): 1–14.

Tasiemski, A., M. Salzet, H. Benson, G. L. Fricchione, T. V. Bilfinger, Y. Gouman, M. H. Metz-Boutiguek, D. Aunis, G. B. Stefano. "The presence of antibacterial and opioid peptides in human plasma during coronary artery bypass surgery." *Journal of Neuroimmunology* 109 (2000): 228–35.

Thomas, K. B. "General Practice Consultations: Is There Any Point in Being Positive?" *British Medical Journal Clinical Research* 294 (1987): 1200–2.

Tilley, B. C., G. S. Alarcon, S. P. Heyse, D. E. Trentham, R. Neuner, D. A. Kaplan, D. O. Clegg, J. C. Leisen, L. Buckley, S. M. Cooper, H. Duncan, S. R. Pillemer, M. Tuttleman, and S. E. Fowler. "Minocycline in Rheumatoid Arthritis: A 48-week, Double-Blind, Placebo-Controlled Trial." *Annals of Internal Medicine* 122 (1995): 81–89.

Traut, E. F., and E. W. Passarelli. "Placebos in the Treatment of Rheumatoid Arthritis and Other Rheumatic Conditions." *Annals of the Rheumatic Diseases* 16 (1957): 18–22.

Turner, J. A., R. A. Deyo, J. D. Loeser, M. Von Korff, and W. E. Fordyce. "The Importance of Placebo Effects in Pain Treatment and Research." *Journal of the American Medical Association* 271 (1994): 1609–14.

VanderArk, S. D., and D. Ely. "Biochemical and galvanic skin responses to music stimuli by college students in biology and music." *Perception and Motor Skills* 74 (1992): 1079–90.

———. "Cortisol, biochemical, and galvanic skin responses to music stimuli—different preference values by college students in biology and music." *Perception and Motor Skills* 77 (1993): 227–34.

Chapter 11: The Sixth Peak—Transcendence

Atchley, R. A., M. Keeney, and C. Burgess. "Cerebral hemispheric mechanisms linking ambiguous word meaning retrieval and creativity." *Brain Cognition* 40 (1999): 479–99.

Augustine, Saint. *Confessions.* New York: Sheed & Ward, 1942.

"Born-Again Christians." Barna Research Online, February 26, 2002. www.barna.org.

Chambers, Oswald. *My Utmost for His Highest.* New York: Dodd, Mead & Company, 1935.

Dumond, D. L. *Antislavery Origins of the Civil War in the United States.* Ann Arbor: University of Michigan Press, 1960.

James, W. *Varieties of Religious Experience.* New York: The Modern Library, 1902, 1929.

Jastrow, R. *God and the Astronomers.* 2nd ed. New York: W. W. Norton, 1992/2000.

Jausovec, N., and K. Jausovec. "Differences in resting EEG related to ability." *Brain Topography* 12 (2000): 229–40.

———. "EEG activity during the performance of complex mental problems." *International Journal of Psychophysiology* 36 (2000): 73–88.

McCann, J., ed. and trans. *The Rule of Saint Benedict in Latin and English.* London: Burns Oates, 1952.

New American Standard Bible. Cambridge study ed. Cambridge, U.K.: Cambridge University Press, 1977.

Parker, P. L., ed. *The Journal of John Wesley.* Kent, England: STL Productions, n.d.

Potter, D. M., and T. G. Manning. *Nationalism and Sectionalism in America.* New York: Holt, Reinhart and Winston, 1949, 1961.

Princeton Religion Research Center. "Emerging Trends." Gallup Polls analyzed from 1939–2001. www.gallup.com.

"What Do Americans Believe?" www.christianitytoday.com/leaders/newsletter/ 2001.

Chapter 12: The Power of Intrinsic Belief

Benson, H., J. W. Lehmann, M. S. Malhotra, R. F. Goldman, J. Hopkins, and M. D. Epstein. "Body temperature changes during the practice of g tum-mo (heat) yoga." *Nature* 295 (1982): 234–36.

Benson, H., M. S. Malhora, R. F. Goldman, G. D. Jacobs, and P. J. Hopkins. "Three case reports of the metabolic and electroencephalographic changes during advanced Buddhist meditative techniques." *Behavioral Medicine* 16 (1990): 90–95.

Brody, J. E. "Taking Action Before the Verdict Is In." *New York Times,* June 13, 2000, D8.

Foster, R. J. *Celebration of Discipline.* San Francisco: Harper & Row, 1978.

Groeschel, B. J. *Spiritual Passages.* New York: Crossroad, 1986.

Hesse, H. *Siddhartha.* New York: New Directions Paperbook, 1951, 1957.

His Holiness the Dalai Lama. *How to Practice.* New York: Pocket Books, 2002.

James, W. *Varieties of Religious Experience.* New York: The Modern Library, 1902, 1929.

John of the Cross. *Dark Night of the Soul.* New York: Doubleday, 1959.

Julian of Norwich. *Enfolded in Love.* New York: Seabury Press, 1981.

Kass, J. D., R. Friedman, J. Leserman, P. C. Zuttermeister, and H. Benson. "Health Outcomes and New Index of Spiritual Experience." *Journal for the Scientific Study of Religion* 30 (1991): 203–11. Addendum: "Questionnaire on Spiritual and Religious Attitudes."

Koenig, H. G. *Handbook of Religion and Mental Health.* San Diego: Academic Press, 1998.

Lawrence, Brother. *The Practice of the Presence of God.* New York: Doubleday, 1977.

Nouwen, H. *The Way of the Heart.* New York: Ballantine Books, 1981.

Teresa of Avila. *Interior Castle.* New York: Doubleday, 1944, 1961.

The End . . . and the Beginning:
Realizing the Promise of the Breakout Principle

James, W. *Varieties of Religious Experience.* New York: The Modern Library, 1902, 1929.

INDEX

AAOHN Journal, 230
Aaron, 245–46
actors, 139–41
Adams, John, 224
adrenal glands, 57
aerobic sports, 201–6
    anaerobic sports vs., 201
    benefits of, 203, 204
    lactate buildup in, 203
    relaxation response and, 201–3,
        204, 205
AIDS, 73
Albright, Tenley and Nile, 210
Allen, Robert L., 33–34
altruistic activities, 16, 18, 43, 88,
    97–98, 100–101, 137, 228
*American Journal of Hospital
    Palliative Care,* 229
American Journal of Psychology, 168
American Journal of Public Health,
    162, 216
*American Sphinx: The Character of
    Thomas Jefferson* (Ellis), 225
anaerobic sports, 201

analytical thinking, *see* linear
    (analytical) thinking
anger, avoidance of, 231
angina pectoris, 53, 223
animals, 188–90, 284–85
    as triggers, 43
Annals of Internal Medicine, 227
antibacterial peptides, 218
antibiotics, natural, 218–19
antinomy principle, 133, 135
*Antislavery Origins of the Civil War in
    the United States* (Dumond), 253
anxiety, 5, 11–12, 14, 16–17, 20, 32,
    33, 35, 58, 74–76, 79–80, 81,
    138, 211
    athletic preperformance, 206–9
Archimedes, 47–48
art, 17, 41, 63–64, 287
arthritis, 116–18, 223
artificial intelligence research, 49
Asian vs. Western thinking, 133–37,
    157–58
    see also holistic (dialectical) thinking;
        linear (analytical) thinking

asthma, 54, 223
athletes, athleticism, 5, 14, 15, 24,
    173, 181, 182–209, 284, 287
    animals and, 188–90
    average, 195–98
    brain coherence in, 129
    corporate, 165–66
    "in the zone," *see* "zone," athletic
    IZOF of, 207–8, 209, 246
    mind-body fitness of, 190–95
    muscle motor memory of, 99, 185,
        186–87, 192, 196
    Olympic, 190–95, 208, 209, 210
    preperformance anxiety of, 206–9
    preperformance rituals of, 191–93,
        208–9
    release stage of, 183, 184, 209
    struggle stage of, 29–31, 182–83,
        184, 185, 191, 192, 206, 209
    visual focus of, 41, 98–99, 186–88,
        196–97, 198, 199, 200
    visualization technique for,
        191–93
    see also aerobic sports
athletic triggers, 41–42
attitudes, basic, 108, 116–18
Augustine, Saint, 11, 250
Australia, 204
Austria, 129
autonomic nervous system, 73, 74, 79,
    80
axons, 69

backing off, 19, 26–27, 34, 36, 40, 58,
    91, 255
    see also release, stage of
Baiul, Oksana, 194
Barger, A. Clifford, 53
Barna Research, 247–49
baseball players, 5
    batting of, 182–86, 189, 200
    "in a groove," 185–86
basketball players, 5, 200, 201, 206
    struggle stage of, 29–31
Beatles, 108–10
Beaufort, Abbé Joseph de, 276

Becca Orchard and Associates, 153–54
Behavioral Medicine, 269
beliefs, personal, *see* personal belief
    system
Benedict, Saint, 238–39
Bernick, Carol, 176
Beyond the Relaxation Response
    (Benson), 268–69
Bible, 22, 65, 244–48, 249–51, 255
bicycling, 41, 201–3, 204, 206
biochemistry, 14, 38, 45, 46–68,
    160–61
    neurotransmitters in, 27, 49–50, 60,
        61, 62, 63, 64, 90–91, 128, 199,
        205–6, 229, 240
    of "new-normal" state, 62–63
    of peak experience, 61–62
    of release stage, 58–61, 63–64
    spirituality and, 65–67
    stress hormones in, 21, 52, 57–58,
        59–60, 70, 185, 211, 222, 239,
        284
    of struggle stage, 57–58
    see also nitric oxide; relaxation
        response
biofeedback, 191
Biology and Psychology, 204
blood analysis, 27
blood flow, 50, 129–30
blood pressure, 20, 21, 70, 73, 74
    hypertension, 12, 53, 54–55, 73,
        212, 216
Bloomberg, Stu, 8
Bock, Hal, 198
Boeing, 177–78
Böhler, Peter, 254, 255
born-again Christians, 241, 247–56
    biblical definitions of, 249–51
    Charles Finney, 251–53, 256, 258,
        267
    John Wesley, 251, 253–56, 258,
        267
    number of, 247–49
    sociological definitions of, 248–49
Boston Globe, 7–8, 49
Boston Globe Magazine, 194

brain, 21, 49–50, 51, 60–61, 69–86,
91, 128, 160–61, 221, 285–86
athleticism and, 186–87, 200
brain stem of, 73, 79, 80, 82
calm commotion in, 70, 74, 81–82,
199, 240, 272
cerebellum of, 79
coherence in, 128–29, 135, 137,
143, 241
functioning of, 78–83
limbic system of, 73
mind's relationship to, 72, 83–86
music's effect on, 144
primitive (reptilian), 79–80, 81–82
psychosis and, 211
regional blood flow in, 129–30
in release stage, 73–74, 81–83
in struggle stage, 79–80
thinking and, 79
see also biochemistry
Brain Cognition, 128, 241
brain-mapping, 14, 56, 68, 69–86, 240
fMRI in, 21, 27, 70–74, 79, 84,
173, 193, 268, 269, 272
see also biochemistry; brain
Brain Research Reviews, 21, 56, 59,
85–86, 94, 222
brainstorming, 138, 158, 159–62
electronic, 172
individual, 161, 172
brainstorming triggers, 43
Brain Topography, 128, 241
brain waves, 69, 144
Breakout Networks, 23, 43–45,
147–81
biological changes and, 148, 157,
160–61
brainstorming vs., 158, 159–61
cordial disagreement in, 153
corporate athletics in, 165–66
corporate culture and, 149–50, 151,
164, 176–77
as creative organism, 173
definition of, 147–48
dissimilar participants in, 150–51,
156, 160

divergent thinking styles in, 152,
156, 157–58, 160, 161, 169
dominant individuals in, 153, 156,
159
elderly people in, 150
electronic brainstorming in, 172
examples of, 44–45, 173, 174–80
exchanging roles in, 165
fresh graphic aids in, 166–68
grating paradox in, 152–58, 160,
162
group facilitators in, 159, 164, 169
holistic thinking in, 156, 157–58,
160, 169
humor in, 163–64
language translator software and,
174–76
linear swordplay in, 169–72, 180
linear thinking in, 156, 157–58, 160
living companies and, 148–50, 151
in medicine, 154–55
moonshine shop and, 177–78
mutual respect as rule of, 156–57
optimum size of, 155–56
organizational agility engendered
by, 181
participative culture and, 149–50,
151
personal Breakouts achieved in,
151–52
prior mental patterns severed in,
151, 162, 163
recording ideas in, 159–60
relaxation-response breaks in,
163–64
research evidence and, 148–52
for self-awareness, 119–23
sensory stimulation in, 167–68,
178–79
session length of, 159
storytelling in, 168–69
switching roles in, 165
synchronization in, 150–52
synthesis in, 170–71
teaching in, 164–65
thesaurus in, 171–72

Breakout Networks (*cont.*)
time required by, 157
triggering strategies for, 161–72
Breakout Principle, 3–25, 87–88,
160–61, 206, 209, 283–88
animals and, 284–85
biology of, 20–21, 46–68, 148, 157,
160–61, 199, 222, 252, 267,
284–85; *see also* biochemistry;
brain
components of, 14–24
as cross-cultural phenomenon,
136–37
definition of, 4–6
stages of, 18–21, 27–28, 195, 217
as ultimate self-help principle, 4,
87, 283
volitional steps required by, 285–86
breathing, 12, 42, 89–90, 192, 196,
269, 273, 274
Brigham and Women's Hospital, 49
British Journal of Sports Medicine,
203, 208
British Medical Journal, 225
Buddhists, 146, 268–72
Bush, George W., 37–38
business leaders, 33–34, 208
Button, Dick, 194

calm commotion, paradox of, 70–74,
81–82, 199, 240, 272
Canada, 172, 221–22, 253
Canadian Family Physician, 138
cancer, 73
Cannon, Walter, 53
Capriati, Jennifer, 198
Celebration of Discipline (Foster), 281
Chambers, Oswald, 239
Chicago School of Public Health, 228
chi gong, 40, 52, 230
Chile, University of, 150
Chinese-Americans, 225
Christians, born-again, *see* born-again
Christians
Christian Scientists, 224
Christmas Carol, A (Dickens), 140–41

Circulation, 231
Cleveland Clinic Foundation, 192–93
CNN, 222
Cohen, Leonard, 145–46
coherence, brain, 128–29, 135, 137,
143, 241
Columbia University, 227
Comprehensive Therapy, 230
computers, 49
electronic brainstorming on, 172
language translator software for,
174–76
Confessions (Saint Augustine), 250
conversions, religious, 241, 242, 247–56
see also born-again Christians
coronary bypass surgery, 50, 218
coronary heart disease, 231
corporate athletics, 165–66
corporate culture, 164, 176–77
participative, 149–50, 151
cortisol, 52
creative abrasian, 152–53, 155, 158
creative intelligence, 129–31
creative thinking, 129, 130, 131–38
cultural factors in, 134–37
holistic thinking in, 131, 133,
134–38
linear thinking vs., 131, 132,
133–35, 137–38
synthesis in, 135
creativity, 4, 11, 14, 15, 23, 27, 34, 55,
125–46, 147, 287
of actors, 139–41
antinomy principle and, 133, 135
biology of, 125, 127–31
blocked, 5, 11, 125–26, 137–38
cerebral blood flow and, 129–30
coherent brain activity in, 128–29,
135, 137, 143
incubation period in, 142, 143
intelligence vs., 130
of musicians, 109, 144–46
scenarios of, 139–46
of scientists, 142–44
of writers, 125–27, 137–38
see also Breakout Networks

creativity tests, 129–30
cricket players, 186–87
cross-country skiing, 201
Crowe, Russell, 8
cults, 281
cultural triggers, 41, 63–64

Dalai Lama, 270–72
Dark Night of the Soul (John of the
    Cross), 275–76
Deaconess This Month, 190
death, 108
    fear of, 121, 123, 254
    of loved ones, 18, 29
    number four and, 225
    time of, 224–25
de Geus, A., 148–49
dendrites, 69
Denmark, 220, 221
depression, 14, 50, 73
dermcidin, 219
desensitization training, 122
Dickens, Charles, 140–41
difficult people, 35, 213–18
directors, spiritual, 280–81
disability paradox, 228
divorce, 18, 45
Dodson, John D., 32
"Don't homogenize, synchronize"
    (Sawhney), 150
dopamine, 27, 50, 60, 61, 128, 199,
    222, 240
Dorsey, Thomas, 214
drumming, 42
Dumond, Dwight Lowell, 253
duodenal ulcers, 54, 223

Eastern movement therapies, 230–31
Eastern Orthodox Church, 278
Eccles, Sir John C., 85, 142–43
Einstein, Albert, 142, 143–44
Einstein in Love (Overbye), 144
elderly people, 150
electroencephalograms (EEGs),
    128–29, 173
electronic brainstorming, 172

Eliot, T. S., 46
Ellis, Joseph, 225
emotional obstacles, 14–15
endorphins, 27, 50, 60, 61, 128, 199,
    204, 205–6, 222, 229, 240
enkelytin, 61
environmentalism, 92–93
Ephesians, Letter of Paul to the, 250
epinephrine, 52, 57–58, 185, 239, 284
estrogen replacement therapy, 50
eureka events, 47–48
evangelical Christians, 242, 248–49
    see also born-again Christians
*Evolution of the Brain: Creation of the
    Self* (Eccles), 85, 142–43
Exodus, Book of, 244–48
extradimensional reality, 66, 83–84
extrinsic beliefs, 258
eyewitness memory, 33

faith factor, 89–90
family problems, 12, 34, 44–45
Faulk, Marshall, 199
FedEx, 179–80
Fénelon, François de Salignac de la
    Mothe, Archbishop, 11
fight-or-flight response, 52
    physiologic changes in, 57–58, 211,
        245, 284
figure skaters, Olympic, 190–95, 209,
    210
Finney, Charles, 251–53, 256, 258,
    267
fireflies, 49
fishing, 42
fMRI (functional magnetic resonance
    imaging), 21, 27, 70–74, 79, 84,
        173, 193, 268, 269, 272
football players, 199
Forbes, 178, 179
Foster, Richard, 281
four, negative beliefs about, 225
Four Quartets (Eliot), 46
France, 218
Franklin Institute Online, 193
free association, 43

Fricchione, Gregory L., 21, 56
FSB, 180
Fuente-Fernández, Raúl de la, 60

Galatians, Letter of Paul to the, 251
Gallup polls, 227, 238, 247–48
    Princeton Religion Research Center
        of, 248
Germany, 218–19
God and the Astronomers (Jastrow),
        66, 235
graphic aids, 166–68
grating paradox, 152–58, 160, 162
    definition of, 153
Great Britain, 49
Greek language, 22, 65, 249
Greeks, ancient, 47–48
Green Mountain Coffee Roasters,
        178–79
grief, 14, 36
Groeschel, Benedict J., 273–74
    spiritual mentoring advocated by,
        280
group memory activities, 150
group zone, 173
growth development leaders (GDLs),
        176
gTum-mo yoga, 268–69
Gwynn, Tony, 185, 186

Hamilton, Scott, 194
Harding, Tonya, 194
Harrison, George, 108–10
Harvard Business Review, 33–34,
        148–49, 150, 152–53, 154, 158,
        162, 164, 165, 166, 167, 176,
        181
Harvard Medical Alumni Bulletin, 53
Harvard Medical School, 13, 21, 25,
        52, 67, 70, 71–74, 158, 191,
        193, 201–2, 204, 210, 217, 222,
        231, 268, 272
Harvard Physiological Laboratory, 32
headaches, 58, 212, 213–18
health, see rejuvenation
Health and Psychology, 203

health problems, 219, 224, 259
    personal belief system and, 223–24
    self-awareness and, 116–18
    stress in, 212, 213–18, 227
    visualization for, 191
hearing, sense of, 99, 167–68
heart rate, 20, 21, 70, 73, 74
Hebrew language, 22, 65, 245, 249
Hegel, G. W. F., 135
herpes simplex, 54, 223
Hesse, Hermann, 220
Hieron II, king of Syracuse, 47
Hippocrates, 15, 211
holistic (dialectical) thinking, 174–75,
        216, 229, 286
    in athletic "zone," 188–90, 194–95,
        197
    in Breakout Networks, 156,
        157–58, 160, 169
    in creative thinking, 131, 133,
        134–38
    intrinsic belief and, 270, 272
    music and, 229–30
    transcendence and, 235, 243
Hollis Albright Annual Symposium,
        210–11, 218
Holmes, Oliver Wendell, 53
Holmes, Thomas, 227
Holmes-Rahe "social adjustment
        scale," 18–19
Holt, Jim, 144
housework triggers, 18, 42
"How Culture Molds Habits of
        Thought" (Nisbett), 134
How to Practice (Dalai Lama),
        270–72
Hudson, Katherine, 164
humor, 163–64
hypertension, 12, 50, 53, 54–55, 73,
        212, 216

Illinois, University of, 228
immune system, 51, 203, 222, 227
impetigo, 219
impotence, 51
India, 33, 71, 268–69

individual brainstorming, 161, 172
individual zone of optimal functioning
    (IZOF), 207–8, 209, 246
insomnia, 13, 32, 53, 54–55, 58, 73,
    74, 224
INSPIRIT scale, 259–66
intelligence tests, 130
Interior Castle (Teresa of Avila), 275,
    280–81
*International Journal of
    Psychophysiology*, 128, 129,
    241
intrinsic beliefs, 25, 93–94, 219, 256,
    257–82, 286
    definition of, 258–59
    enhancement of, 266–67
    extrinsic beliefs vs., 258
    Far Eastern expression of, 268–72
    features of, 258–66
    historical testimony to, 268–79
    INSPIRIT scale of, 259–66
    negative, 279–82
    Roman Catholic expression of,
        272–79
investment bankers, 110–12
ischemia, 50
"Is the Placebo Powerless? An Analysis
    of Clinical Trials Comparing
    Placebo with No Treatment"
    (Hrobjartsson and Gotzsche),
    220

Jacobs, Sue C., 191, 193
jail term, 18
James, William, 53, 240, 283–84, 287
    on Charles Finney, 251–52
    on conversions, 241, 242
Japan, 136, 154–55, 172
Japanese-Americans, 225
Japanese Journal of Clinical Oncology,
    155
Jastrow, Robert, 65–66, 235
Jefferson, Thomas, 224–25
Jesus, 249, 250
jogging, 11, 17, 41, 59, 166, 188–90,
    201

John, Gospel According to, 249
John Adams (McCullough), 224
John of the Cross, Saint, 273, 275–76
journal, personal, 39
*Journal for the Scientific Study of
    Religion*, 259
Journal of Applied Psychology, 172
Journal of Business Strategy, 149
Journal of Cardiovascular Nursing,
    190, 216
*Journal of Experimental Psychology,
    Human Perception, and
    Performance*, 168
Journal of Human Stress, 202
Journal of John Wesley, The (Parker,
    ed.), 254
*Journal of Nervous and Mental
    Disease*, 224
Journal of Neuroimmunology, 218
*Journal of Neuropsychiatry and
    Clinical Neuroscience*, 168
Journal of Psychosomatic Research,
    18, 203, 204
*Journal of Sports Medicine and
    Physical Fitness*, 199
Journal of Sports Science, 207
Julian of Norwich, Lady, 274–75

Kanter, R. M., 154
Kass, Jared D., 258–59
Kennedy, Father Isidore, 273–74
Kerrigan, Nancy, 190–95, 198
    attack on, 193–94
    mind-body training of, 190–91,
        193
King, Stephen, 125–27
knitting, by men, 7–8

lactate buildup, 203
language translator software, 174–76
Latin, 15, 53
Lawrence of the Resurrection, Brother,
    276–77
lawyers, 12–13, 74–83, 94–95
Lazar, Sara W., 21, 71
learning ability, 27, 50

Leonard, D., 152–53, 158
Lerner Research Institute, 192–93
letting to, 19, 26–27, 30, 31, 58, 91,
    127, 250, 255
  see also release, stage of
Lewis, C. S., 67
life events, *see* traumatic life events
linear swordplay, 169–72, 180
linear (analytical) thinking, 131, 132,
    133–35, 137–38, 174–75
  athleticism and, 188, 189, 194,
    197
  in Breakout Networks, 156,
    157–58, 160
  characteristics of, 134
  circular obsessive patterns of, 5, 16,
    26, 95, 216
  economic, 149
  intrinsic belief and, 270, 271–72
  in medicine, 154–55
  music and, 229–30
living companies, 148–50, 151
  average short-lived companies vs.,
    149
Loehr, J., 166
London Business School, 148–49
Los Angeles Rams, 199
Lund University, 129–30
Luther, Martin, 256

McCann, Justin, 239
McCullough, David, 224–25
Mackie, Bob, 8
management consultants, 6–10,
    171–72
Manning, Thomas G., 253
marital separation, 18
Mark, Gospel According to, 250
marketing executives, 63–64
Martz, Mike, 199
Maslow, Abraham H., 22
Massachusetts, University of, 203
Massachusetts General Hospital, 21
massages, 99
mass psychogenic illness, 279
Masuda, Takahiko, 136

Medical Education, 169
Medical Science, Sports and Exercise,
    203, 204, 208
medicine, 231–32
  linear thinking in, 154–55
meditation, 40, 42, 52, 65, 75, 77,
    100, 209, 214, 216, 257,
    268–79
  Buddhist, 268–72
  calm commotion in brain produced
    by, 70–74
  Eastern Orthodox, 278
  lactate buildup reduced by, 203
  nocebo effect and, 281–82
  Roman Catholic, 272–79
  runners and, 203, 204
  of Sikhs, 71–74, 84, 90, 240, 268,
    272
memory, 27, 50
  eyewitness, 33
  muscle motor, 99, 185, 186–87,
    192, 196
  in placebo effect, 221
Men at Work: The Craft of Baseball
    (Will), 185–86, 189
menopause, 50
menstrual stress, 33
mentors, spiritual, 280–81
Methodist Church, 242, 251, 256
middle management, 154
mind, 51
  brain's relationship to, 72, 83–86
mind-body connection, 116–18, 184,
    212, 222, 224, 279
mind-body fitness, 190–95
Mind/Body Medical Institute, 190–91,
    193, 215–16, 224, 259
mindfulness, 271
Miracles (Lewis), 67
molecular biology, 14
moonshine shop, 44, 177–78
Moses, 244–48, 256, 258, 267
movement, repetitive, *see* repetitive
    physical activities
movement therapies, Eastern, 230–31
movies, 99–100

muscles:
    motor memory of, 99, 185, 186–87,
       192, 196
    progressive relaxation of, 12, 52,
       191–92
    visualization's effect on, 192–93
music, 144
    in stress reduction, 229–30
musical triggers, 41, 58, 59, 99, 142,
    143
musicians, 50, 108–10, 284
    creativity of, 109, 144–46
    motor memories of, 187
music therapy, 229
mystery, sense of, 242
My Utmost for His Highest
    (Chambers), 239

*Nationalism and Sectionalism in
    America* (Potter and Manning),
    253
natural healing powers, *see* self-
    healing, natural powers of
Natural Neuroscience, 187
Nature, 269
Nature Immunology, 218–19
nature triggers, 42, 59, 237–38, 239
needlepoint, 6–10, 18, 42
negative personal beliefs, 225–27
    about number four, 225
    avoiding pitfalls of, 279–82
    stress and, 226–27
    see also nocebo effect
Neuropsychologia, 130
Neuro-Report, 21, 71, 84–85
neurotransmitters, 27, 49–50, 60, 61,
    62, 63, 64, 90–91, 128, 199,
    205–6, 229, 240
Newberg, Andrew B., 85
newborn babies, 50, 229
New England Journal of Medicine,
    220, 221
"new-normal" state, stage of, 19–20,
    27, 28, 217
    maintenance of, 62–63
    personal beliefs in, 63

    of transcendence, 241, 244,
       250–51, 253, 256
New Testament, 22, 65, 247, 249–51,
    255
Newton, Isaac, 142–43
New York Times, 49, 71, 108, 134,
    136, 140, 141, 146, 199, 229
New York Times Book Review, 144
Nisbett, Richard, 134, 136
nitric oxide (NO), 27, 48, 49–51, 56,
    57–64, 90–91, 94, 128, 199,
    222, 240
    in artificial intelligence research,
       49
    benefits of, 50–51, 61, 62
    in fireflies, 49
    mind's connection with, 51
    as modulatory neurotransmitter,
       49–50
    in release stage, 21–22, 58–61, 62,
       63, 64
    as "spirit," 22, 65, 249
Nividia, 180
nocebo effect, 225–26, 279
    spiritual practices tainted by,
       281–82
nonlinear thinking, *see* holistic
    (dialectical) thinking
norepinephrine, 21, 52, 57–58, 59–60,
    185, 211, 222, 239, 284
Norway, 203
Nouwen, Henri J. M., 277–78

Oberlin College, 251, 253
occupational health nurses, 230
Ochanomizu University, 172
Old Testament, 22, 65, 244–48
Olympic athletes, 190–95, 208, 209,
    210
On Writing (King), 125–27
optimum-anxiety portal, 206–8
Orchard, Becca, 153–54
organigraphs, 167
Organization Dynamics, 149
Overbye, Dennis, 144
Oxford University, 186

pain reduction, 223, 229, 230
panic attacks, 13, 119
pantomime plays, 150
paradox of calm commotion, 70–74, 81–82, 199, 240, 272
Parker, Percy Livingstone, 254
Parkinson's disease:
common medications for, 61, 222
dopamine and, 50, 60, 61
placebo effect in, 60–61, 221–22
participative corporate culture, 149–50, 151
peak experiences, 17, 19, 20, 21, 22–24, 27, 28, 31, 39, 45, 57, 65, 77, 82, 91, 105–256, 283–84
biochemistry of, 61–62
brain-mapping and, 74
as eureka events, 47–48
ineffability of, 46–47, 198
neurotransmitters in, 50
see also athletes, athleticism; creativity; productivity, organizational; rejuvenation; self-awareness; transcendence
peptides, antibacterial, 218
Perception, 186, 187
Perception and Motor Skills, 203, 230
performance pyramid, 166
personal belief system, 13, 24–25, 53, 62, 287
environmentalism in, 92–93
health problems improved by, 223–24
immersion in, 59, 88, 92–94, 100–101, 137, 212, 216, 228, 279
negative, *see* negative personal beliefs
"new normal" state in, 63
nonrepetitive exposure to, 257
in rejuvenation, 212, 214, 216, 218, 219–27, 228
repetitive mental activity linked to, 37, 55, 59, 67, 72, 89–90, 100, 214, 216, 257, 272–74, 277–78

time of death affected by, 224–25
see also intrinsic beliefs; placebo effect
Peters, Ruanne K., 162–63
pet triggers, 43
phobias, 14, 18, 119
Physical and Medical Rehabilitation Clinics of North America, 230
placebo, 53
placebo effect, 51, 52, 53–57, 59, 89, 220–23
components of, 54, 221, 225–26
doubtful existence of, 220, 221
in Parkinson's disease, 60–61, 221–22
patient-provider relationship in, 54, 221
in rejuvenation, 220–23
as remembered wellness, 54, 94, 220–21, 258
scientific definition of, 54
see also nocebo effect
pneuma, 22, 65, 249
Polkinghorne, John, 85
positron-emission tomography (PET) scans, 60, 84, 85
post-traumatic stress disorder (PTSD), 36, 118–24
symptoms of, 118–19
Potter, David M., 253
Practice of the Presence of God, The (Lawrence of the Resurrection), 276–77
prana, 269
prayer, 18, 24, 25, 37–38, 40, 42, 52, 59, 65, 70, 77, 208, 209, 216, 239
nocebo effect and, 280–81
as repetitive mental exercise, 257, 272–74, 277–78
in struggle stage, 245, 246
predictive saccades, 186
premenstrual syndrome (PMS), 73
preperformance anxiety, 206–9
preperformance rituals, 191–93, 208–9

Index

Princeton Religion Research Center, 248

prior mental patterns, severance of, 4, 5, 15–18, 19, 26–27, 38, 43–45, 59, 63–64, 77, 81, 88, 286
  in athleticism, 196, 197, 206
  in Breakout Networks, 151, 162, 163
  intrinsic beliefs and, 257–58, 266–67, 271, 274, 278
  in rejuvenation, 216, 218, 228, 229
  in transcendence, 252, 255, 256

Proceedings of the National Academy of Sciences, 144

productivity, organizational, 5, 14, 15, 23, 27, 34, 55, 147–81, 271, 287
  brain coherence in, 129
  innovation in, 149, 152, 154, 165, 176
  of middle management, 154
  organigraphs in, 167
  see also Breakout Networks

progressive muscle relaxation, 12, 52
  technique of, 191–92

Psalms, Book of, 37, 250

psychedelic drugs, 22–23

Psychiatry, 52

Psychological Bulletin, 33

Psychological Reports, 33

Psychology of Religion (Starbuck), 283–84

psychotic surgical patients, 210–11

public speakers, 6, 16–17, 50
  lawyers as, 12–13, 74–83
  in profound connection with audience, 17, 77, 83

pulmonary hypertension, 50

"Putting your company's whole brain to work" (Leonard and Straus), 152–53, 158

Quarks, Chaos, & Christianity (Polkinghorne), 85

Queen's University, 172

rehabilitation clinics, 230

rejuvenation, 24, 210–32
  brain coherence in, 129
  definition of, 211–12
  medical intervention in, 231–32
  natural self-healing power in, 211, 212, 218–19, 232
  personal belief system in, 212, 214, 216, 218, 219–27, 228
  placebo effect in, 220–23
  relaxation response in, 214, 222, 228, 230
  stress reduction in, 228–31
  struggle stage of, 214, 216–17
  trigger mechanisms in, 212–18, 228–31

relaxation exercises, 7, 12, 21, 52, 70, 73, 209
  see also progressive muscle relaxation

relaxation response, 13, 14, 21, 51, 52–57, 59, 61, 62, 174–75
  athletic "zone" and, 191–92, 201–3, 204, 205, 208–9
  brain-mapping and, 70, 71, 72
  diminished anger in, 231
  evocation of, 54–55, 77, 89, 116, 191–92, 201–3, 208–9, 212, 271, 277
  physiologic signs of, 52
  in rejuvenation, 214, 222, 228, 230
  volitional act in, 52, 285
  see also placebo effect

Relaxation Response, The (Benson), 53, 174–75

relaxation-response breaks, 163–64

release, stage of, 8, 19, 20, 26–27, 28, 30, 48, 77, 91, 145
  of athletes, 183, 184, 209
  biochemistry of, 58–61, 63–64
  brain in, 73–74, 81–83
  nitric oxide in, 21–22, 58–61, 62, 63, 64
  of transcendence, 239–40, 244, 250, 252, 255, 270, 271, 278

remembered wellness, 54, 94, 220–21, 258
repetitive mental activities, 12, 40, 42, 54–55, 75, 77, 191, 271
  as basic triggering mechanism, 88, 89–91, 100, 137, 192, 197, 212, 228
  formal technique for, 89–91, 100, 116, 117
  personal belief system linked to, 37, 55, 59, 67, 72, 89–90, 100, 214, 216, 257, 272–74, 277–78
  as portal to athletic "zone," 192, 197, 201–6, 208–9
repetitive physical activities, 9, 41, 42, 77, 113–16, 126–27, 255
  as basic triggering mechanism, 88, 91, 100, 137, 212, 228, 230–31, 279
  in corporate athletics, 165–66
  as portal to athletic "zone," 200–203, 204
repetitive practice, 42
Research Questions in Exercise and Sports, 208
restaurant triggers, 18, 43, 96
rest-room triggers, 41
Revelations of Divine Love, The (Lady Julian of Norwich), 274–75
Review of Medicine in Chile, 150
Rickey, Branch, 186
robots, 49
role-playing, 138
Roman Catholics, 272–79
Romans, Letter of Paul to the, 250, 256
ruah, 22, 65, 249
Rule of Saint Benedict in Latin and English, The (McCann, ed.), 239
runners, 203
  distance, 201, 202, 204, 205–6
runner's high, 50, 60, 205–6

Salt Lake City Olympics, 194
San Diego, University of, 225

San Diego Padres, 185
sat nam, 72, 90, 272
Sawhney, M., 150
Scandinavian Journal of Medical Science and Sports, 207
Schwartz, T., 166
Science, 60, 222
scientists, 142–44, 234–35
self-actualization, 22
self-awareness, 15, 23, 35, 37, 39, 105–24, 237, 286
  asking fundamental questions in, 107–8, 110–24
  benefits of, 123–24
  Breakout Network for, 119–23
  changing basic attitudes in, 108, 116–18
  definition of, 106–7
  as first step in transformation, 106–7, 124
  of George Harrison, 108–10
  health problems and, 116–18
  inner exploration in, 105–6, 107
  self-discipline in, 108, 112–16
  understanding traumatic events in, 108, 118–24
  "Who am I?" question in, 107, 110–12
self-discipline, 108, 112–16
self-focus, avoidance of, 16, 30–31, 43, 82, 97–98
self-healing, natural powers of, 14–15
  in rejuvenation, 211, 212, 218–19, 232
self-help programs, 3–4
Senate, U.S., 204, 205
sensory impressions, focus on, 88, 98–100, 167–68, 228, 229–30
sensory stimulation, 167–68, 178–79
  synesthesia in, 168, 179
September 11th terrorist attacks, 18, 36–39, 118–24
septic shock, 51
Shinrigaku Kenkyu, 172
showering, 18, 41, 99, 132
Siddhartha (Hesse), 270

sight, sense of, 98–100, 167–68
    in athletes' visual focus, 41, 98–99,
        186–88, 196–97, 198, 199, 200
significant personal encounters, 88,
        95–97, 100, 228
Sikhs, 71–74, 84, 90, 240, 268
skin problems, 219, 224
skin temperature, 268–69
Slingsby, Brian, 21
Slovenia, 128, 240–41
smell, sense of, 99, 167–68, 178–79
Smith, Fred, 179–80
Social Science and Medicine, 228
Society for Neuroscience, 192–93
Solomon, Jerry, 194
space-time transcendence, 83, 133,
        234–35, 287
"spirit," 22, 65, 249
spirituality, 5, 11–12, 13, 14, 15,
        24–25, 35, 37–38, 44, 65,
        286–87
    biochemistry and, 65–67
    brain coherence in, 129
    extradimensional reality and, 66,
        83–84
    INSPIRIT scale of, 259–66
    physical expressions of, 267
    science vs., 25, 236–44, 287
    source of, 67
    see also intrinsic beliefs;
        transcendence
spiritual mentors, 280–81
Spiritual Passages (Groeschel), 273–74,
        280
spiritual triggers, 44
sports psychology, 194
sprinting, 201
Stand, The (King), 125–27
Starbuck, Edwin, 283–84, 287
Star Trek: The Next Generation, 139
Stefano, George B., 21, 56, 222
Sternberg, Esther, 222
Sternberg, R. J., 158
Stewart, Eileen M., 216
Stewart, Patrick, 139–41
Stiller, Robert, 178–79

Stora, 149
storytelling, 168–69
Straus, S., 152–53, 158
stress, 4, 5, 11–12, 14, 80, 89, 94, 245
    in business leaders, 33–34, 208
    in efficiency and performance, 7,
        32–34, 58, 80, 206–8
    excessive, physiologic signs of,
        20–21, 74–75
    in health problems, 212, 213–18,
        227
    menstrual, 33
    negative beliefs and, 226–27
    physiologic signs of, 20–21, 74–75
    prevalence of, 227
    warning signs of, 58
    see also fight-or-flight response;
        traumatic life events
stress hormones, 21, 52, 57–58, 59–60,
        70, 185, 211, 222, 239, 284
stress reduction, 5, 7, 13, 14, 75, 89,
        91, 116, 164, 228–31
    avoiding anger in, 231
    disability paradox and, 228
    Eastern movement therapies in,
        230–31
    intrinsic beliefs and, 271–72
    music in, 229–30
    needlework in, 6–10
    triggering mechanisms in, 228
    see also relaxation exercises;
        relaxation response
stroke, 50
struggle, stage of, 18–19, 20, 27–40,
        48, 63, 77, 89, 126
    of athletes, 29–31, 182–83, 184,
        185, 191, 192, 206, 209
    biochemistry of, 57–58
    brain in, 79–80
    of Breakout Networks, 155, 160
    involuntary initiation of, 28–29, 35,
        36–39
    of Moses, 244, 245
    physiologic responses in, 20–21
    prayer in, 245, 246
    recognizing opportunities in, 34–35

struggle, stage of (*cont.*)
  of rejuvenation, 214, 216–17
  scientific research on, 32–39
  stress hormones in, 57–58
  of transcendence, 238–39, 243,
      244, 250, 251–52, 253–55, 270,
      271, 278
  ultimate objective of, 39–40
  voluntary initiation of, 28, 35
  of weight loss, 113
  of writers, 126
substance abuse, 24–25
Sufis, 278
surgery, 210–11, 223
  coronary bypass, 80, 218
surrender to sense of total abandon,
      76–78, 88, 94–95, 127, 197,
      200, 228
surrender triggers, 42
Sussex, University of, 49
sweat, human, 218–19
Sweden, 33, 129–30, 149
swimming, 17, 41, 201, 209
synapses, 69
synchronization, 150–52
synesthesia, 168, 179
synthesis, 135, 170–71

tai chi, 40, 52, 230
teaching, 164–65
television, 99–100
Ten New Songs (Cohen), 145–46
tennis players, 5, 10–11, 195–98, 209
Teresa of Avila, Saint, 273, 275
  spiritual mentoring advocated by,
      280–81
Texas, 172
theological problems, 132–33, 135
thesaurus, 171–72
Tibetan Buddhist monks, 268–69,
      270–72
Tichy, Noel M., 165
time, 157
  altered perceptions of, 5, 199, 242
  of death, 224–25
  space-, 83, 133, 234–35, 287

Timeless Healing (Benson), 224, 232
total abandon, sense of, 76–78, 88,
      94–95, 127, 197, 200, 228
touch, sense of, 99, 167–68
touch typists, 187
transcendence, 15, 24, 25, 232,
      233–56, 257–58, 282, 286–88
  biology of, 236, 239, 240–41, 245
  conversions and, 241, 242, 247–56,
      286; *see also* born-again
      Christians
  definition of, 233–34
  experiences of, 237, 240, 241–43,
      252, 254, 275
  life-changing, 236–38, 242, 256, 267
  meaningful insights in, 242–43
  meditation and, 268–79
  of Moses, 244–48, 256, 258, 267
  in natural settings, 237–38, 239
  of nonreligious people, 236–38
  scientists' view of, 234–35
  sense of mystery in, 242
  sense of unity in, 241–42, 273, 275,
      276
  source of, 238
  space-time, 83, 133, 234–35, 287
  stages of, 238–41, 243–56, 270,
      271, 278
  time perceptions in, 242
  see also intrinsic beliefs; spirituality
traumatic life events, 4, 18–19, 28–29,
      34, 35, 36–39
  understanding of, in fear
      management, 108, 118–24
triggering mechanisms, basic, 88–101,
      209, 269
  altruistic activities, 16, 18, 43, 88,
      97–98, 100–101, 137, 228
  combinations of, 100–101, 212–18
  focus on sensory impressions, 88,
      98–100, 167–68, 228, 229–30
  immersion in personal belief system,
      59, 88, 92–94, 100–101, 137,
      212, 216, 228, 279
  negative beliefs and, 279
  in rejuvenation, 212–18, 228–31

repetitive mental activities, 88, 89–91, 100, 137, 192, 197, 212, 228

repetitive physical activities, 88, 91, 100, 137, 212, 228, 230–31, 279

significant personal encounters, 88, 95–97, 100, 228

in stress reduction, 228

surrender to sense of total abandon, 76–78, 88, 94–95, 127, 197, 200, 228

triggers, 5, 15–18, 23, 25, 26–45, 71

altruistic, 43

animal/pet, 43

athletic, 41–42

biological, 15

brainstorming, 43

in Breakout Networks, 161–72

cultural, 41, 63–64

description of, 27–32

housework, 42

musical, 41, 58, 59, 99, 142, 143

nature, 42, 59, 237–38, 239

personal belief, 24–25

pulling of, *see* release, stage of

range of, 10–13

restaurant, 18, 43, 96

rest-room, 41

selection of, 39–44, 58–59

spiritual, 40

surrender, 42

water-related, 41, 58, 99

yardwork, 42

see also prior mental patterns, severance of; repetitive physical activities

tuberculosis, 227

Tufts University, 49

UCLA, 141

Underground Railroad, 253

unity, sense of, 241–42, 273, 275, 276

Varieties of Religious Experience (James), 240, 241, 242, 252, 283–84

Veterans Administration Normative Aging Study, 231

vis medicatrix naturae, 15, 211, 218–19, 232

visualization, 189, 208, 209

muscles strengthened by, 192–93

technique of, 191–93

voodoo, 279

Wadsworth Theater, 141

walking, 11, 17, 41, 58, 59, 114–16, 126–27, 142, 143, 166, 201

"Walking onto a Bare Stage (and into Scrooge's skin)" (Stewart), 140, 141

Wall Street Journal, 177–78

Washington Post, 193

water-related triggers, 41, 58, 99

Way of the Heart, The (Nouwen), 277–78

weight loss, 112–16, 223

Weld, Theodore, 253

Wesley, Charles, 255

Wesley, John, 251, 253–56, 258, 267

Western vs. Asian thinking, 133–37, 157–58

see also holistic thinking; linear (analytical) thinking

"Who am I" question, 107, 110–12

Why God Won't Go Away (Newberg et al.), 85

Will, George F., 185–86, 189

worst-case scenarios, 42, 80, 95

wrestlers, Olympic, 208

writers, 6, 11, 125–27, 137–38

yardwork triggers, 42

Yerkes, Robert M., 32

Yerkes-Dodson Law, 7, 32–34, 58, 80, 208

yoga, 40, 52, 230

"bliss state" of, 269

gTum-mo, 268–69

Zen Buddhism, 146

Zohn, Ethan, 8

"zone," athletic, 8, 11, 24, 29, 50, 55, 129, 181, 197–209
    experience of, 5–6, 31, 183–84, 185–86, 196–97, 198
    holistic thinking in, 188–90, 194–95, 197
    mental repetition portal to, 192, 197, 201–6, 208–9
    optimum-anxiety portal to, 206–8
    physical repetition portal to, 200–203, 204
    physiology of, 5–6
    portals to, 200–209
    relaxation response and, 191–92, 201–3, 204, 205, 208–9
    runner's high in, 50, 60, 205–6
    time perception in, 5, 199, 242
    total abandon in, 197, 200

About the Authors

HERBERT BENSON, M.D., is the Mind/Body Medical Institute Associate Professor of Medicine at the Harvard Medical School and is also the founding president of the Mind/Body Medical Institute. He has conducted some of the world's most significant mind-body research during the past thirty years. Dr. Benson is the author of the mega-bestseller *The Relaxation Response* and five other books, which have sold more than 4 million copies.

WILLIAM PROCTOR, a graduate of Harvard College and Harvard Law School, has authored, coauthored, or ghostwritten more than eighty books, including the international bestsellers *The G-Index Diet* with Dr. Richard N. Podell, *Controlling Cholesterol* with Dr. Kenneth H. Cooper, and *Beyond the Relaxation Response* with Dr. Herbert Benson. He has also written books with discount broker Charles Schwab, car-rental founder Warren Avis, and mutual-fund magnate Sir John Templeton, as well as bestsellers in the Christian market.

PEW

Norman   Dershowitz
    Finkelstein
the   Nation Mag,
Case for Israel

The Holocaust Industry

    Films
180 on holocaust
NY Times
220 articles - 1999

Politics of memory